HISTORY OF
ENGLAND

HISTORY OF
ENGLAND

JEREMY BLACK

BISON GROUP

First published in 1993 by

Bison Books Ltd
Kimbolton House
117A Fulham Road
London SW3 6RL

ISBN 1-86124-785-X

Printed in Hong Kong

The right of Jeremy Black to be identified as the
author has been asserted by the same in accordance
with the Copyright, Designs and Patents Act 1988.

FOR STEPHEN

Page 1: Coin issued by Edward the Confessor (1042-66).
Page 2: Portsmouth, by Dominic Serres *c.*1782; Portsmouth, Britain's leading naval base, is shown at the close of the War of American Independence. The career of the painter, Dominic Serres (1722-93), as well as his subject, illustrates British naval power. A Frenchman, he was captured by a British frigate in the Seven Years War, settled in England and became a leading painter of naval pieces. One of the founding members of the Royal Academy in 1768, Serres exhibited 105 works there, many of them scenes of imperial triumph, such as *The Siege at Fort Royal, Martinique* (1769). He was appointed Marine Painter to George III.

PREFACE

IN SOME RESPECTS this has been the most interesting and most difficult book that I have attempted. Most interesting because I have had to read so widely, most difficult because of the discipline of writing in accordance with particular guidelines and to a tight word-limit. What has been discarded in endless redrafting could have made several books, which shows not only the richness and variety of English history, but also the different ways in which it can be approached.

This book is dedicated to my brother Stephen in love and friendship, but while writing it my thoughts have often turned to those who taught me English history: to David Griffiths at Haberdashers'; to Tim Blanning, Martin Brett, Marjorie Chibnall, John Morrill, Jonathan Riley-Smith and John Walter at Cambridge. I am most grateful to Ian Archer, Stuart Ball, Chris Bartlett, Sarah Black, John Blair, John Bourne, P. J. Casey, John Davis, John Derry, George Boyce, Duncan Bythell, Robin Frame, Steve Gunn, Paul Harvey, Alan Heesom, Jon Parry, John Plowright, Bernard Porter, Michael Prestwich, David Rollason, Nigel Saul, Geoffrey Searle, Henry Summerson and John Young for commenting on sections of earlier drafts, Wendy Duery for all her help and my editor, Jessica Hodge. Aside from thus thanking my best critic, my wife Sarah, as well as a number of scholars whose work I admire greatly, including three friends from student days at Cambridge and Oxford, it is a particular pleasure to be able to express my gratitude to six colleagues from the History Department at the University of Durham, of which I have been fortunate to be a member since 1980, and in thanking them to record my gratitude for support and acceptance to the entire department and to the University.

Jeremy Black 28 September 1992

CONTENTS

1
ROMAN BRITAIN

NGLAND WAS FIRST UNITED as a result of
conquest, conquest by the most powerful
and extensive empire in the history of
Europe, that of Rome. The direct Roman impact
on England lasted for a half-millennium, for 330
years of which (AD 78-409) the whole of England
and Wales was ruled by imperial Rome. This
period is a good starting point for the history of
England, not only because of its political unity,
but also because the nature of the historical
sources changes substantially with the addition of
written to archaeological remains. Furthermore,
the development of closer links between the
British Isles and the Continent was of considerable importance, not least because of the spread
of Christianity, which was introduced in the late
second century and organized into dioceses by the
early fourth century, though its impact before the
fourth century should not be over-stated.

The societies that the Romans conquered are
somewhat obscure to us, because of the dearth of
historical records. This is especially true of western and northern England, as well as of Ireland,
Scotland and Wales, a contrast in terms of evidence that was to last well into the Middle Ages.
Nevertheless, the Celts who lived in late-Iron-
Age Britain were clearly far from being savages,
even if the nature of their societies was different
from that of Rome. They lacked a developed
urban civilization, a sophisticated governmental
system with differentiated administrative functions, a permanent army or a literary culture.

Being different was (and is) not, however, the
same as being primitive. Agricultural activity was
both varied and extensive. Arable and pastoral
farming were practised; much of the woodland
had been cleared, especially in areas with light
soils, and ploughs with mould-boards may have
been used, but poorly-drained terrain, of which
there was much, was of little use. A high and increasing level of settled population was supported; and the surplus helped to sustain an aristocratic society. Identifiable tribes existed,
especially in southern Britain, where the influence of Belgic peoples from northern France
helped to produce 'states' with monarchical patterns of government; the use of coins, which was
restricted to south-east Britain and the Midlands;
and the development of proto-towns, both hillforts and low-lying centres such as Camulodunum
(Colchester), capital of the Trinovantes of Essex.
As with earlier Celtic immigration, the impact of
the Belgic peoples indicated the close and important links that existed between Britain and
the Continent. If one of the classic themes of
nineteenth-century British historiography was
the independence of 'sea-girt' Britain, then it is
also important to note that close continental
links, political, economic and cultural, were a
central feature from before the period of recorded
history. Indeed for much of British history, especially the period from the late Iron Age to the loss
(bar Calais) of empire in France in 1453, links between southern England and northern France

Below: Ptolemy's map.
Claudius Ptolemaeus, who
worked in Alexandria,
compiled his *Geography* in
about 150 AD. He included
the latitude and longitude
of many places, and maps
were drawn on the basis of
this information. A text
with maps was translated
from Greek into Latin in
about 1406, and many
fifteenth-century copies
survive. This is a portion of
the world map from the
edition published at Rome
in 1478.

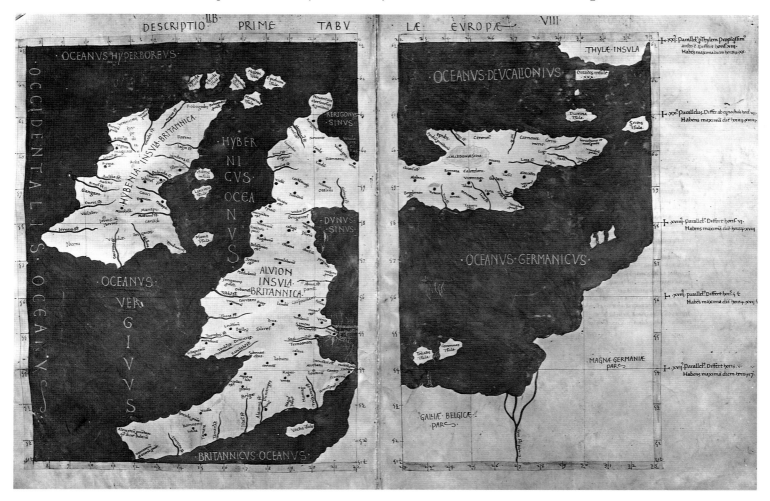

were in many respects closer than those within the British Isles.

Although there was quite a lot of contact at the aristocratic level with the Roman world before the Roman conquest, relations with the Continent in the late Iron Age had not been imperial in character. The Romans were to change this, and to introduce a political world in which events elsewhere in Europe had a continuous and direct impact in Britain. This was most obvious with the invasions and eventual conquest of England. Julius Caesar claimed that this was necessary to end British support for the Celts who were resisting his conquest of Gaul, but it was largely personal prestige and the dictates of politics in Rome that led to his expeditions in 55 and 54 BC and that of the Emperor Claudius in AD 43. Caesar needed to show that the invasion was necessary for him to remain in control of the army in Gaul, the basis of his power. England was a formidable military challenge, requiring a major amphibious expedition across tidal waters, a task of which the Romans had little experience; but, once landed, the Romans enjoyed the military advantage. The disciplined infantry, with their body-armour, javelins and short swords, were more effective than the British, whose chariots and hillforts were vulnerable to Roman archers and siegecraft respectively. British infantry had little body armour and lacked effective missile power. Nevertheless, surprise, numbers and favourable terrain could sometimes combine to bring the British victory. They were possibly most at a disadvantage in lacking specialized armies: unlike the Romans, British farmer-soldiers could not afford to be soldiers all the time, and their farming also made them vulnerable to Roman devastation. In contrast, the British of highland Caledonia, who were never fully subdued by the Romans, were probably primarily pastoralists, living in defended homesteads and better able

Land height in metres

100 - 1000

less than 100

and more used to serving as soldiers for long periods. The Roman conquest, even as it united much of Britain, also demonstrated a central feature of British history: a lack of uniformity that in part reflected a variety of local socio-economic systems stemming from an extraordinary geological and geomorphological range for a country of its size.

Caesar's first expedition, in which he did not move far from his beachhead in Kent, witnessed Roman victories in hard fighting, but the damage done to Caesar's ships by equinoctial gales and the scale of the resistance encouraged him to come to terms with the local tribes. A larger force the following year made an unopposed landing, marched through Kent, winning a victory near Canterbury, defeated tribal leader Cassivellaunus, and crossed the Thames. Cassivellaunus' capital, possibly Wheathampstead, was seized, an attack on the Romans' Kent beachhead was beaten off, and Caesar reached a settlement with Cassivellaunus. Hostages and tribute were

Above: Physical map of England, showing uplands, lowlands, towns and rivers. Geographical and geological diversity is a continuous theme in English history.

Left: The civil engineering of the Roman Empire was technically sophisticated, as befitted an imperial power. Eboracum (York) was the centre of Roman power in northern England, a legionary fortress and, by 216 AD, capital of the province of Britannia Inferior (the more northern British province); the Roman sewer in Church Street is made of huge millstone grit blocks and was used to serve the legionary bath buildings nearby.

planned an invasion of Britain and, in search of military reputation, Claudius launched one. It was to be no mere raid. A military force of about 40,000 men, approximately twice the size of Caesar's army in 55 BC but about the same as that of 54 BC, made an unopposed landing, probably in Kent, and defeated a confederation of forces in three battles, two of which were caused by contested crossings of the Medway and the Thames. Claudius then arrived, with the first elephants seen in Britain, and received the surrender of Colchester. He decided to make Britain a Roman province, and the Romans rapidly overran southern Britain. The current leader of the Catuvellauni, Caratacus, continued resistance from Wales, but was eventually defeated in c. AD 50-1 and fleeing north, was handed over to the Romans by Cartimandua, queen of the Brigantes of Yorkshire. In return for accepting Roman suzerainty, she had become a client ruler. Similar status was granted to the Iceni of East Anglia, and the Atrebates of Surrey, Sussex and Hampshire under Cogidubnus. By AD 49 most of lowland England was under Roman control. The hillforts of the West Country had been overrun, the future emperor Vespasian destroying more than 20, including Maiden Castle, when he conquered the Durotriges of Dorset and Somerset. The governor Suetonius Paulinus was campaigning in north Wales when the Iceni under Boudica (Boadicea is a later corruption of the name), enraged by vicious mismanagement and expropriation by the Romans and by the abuse of her family, including the flogging of Boudica herself and the rape of her daughters, rose in rebellion (AD 60-1). The Iceni were backed by the Trinovantes, much of whose land had been confiscated to support the colony

Above: An Iron Age tribal boundary? This dramatic hill-carving of a white horse at Uffington, on the Ridgeway in south Oxfordshire, may have been a signal of control by the Dobunni or the Atrebates, and is carved in a flowing, stylized manner that is typical of Celtic art before the Roman invasion.

promised by the local rulers and a client ruler installed for the Trinovantes of Essex, but rebellion in Gaul, followed by civil war, prevented the Romans from following up Caesar's expeditions during the last years of the republic.

Although intervention in Britain may have been contemplated by Augustus Caesar, the German frontier was a higher priority. Caligula also

Right: Avebury in Wiltshire is the largest stone circle in the world, 1200 feet in diameter, dating from around 1750 BC. A circular bank of chalk surrounds a circle of sandstone pillars, while an avenue of standing stones leads to what was a temple site a mile away.

of Roman veterans at Colchester. The major Roman settlements, Camulodunum, Londinium and Verulamium (Colchester, London and St Albans), were stormed, and their inhabitants slaughtered with great cruelty. At a battle somewhere in the Midlands, Paulinus crushed Boudica, who died, probably by suicide, and the Iceni and their allies were then 'pacified' with typical Roman brutality.

After Roman Britain had been restored, the Roman civil war that began with Nero's suicide in AD 68 was the first of a series of conflicts within the Roman elite that periodically weakened the Roman military effort and presence in Britain until the eventual fall of the empire. Nevertheless, the pace of advance resumed in AD 71 with the subjugation of the Brigantes of northern England (71-73/4), the subjugation of most of Wales (73/4-6) and, during the governorship of Agricola (77-83), the completion of the conquests of Wales and northern England and the invasion of Scotland, leading to his victory at Mons Graupius. Southern Scotland and the agricultural lands to the east of the Highlands had now been conquered, and the Romans had advanced at least as far as the river Spey.

The Romans were not to persist in this first attempt to unite Britain militarily. Agricola's proposal for an invasion of Ireland was ignored, and the competing demands of the vulnerable Danube frontier meant a reduction in the considerable military effort devoted to Britain, just as earlier Nero had withdrawn troops in preparation for campaigning on the Asian frontier of the empire. By the early years of the second century the Romans had abandoned their occupation of southern and central Scotland, instead they

developed a frontier at the narrowest part of the island, the Tyne-Solway line. This was consolidated by the construction of Hadrian's Wall from about 122. This most impressive of structures, eventually comprising a stone wall 70 miles long with supporting forts such as Housesteads, did not mark the end of Roman attempts to extend the empire. Hadrian's successor, Antoninus Pius, ordered a fresh advance north. Eastern Scotland was occupied as far north as the river Tay, and a wall of turf on a stone base was built from the Forth to the Clyde (c. 140). That line was held until c. 163 or later, when Hadrian's Wall again became the frontier, though the Antonine wall had already been briefly abandoned in c. 155-8 for reasons that are unclear. The Emperor Septimus Severus advanced into Scotland in 209-10, but thereafter the frontier stabilized on the Tyne-Solway line.

Roman Britain displayed the characteristics of other imperial provinces, albeit with the addition of the expensive military presence that typified

Above: This gold coin of King Cunobelinus (flourished about 10 BC – about 41 AD) of the Catuvellauni/Trinovantes federation bears the mint mark of his capital CAMU[LODUNUM] (Colchester). He also issued coins from Verulamion (St Albans; the more normal Roman spelling is Verulamium). The volume of his gold and silver coinage suggests that he was both wealthy and influential, and the Latin inscription bears testimony to a degree of romanization in Celtic Britain before the Claudian invasion.

Left Maiden Castle, an Iron Age hillfort outside modern Dorchester, Dorset, belonged to the Durotriges and was captured, in the Romans' initial drive west, by the future Emperor Vespasian, commanding the II Augusta legion. The serried banks were calculated to break up an attacking charge; the innermost bank carried a palisade.

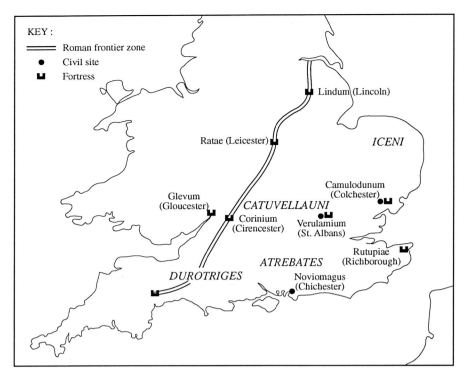

KEY :
═══ Roman frontier zone
●   Civil site
◼   Fortress

Lindum (Lincoln)

Ratae (Leicester)

ICENI

Camulodunum
(Colchester)

Glevum
(Gloucester)

CATUVELLAUNI

Corinium
(Cirencester)

Verulamium
(St. Albans)

Rutupiae
(Richborough)

ATREBATES

DUROTRIGES

Noviomagus
(Chichester)

Above: The Roman
conquest of lowland
Britain, 43-47 AD.

frontier provinces. The settlement of people from
elsewhere in the empire, many of them ex-
soldiers, was matched by the romanization of the
British elite. Towns developed as centres of administration and integration, many of them on
the sites of modern cities. The administrative
hierarchy and military system were not unchang-
ing, but by the mid-second century London, the
major port of Roman Britain and thus its crucial
link with the rest of the empire, and the lowest
bridging point on the Thames, was the provincial
capital. York, Chester and Caerleon were the
permanent bases of three legions, while Colchester, Lincoln and Gloucester were *coloniae*,

towns founded for veterans. Provincial capitals
included Canterbury, Chichester, Winchester,
Dorchester, Exeter, Cirencester, St Albans,
Leicester and Carmarthen. Rectilinear grid street
plans, centred on fora and basilicas, developed in
these towns. The towns were linked by roads,
some of which are still used today: the A5, for
example, follows the route of Watling Street.
Roads were built to a high standard, with stone
foundations and gravel surfaces, and were often
straight. They constituted a planned network,
testimony to the impact of a powerful governmental structure that also organized a large-scale
drainage scheme in East Anglia, brought economic changes designed to supply the army and
introduced effective taxation.

As goods and money were moved in a regular
fashion across greater distances, and also to and
from the Continent, inter-regional contact increased and new fashions and designs were dis-
seminated, as in the pottery industry. The population increased, agriculture improved with the
introduction of scythes, and villas – houses in the
country constructed in a Roman style and heated
from under the floor by a hypocaust system –
appeared. The greater quantity of archaeological
material surviving from the Roman period suggests a society producing and trading far more
goods than its Iron Age predecessors. Roman religious cults spread, though assimilation with
native Celtic beliefs was important. When Christianity became the state religion, this brought
more systematic cultural links between England
and the Continent; the pre-Roman druids, whom
the Romans stamped out, and the cults of the
Olympian gods which they introduced had lacked
both diocesan structure and doctrinal regulation.
Pagan practices continued, however, and outside

Right: Model of Fishbourne,
a palatial Romano-British
villa near Chichester,
Sussex, and the site of a
major excavation
programme. It was probably
the property of
Cogidubnus, a client ruler
who was appointed king
over the Atrebatic
kingdom by the Romans.
He remained loyal during
the Boudican revolt of 60
AD and continued to rule
into the 70s.

the lowland towns, the centres of consumption, authority and Roman culture, Britain was not as thoroughly romanized as other provinces of the empire, such as Gaul.

Roman Britain was weakened by the inability of the Roman empire to devise a consistently accepted system of imperial succession, and by the willingness of military units to support their commanders in bids for power. Although such bids were not continual, they dramatically weakened the empire. In 296 Britain had to be invaded in order to defeat a rebel Roman leader. These

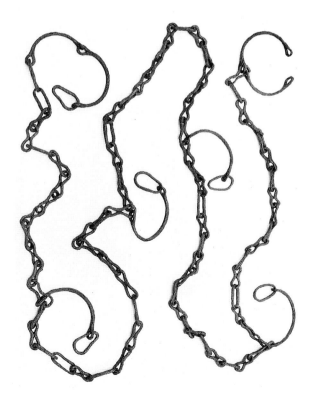

Above: Roman mosaic work varied from simple to sophisticated. This high-quality floor from Fishbourne villa, dating from the second century AD, combines geometrical and representational motifs, including a boy on a dolphin.

Right: Roman coastal defences at Porchester, Dorset, constructed by 285, one of the 'Saxon Shore' forts built or refortified in the third and fourth centuries along Britain's vulnerable southern coast. It was the westernmost of what, by 370, formed a chain of ten forts beginning at Brancaster, Norfolk. Most, like Porchester, had bastion towers and were designed to protect harbours and estuaries.

Far right: Roman road over Wheeldale Moor, North Yorkshire. The road network constructed by the Romans facilitated both communication and control.

367 led to widespread devastation. Order was restored by Theodosius in 368-69. The construction of town defences from the third century indicated an attitude of growing defensiveness.

Civil war in the empire and barbarian invasions led to renewed problems in the 400s. In 406 Gaul was invaded by a vast number of barbarians. Britain, threatened with being cut off from the rest of the empire, created its own Emperor, who took a significant part of the island's military forces to counter the barbarian threat. They did not return. In 410 the Britons, disillusioned with the rebel Constantine III's activities, expelled his administrators and appealed to the true Emperor, Honorius, for the restoration of legitimate rule. He, hard pressed in Italy by Alaric, the Visigothic leader who captured Rome that year, could do no more than tell them to look to their own defence. This was the end of the Roman empire in Britain, but not of Roman Britain. Indeed the very break with Rome and the subsequent, initially successful, resistance to Saxon attack may be seen as evidence of the vitality of the Romano-Britons.

The fifth century is a particularly obscure period, but it seems clear that a measure of continuity can be stressed. Rather than being a period simply of conquest and resistance, the collapse of one regime and the rise of another separate one, it is likely that the situation was far more complex. Romanized town and villa life, and the practice of Christianity, did not cease abruptly, and archaeological evidence of violent destruction is limited. Nevertheless, as elsewhere in

upheavals interacted cumulatively with the burden of defending Roman Britain from outside challenges, including Picts from Scotland, Scots from Ireland and Saxons from northern Germany and southern Scandinavia. Their attacks became serious in the 350s, while a successful invasion in

in western Europe, 'barbarian' mercenaries were hired and came to demand power for themselves. Alongside continuity in, for example, the boundaries of some political units, such as possibly Kent and Lindsey, there was Germanization, not least linguistically. Romano-British resistance was not uniformly unsuccessful, however, and in about 500 it achieved a major victory, possibly under a warrior called Artorius (Arthur) at Mons Badonicus. It has been suggested that a large hall on the summit of the hillfort at South Cadbury in Somerset may have been the feasting hall of a warrior leader of the period, the source of the legend of Arthur's Camelot. Unlike in the fourth century, however, the defenders of Britain could not call for assistance from the Continent and were themselves divided into warring kingdoms, while their assailants benefited from bases in lowland England. According to *The Anglo-Saxon Chronicle* (Saxon annals written considerably later, probably first in Alfred's reign), Jutes under the possibly mythical Hengist and Horsa founded the kingdom of Kent in the 450s. The sources for the invasion period are, however, scanty and sometimes contradictory. The Germanic invaders were illiterate, and Bede and other later written sources provide a rather different account from the archaeological evidence. The latter has to be used with care because of the difficulty of interpreting evidence and its uneven spread, reflecting in part the varied pattern of excavation and fieldwork activity. Nevertheless, such evidence suggests that there was already a substantial Germanic presence in eastern England before the

450s. The invaders, Angles, Saxons and Jutes, came from Denmark and northern Germany, the Jutes establishing themselves in Kent, the Isle of Wight and parts of Hampshire. Wessex, the kingdom of the West Saxons, was founded in the Upper Thames Valley, around Dorchester-on-Thames, and expanded its power into Hampshire. A new political geography, born of conquest and tribal differences, was being created.

Above: This stone relief of the triple dwarf-gods, called Genii Cucullati because they are usually shown as wearing a *cucullus* or hooded cloak, was found at Housesteads fort on Hadrian's Wall and dates from about the third century AD.

2
ANGLO-SAXON ENGLAND

Left: Crown and Church; the house of Wessex was closely associated with the development of the Church in the tenth century. King Edgar, standing between the Virgin Mary and St Peter, is shown offering Christ the codex containing the charter of 966, which marked the transformation of the New Minster at Winchester into a Benedictine monastery. A product of the Winchester school of manuscript illumination.

THE SIXTH CENTURY saw the retreat of sub-Romano-British power. The Wessex Saxons spread west and north, while the Angles established kingdoms in the Midlands (Mercia), Yorkshire (Deira), north of the Tees (Bernicia) and East Anglia. Bernicia was probably established at or near Bamburgh in the mid sixth century; Deira, to the north of the Humber, in the late fifth century. For over three centuries, as the invaders spread their power, struggle can be seen as a central theme of English history, although it did not prevent a measure of assimilation and, at times, political co-operation. Bernicia expanded greatly under Aethelfrith (593-616), reaching as far as Lothian, and also probably pushed back the frontier of North Wales, while Deira gained the vales of York and Pickering. The British kingdoms of Elmet, centred on Leeds, and Rheged, around the Solway estuary, were absorbed by Northumbria (created from Bernicia and Deira) in the late sixth and seventh centuries, although Strathclyde survived and the

Below: Anglo-Saxon England c.700.

Right: The helmet from the Sutton Hoo ship burial c.630. The burial, near Woodbridge, Suffolk, probably contained the tomb of King Raedwald of East Anglia, fourth on Bede's list of Bretwaldas (over-kings). The helmet is of late Roman Spangenhelm form and is made of iron inlaid with silver and with gilded and tinned ornaments.

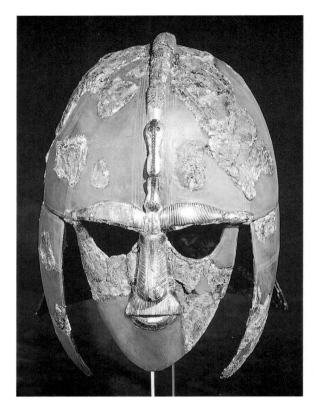

history of Rheged is particularly obscure. Elsewhere, the process of expansion was far from continuous: the Saxon occupation of Dorset was delayed until the late sixth or seventh centuries; Cornwall was only conquered by Wessex in 838; and the kingdoms in Wales were never conquered.

It is likely that the population of England fell dramatically, not least because of plague, and that in those areas that were conquered the Romano-Britons largely fled or survived as slaves and peasants, although the latter could lead to a significant level of both survival and continuity with Anglo-Saxon settlement. The present archaeological evidence permits the tentative conclusion that Anglo-Saxon settlers continued the Romano-British pattern of generally neglecting clay lands in favour of lighter soils on gravel, sand and chalk, and thus occupied an already managed landscape. British language and culture were largely lost in England but in Wales Christianity flourished, while Anglo-Saxon civilization owed much to that of its predecessors. These centuries of plague and violence, a period characterized by a subsistence economy with few ceramics or coins, have left scant trace in the archaeological record, certainly compared to Roman Britain. Within the former Roman empire the loss of language, towns and religion was unique to Britain: it did not happen in Gaul, Italy, Spain or North Africa. On the other hand, the rich and ornate goods, many from the Continent and Byzantium, found in the ship burials at Sutton Hoo (c. 630), and, to a lesser extent, at Snape and in the Kentish cemeteries of these years, testify to the wealth of the East Anglian and Kentish dynasties and the importance of commercial links with the Continent.

Left: This purse-lid of gold and garnets from the Sutton Hoo ship burial reflects the exceptional quality of the ornamental work found with the burial. Evidence of the wealth and splendour of some elements of seventh-century society, the treasures in the funerary ship also prompt speculation about the riches of Anglo-Saxon civilization that have been lost.

Below: Decorated initial from the Lindisfarne Gospel, one of the great works of Northumbrian monasticism. Illuminated between 689 and 721, it reveals Irish influence in its script and ornamentation. The monastery of Lindisfarne was founded in the seventh century by St Aidan and King Oswald of Northumbria.

Politically the Anglo-Saxon kingdoms were in a state of flux as far as both their frontiers and their inter-relationships were concerned. The numerous small kingdoms of the sixth century took a long time to coalesce. The process can be seen in cellular terms, with small units, based no doubt on successful warbands, being gradually brought together into larger units. Penda of Mercia (*c.* 632-654) was said to have had an army which included forces contributed by thirty subordinate leaders, many of whom would once have been the independent rulers of small territories. Chance, not least the personalities of rulers, helped to explain why some areas ceased to be independent kingdoms, while others flourished. The West Midland kingdoms of the Hwicce and the Magonsaetan were absorbed by Mercia which, after the death of King Anna (654), dominated hitherto independent East Anglia. Overkings, rulers who enjoyed hegemony over other kings, found their success short-term. Aethelbert of Kent was one such in the 590s, but for much of the seventh century the position belonged to the rulers of Northumbria. Oswald (634-41), Oswin (641-70) and Egfrith (670-85) ruled the lands between the Humber and the Forth on the eastern side of Britain, and between the Mersey and the Ayr on the west, and were at times treated as overlords by the rulers of Mercia, Wessex, Strathclyde and the Pict and Scottish territories. This hegemony was ended as a result of defeats at the hands of Mercia (678) and the Picts (685), and thereafter Northumbria ceased to be the most dynamic and powerful of the Anglo-Saxon kingdoms. This position was taken by Mercia, while Wessex became more dominant in southern England, conquering the Isle of Wight in 685.

Right: The Bewcastle Cross, Cumbria, Anglian cross, late eighth century, with runic inscriptions. A far-flung outpost of the Celtic mission to Northumbria. Christianity provided new media for the Anglo-Saxon artist in the form of stone sculpture and manuscript illumination, but many of the decorative motifs used had their roots in pagan Saxon art, as found, for example, in the Sutton Hoo ship burial. The great Anglo-Saxon crosses, of which this and the Ruthwell Cross are the best examples, probably served as funerary monuments or sanctuary markers. The principal carved decoration presents a series of sophisticated and literate scenes from the life of Christ, including the Visitation, the Annunciation and Christ healing the blind man. The Ruthwell Cross also bears, in runic lettering, a version of the Anglo-Saxon poem *The Dream of the Rood*, a powerful account of the crucifixion as told by the cross.

Though evidence of social developments is limited, settlement in the Middle Saxon period (*c.* 650-850) seems to have been widespread but scattered, apparently mainly in farmsteads and small hamlets; the nucleated villages of high medieval England still lay in the future. Anglo-Saxon place-names, such as *ham, tun* and *worth*, were thereafter to be the most important in rural England, matching the *chesters* and *cesters* that denote Roman towns. A small number of major ports (Ipswich, London, Southampton, York) developed spectacularly in the eighth century, and by the tenth century a more extensive urban network was in place.

Christianity spread again across England. In 597 a mission from Pope Gregory the Great under a monk called Augustine reached Canterbury, the capital of Aethelbert's Kent, and had some success in the south-east, but it was the church of Ireland that was the base for the conversion first of Scotland and then, via Northumbria, of most of England. There was a pagan reaction in Northumbria (632), but the Christian King Oswald won control there in 634 and, thanks to his influence, Cynegils of Wessex was baptised in 635. Peada, heir to the vigorous pagan Penda of Mercia, followed in 653, but paganism was difficult to extirpate. There was also tension between the Northumbrian church and the authority of Rome but, as a result of the support of King Oswy of Northumbria at the Synod of Whitby (664), Roman customs over the tonsure and the date of Easter prevailed, and the authority of the monastery of Iona over the Northumbrian church was broken. Christianity meant stronger links with the Continent; St Wilfrid (634-709), Abbot of Ripon, who played a prominent role in opposing the Iona rites at Whitby, studied at Rome, ministered in Lyon, and was consecrated bishop at Compiègne.

Such cross-Channel connections were notably beneficial to cultural development, discernible above all in stone carving and manuscript illumination. England was united in religion long before it was united politically, Bede, a Northumbrian monk, writing his *Ecclesiastical History of the English People* in 731, while the canons of the synod of Hertford (672) were issued for and applied to the whole English church. Bishoprics were founded and diocesan boundaries reorganized; and a strong monastic tradition (with houses such as Jarrow, Monkwearmouth and Lindisfarne) influenced the nature of kingship. Many monasteries were founded by or closely associated with the rulers and nobles of the period. From the late seventh century, monastic churches were constructed at important centres, though most local parish churches were probably not founded until the tenth and eleventh centuries. Christianity meant the beginnings of written law, not least to protect churchmen and their property, and the use of written instruments to convey rights in land. It also served as a source of legitimation different to the warrior prowess that had earlier been so important. Nevertheless, military and political strength still determined which of the kingdoms was to prevail. It was responsible for the power of Offa of Mercia (757-96), whose charters may have employed the term 'King of the English', and who controlled such formerly independent kingdoms as Essex, Lindsey, East Anglia, Kent and Sussex; and also for the continued independence of Northumbria and Wessex, though the latter recognized Mercian protection in 786. Feuds within and between royal families and between tribes ensured that society remained violent, the ethos of heroism revealed in the epic poem *Beowulf* being one of glory won through fighting.

Offa is most often linked with the earth dyke built to prevent the Welsh from raiding Mercia, an impressive display of resources and organization, though it is not certain that it was actually Offa who built it. The combined length of this dyke and the related Wat's Dyke was 149 miles, longer than the Antonine and Hadrian's walls, and the building of it must have entailed considerable organization, a testimony to the administrative strength of Mercian England. It was not, however, from Wales that Mercian power was to be challenged decisively. As with the Roman empire, the Anglo-Saxon world was to suffer as a result of internal division and 'barbarian' attack though, unlike the Romans, the Anglo-Saxons did not have a unitary state. Wessex rejected Mercian protection in 802; Mercia was weakened in the 820s by the effort involved in the occupation of north Wales and by dynastic feuds; and in 825, after defeating the Mercians at Wroughton, Egbert of Wessex conquered Kent, Essex, Surrey and Sussex. Mercia fell to Egbert in 829 and Cornwall in 838, and in 829 Northumbria acknowledged his overlordship, but this dominance proved to be transient: effective control was beyond the capability of any one of the kingdoms and Mercia was soon independent again.

Meanwhile the Vikings, raiders from Denmark and Norway, had struck. The limited amount of land available for cultivation in Scandinavia, the opportunities for raiding and settlement in nearby prosperous and fertile lands, and their vulnerability to the seaborne operations that the Scandinavians could mount so well, led to an explosion of activity from the late eighth to the late eleventh centuries. Viking longboats, with their sails and steering rudders, were effective ocean-going ships but could also, as a result of their shallow draught, be rowed in coastal waters and up rivers even if there was only three feet of water. The most dramatic results were the establishment of Swedish power in Russia and Norwegian settlements in Iceland, Greenland and, possibly, Newfoundland (Vinland), but in western Europe the Danes campaigned extensively in northern France, establishing themselves in Normandy, while the British Isles, with their proximity to Scandinavia and their vulnerability to marine raid and invasion, were extensively attacked. The Norwegians overran the Orkneys, the Shetlands, the far north of Scotland and much of its west coast, as well as coastal regions of Ireland.

England had been free from continental invasion for two centuries, but in 789 the Danish ships were first recorded and in 793-94 the pagan Danes brutally sacked the great Northumbrian monastic sites of Lindisfarne and Jarrow. Viking pressure increased in the 830s and 840s, with frequent attacks on southern England. The kings of Wessex played a major role in resisting these attacks. Egbert defeated a joint Viking-Cornish

army at Hingston Down (838); his son Aethelwulf defeated a Danish force at Aclea (851); and the latter's son Alfred was to save Wessex by his efforts. From the mid-ninth century the Vikings came not to plunder, but to conquer and stay. Danish invaders took up winter quarters in Thanet in 850 and Sheppey in 854. The Danish 'Great Army' abandoned operations in northern France and overran East Anglia in 865 and Northumbria in 866-67, and York was stormed in 866. Wessex, which was attacked in 871, owed its survival in part to the skill of King Alfred (871-99), although the struggle was a desperate one and Wessex came very close to total defeat, both in 871 when the Danes won four of the six battles mentioned by name, and in 878. In 871, 876 and 877 Alfred's peace-making with the Danes involved both the paying of tribute and the exchange of hostages. Wessex's resistance encouraged the Danes to turn to the conquest of Mercia. King Burgred fled to Rome in 874, his successor Ceolwulf was appointed by and paid

Above: The organization of the English church *c.* 850, with known or likely diocesan boundaries.

Left: Offa's Dyke. This earth dyke, built to prevent the Welsh from raiding Mercia, implies the existence of impressive resources and organization. The combined length of this dyke and the related Wat's Dyke was 149 miles, longer than the Antonine and Hadrian's walls together, and the building of it is a testimony to the administrative strength of the Mercian state.

tribute to the Danes, and in 877 Mercia east and north of Watling Street became Danish. Extensive Danish settlement is indicated by the large number of Scandinavian place-names ending in *-by* and *-throp*. Church activity was much disrupted where they settled: the bishoprics of Hexham, Lindsey, Elmhan and Dunwich disappeared, while episcopal seats moved from Leicester and Lindisfarne to Dorchester-on-Thames and, eventually, Durham. The Danes also settled in Northumbria in this period, while the Norwegians established a base at Dublin in 841 and in the first two decades of the tenth century colonized the coastline of north-west England, invading the Wirral from Dublin in 902. Scandinavian place-names are quite extensive in Cumbria and coastal Lancashire.

In 878 a sudden attack forced Alfred to flee from Chippenham to the Somerset levels (marshes) at Athelney. His riposte led to victory at Edington (878), which was followed by a treaty leaving the Danes with what became known as the Danelaw; that is, England east and north of a line from Chester to London. London itself was conquered by Alfred in 886. The end of successful Danish attacks enabled Alfred to accumulate

wealth and begin minting good pennies, a clear sign of a well-established kingdom. A further Danish attack in 892-96, as the 'Great Army' returned from France where it had gone after Edington, was unsuccessful.

Alfred then turned to strengthening Wessex, building a fleet, creating a more effective system of military recruitment, and constructing a system of fortified towns. Existing towns had their walls restored or new ones constructed, while new *burhs* were established, a process that was continued by Alfred's successor Edward and by his daughter, Aethelfled, who ruled English Mercia, the area, south and west of Watling Street, not settled by the Danes. Alfred's power and prestige were increased by the earlier destruction of the other Anglo-Saxon ruling houses at the hands of the Danes, and by Alfred's sensitivity in handling the Mercians. Similarly, the Viking invasions of Scotland played a role in the growing power of the kingdom of the Scots. A close relationship between the monarchy of Wessex and the archiepiscopal see of Canterbury was another result of the Danish attacks. As with other kingdoms, a succession of able adult male rulers was crucial. Defence under Alfred was followed by conquest under his heirs. Edward the Elder (899-924), Athelstan (924-39) and Edmund (939-46) conquered East Anglia, eastern Mercia and Yorkshire; the kings of Wessex brought modern England under their authority. Edward overran the Danish bases in eastern Mercia and built forts in the north-west Midlands, including Manchester (919) and Rhuddlan (921), to limit the danger of attack from the Norwegian kingdom of Dublin. The defeated Danes were allowed to keep their lands and the Danelaw retained distinctive features, including its own legal system. English Mercia was absorbed by Wessex after the death of Aethelfled (918). In 923 the rulers of Scotland, Northumbria, Strathclyde and the Welsh kingdoms accepted Edward's lordship, giving the overlordship of Britain some substance. In 927 Athelstan captured York, in 934 he invaded Scotland, and in 937 he defeated a united army of Scots, Strathclyde Britons and Norse (Norwegians) from Ireland at Brunanburh. He formed alliances with leading continental rulers, fixed the Wye as the boundary with South Wales and restricted Cornish power to west of the Tamar. Despite formidable resistance from the Yorkshire Danes, they were finally reduced, Eric Bloodaxe, their last king, being killed in an ambush in 954.

The expanding state, ruled by the house of Wessex, also developed internally, emulating much of the government of Carolingian France. Royal authority was re-established, law and order organized, and a county or shire system consolidated and extended into areas reconquered from the Danes, who were also quick to adopt Christianity. The shires were in turn divided into hundreds and, in Scandinavian areas, wapentakes, responsible for maintaining law and order. Their public courts were a link between rulers and

Below: Early Viking raids on the Northumbrian coast in the eighth century were followed by more wide-ranging attacks on the English coast in the first half of the ninth.

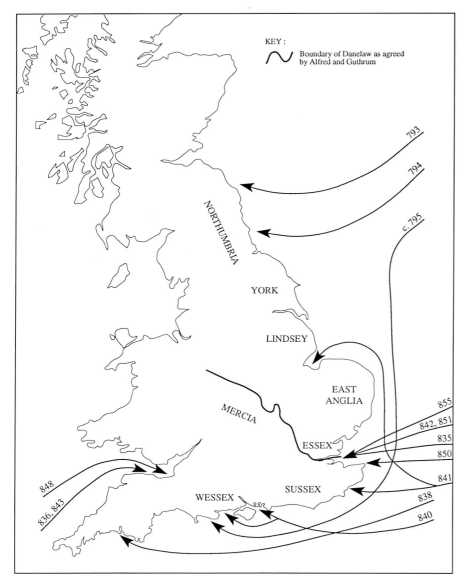

KEY:

∿ Boundary of Danelaw as agreed by Alfred and Guthrum

the fairly numerous free groups in society. Regional groupings or localities, based on and sustained by the practice of administration, thus developed. Government was largely decentralized, through shires and hundreds, though controlled with sophistication through writs. There was also a system of assessment for taxation and military service based on hides, the hide being the amount of land deemed necessary to support a peasant family. The coinage was improved, and under Edmund's son Edgar (959-75) it was reminted on average every six years, a major administrative achievement that was organized from at least 70 mints. The management by reminting of what was effectively a national currency permitted the adjustment of coin weights, with corresponding benefits to the rate of exchange and foreign trade. The state of the coinage indicated both the extent of a cash economy, in which trade, domestic and foreign, played a major role, and the growing use of coin in administration: subjects paying taxes; rulers spending money.

The church was closely linked with royalty, not least in the multiplicity of royal saint-cults, and an ecclesiastical revival took place that was largely monastic in inspiration. Under Edgar there was a continental-style reform of the monasteries, in reaction to the decay of monastic life in the ninth century, and new houses were established that owed much to Dunstan, Archbishop of Canterbury (960-88). Canterbury, Sherborne, Winchester and Worcester all became monastic cathedrals. Bishop Aethelwold of Winchester and Archbishop Dunstan together composed a common monastic rule based on continental Benedictine practice. The church was well endowed, and the total income of monasteries and nunneries in January 1066 was far greater than that

Below: Lindisfarne Priory, Holy Island, Northumberland, was plundered by Vikings in 793. As a result of raids, Lindisfarne was abandoned in 875 and the clergy, with the relics of St Cuthbert, moved first to Chester-le-Street in 883 and then to Durham in 995.

Right: Anglo-Saxon ivory of *c.*1000 showing the Virgin and Child. The flowering of Anglo-Saxon art in the hundred years before the Norman Conquest is associated particularly with Winchester and the reforming work of St Aethelwold, bishop of Winchester 963-84. It is best represented by manuscripts, which survive in some numbers; ivories such as this are more rare, because more fragile.

of the king. In the late seventh and eighth centuries the Anglo-Saxon church provided missionaries, such as Boniface and Willibrord, to help convert Germany and the Low Countries to Christianity, a sign of the vitality of English Christianity, and it sent others to Scandinavia in the late tenth and early eleventh centuries. Monastic revival provided the context for literary and cultural activity, including manuscript illumination, stone carving and embroidery.

By the eleventh century nucleated settlement was widespread in lowland England. The foundation in the tenth and eleventh centuries of numerous local parish churches may have been linked to a greater popular interest in the faith, but can also be attributed to the nucleation of rural settlement, which probably reflected more settled farming systems, and to the growth of local manorial lordship. Hereditary tenure of land developed, alongside a closer definition of the status, rights and duties of *thegns* (nobles), though it is unclear how far some of the developments of the tenth and eleventh centuries may have been anticipated earlier, but emerge more clearly in this period due to the nature of the surviving evidence. Thus bookland, land granted in perpetuity by charter, had been granted to

Right: Britain as represented on the Cotton world map. This tenth- or eleventh-century map was drawn up in England, but is a copy of a world map constructed in the Roman period. Several early-medieval writers also believed that the British Isles lay close to north-west Spain.

secular individuals since at least the reign of Offa. Land was held in return for service in what was very much a service aristocracy: service to the king led to gains of land and status. Alfred had owed much to those whom his adviser and biographer Asser termed his 'noble followers and vassals', and the personal loyalties of the war band were given territorial form, regularity and aristocratic continuity in the tenth century.

This process was not new, but it was given a new range and political complexion by the extent of the kingdom, for Wessex had become what was later termed the Old English monarchy. This state was still very much centred on Wessex. The surviving evidence suggests that Athelstan alone among the tenth-century rulers spent much time in Mercia, and that the kingdom was administered from Hampshire, Wiltshire, Dorset and Somerset, the four heartland shires of Wessex, and the region where the kings spent most of their time. Furthermore, the precariousness of nationhood was indicated in 957 when the Mercians and Northumbrians renounced allegiance to Eadwig in favour of his brother Edgar, although the latter became King of Wessex as well on Eadwig's death in 959. The allegiance of Northumbria to whomever ruled at Winchester remained uncertain until well into the eleventh century. A system of officials, *ealdormen*, sheriffs, port-reeves and hundredmen, linked the ruler and the localities. Land became increasingly important as a sign and source of wealth and power, in part replacing treasure in these functions. The creation in the late ninth and early tenth centuries of a system in which groups of hides were responsible for the maintenance of sections of the defences of *burhs* indicated the strength of the monarchy. Urban defence and revival were organized by the royal government. As a result of agrarian developments, especially the permanent cultivation of common fields from the tenth century and the production of wool and cloth, England became wealthy by the standards of contemporary northern Europe, and a tempting prize to foreign rulers. The power of the Old English monarchy was displayed in 973 when other British rulers made a formal submission to the king at Chester. Soon after, Aelfric, a monk educated at Winchester, wrote:

. . . King Edgar
furthered Christianity, and built many monasteries,
and his kingdom still continued in peace,
so that no fleet was heard of,
save that of the people themselves who held this land;
and all the kings of the Cymry and the Scots
that were in this island, came to Edgar
once upon a day, being eight kings,
and they all bowed themselves to Edgar's rule.

The century after Edgar's death revealed, however, that the governance and cultural life of England were still dependent on its political stability and that, as before, this could be threatened by domestic division and foreign chal-

lenge. The replacement, within England, of the multiple-kingdoms of the fifth to the early tenth centuries by a unitary kingdom was not to be reversed, but it ensured that problems of stability were more obviously national in scale. Furthermore, a single ruler was not the same as a nation state: concepts and practices of national unity were limited. The continuity of able adult leadership was broken with Edgar's death in 975. Both

Above: The assimilation of Cnut the Conqueror. As king, Cnut adopted the practices of the Old English monarchy, including its support for the Church. This miniature depicts the presentation of a large cross to the New Minster at Winchester by Cnut and his wife.

his sons were young; the elder, Edward, succeeded, but was unpopular and was murdered in 978 by supporters of the younger son, Aethelred 'the Unready' (978-1016). Like King John, Aethelred has been somewhat underrated, not least because of the hostile tone of the relevant section of the *Anglo-Saxon Chronicle*. In fact Aethelred made major efforts to improve the state's defences but, like John, he lacked the ability to command or elicit trust, both crucial aspects of kingship in an aristocratic society. This limited his ability to deal with the return of the Vikings.

Like England under the recent kings of Wessex, Scotland under Kenneth MacAlpin (c. 843-58) and much of Wales under the rulers of Gwynedd, the Viking lands had witnessed a measure of state formation that enabled them to organize larger armies. Soon after Aethelred's accession the Danes started mounting major attacks, in one of which they defeated the Essex militia under ealdorman Brihtnoth at Maldon (991). The stress on the loyalty of Brihtnoth's retinue to their lord in the poem inspired by the battle was an example of the sort of allegiance that successful lordship could elicit; a contrast to that received by Aethelred. Aethelred's attempts to buy the Danes off with 'danegeld', which began after Maldon, testify to the wealth and organization of the English state and at least £240,000 was paid, but it was unsuccessful in the long term. The massacre of Danes living in England in 1002 provoked a major response and Aethelred failed in his basic duty of protecting his kingdom, though resistance was sustained for many years. Aethelred probably faced larger armies than those that had attacked Alfred's Wessex. King Swein of Denmark led serious attacks in 1003-6 and 1013, and in 1013

resistance collapsed and Aethelred fled to Normandy. He returned when Swein died in 1014, but Swein's son Cnut continued the struggle, while divisions among the English, especially that between Aethelred and his eldest son, the energetic Edmund Ironside, handicapped the resistance. After Aethelred's death, England was divided between Cnut and Edmund in 1016 by the Peace of Alney, Cnut receiving Mercia and Northumbria. Edmund, however, died and Cnut became king of all England (1016-35). After his older brother Harold, king of Denmark, died in 1019, England became part of a Scandinavian empire. Scandinavian affairs, especially the conquest of Norway, absorbed much of Cnut's attention in the 1020s.

Cnut did not create any administrative structure to weld his empire together and in England he followed the practices of the kings of Wessex, although he introduced a number of Danes into the aristocracy and divided the kingdom into a small number of earldoms. Under his successors these were to become in effect autonomous and to play a role in the instability of the mid-eleventh century, though that was largely due to a series of contested successions. The earldom of Wessex was given to Godwin, an English protégé of Cnut, who married a Danish princess and gave Danish names to four of his six sons, including Harold. An Anglo-Scandinavian aristocracy was being created, as England looked increasingly to Scandinavia.

After the reigns of Cnut's sons, Harold and Harthacnut (1035-42), who faced serious rebellion in Norway, the house of Wessex was restored in the person of Aethelred's surviving son, Edward 'the Confessor' (1042-66). His reign, like

Below: The Norman view of the invasion. In this scene from the Bayeux Tapestry, Harold swears loyalty to William in apparent recognition of his claim to the English throne.

those throughout the entire tenth and eleventh centuries, was a period of demographic growth and agrarian expansion, but it was overshadowed by the problem of the succession, which interacted with that of the powerful earldoms. The childless Edward had little interest in the claims of his great-nephew Edgar or of the Norwegian royal house, and instead favoured the ducal house of Normandy, the family of his mother Emma. He had spent from 1013 to 1041 in Normandy as a refugee from the Vikings. His poor relations with his father-in-law Earl Godwin of Wessex (d. 1053), who had murdered Edward's brother Alfred in 1036 and who resisted Norman influence, led to a confrontation in 1051-52 in which Godwin rebelled and was exiled, but eventually returned and obliged Edward to reinstate him in favour. Edward's Norman friends, including Robert of Jumièges, whom he had made Archbishop of Canterbury in 1051, were driven from England.

Edward's death on 5 January 1066 was followed by the election or recognition of Godwin's oldest surviving son Harold as king by the Witan, the great council of the realm. Harold, Earl of Wessex and, after the king, the largest individual landowner in the country, had acquired considerable prestige from successful campaigning against Gruffydd ap Llywelyn, King of Gwynedd, who had conquered all of Wales and sacked Hereford in 1055. In 1063 Gruffydd was defeated by Harold at Rhuddlan and was soon after murdered by his followers, his head being sent to Harold. Harold claimed that Edward had granted him the kingdom on his deathbed, although Duke William of Normandy argued that Edward had promised him the throne when he visited England in 1051, and that Harold had acknowledged this claim in 1064. Harold initially concentrated his forces along the south coast in order to thwart any invasion by William, who himself began to assemble an invasion force. Contrary winds, however, prevented William from sailing and in September 1066 Harold disbanded his forces and left for London. There he heard that the Norwegians under Harold Hardrada, king of Norway, supported by Harold of England's exiled brother Tostig, had landed in Yorkshire. They defeated the local earls at Gate Fulford (20 September) and seized York, winning a measure of local support, only to be surprised and defeated in their nearby camp at Stamford Bridge on 25 September by Harold, who had marched rapidly north.

William landed at Pevensey on 28 September. Already an experienced warrior, he was, as Duke of Normandy, the head of a warlike people descended from Viking settlers. Harold pressed south in order to attack William before he could consolidate his position, but the English army was weakened by battle and fatigue. On 14 October 1066 they had to fight again, though outnumbered by about 7,000 to 5,000. Harold chose a defensive site on the slopes of a hill, as Caratacus in Wales and Calgacus at Mons Graupius had

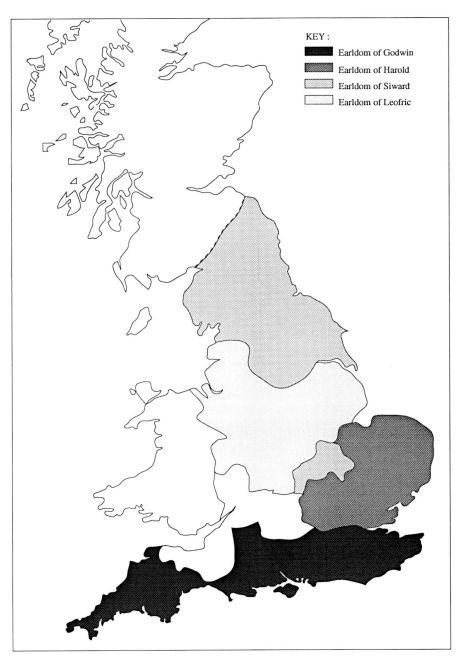

KEY:
- Earldom of Godwin
- Earldom of Harold
- Earldom of Siward
- Earldom of Leofric

done. The position, near Hastings, was a strong one, but it was disturbed by advances designed to exploit real or feigned retreats by the Normans, and after a long battle the shieldwall of the English housecarls was broken and Harold fell, as Hardrada and Tostig had done at Stamford Bridge.

Edgar was now the Anglo-Saxon claimant to the crown, but the victorious William crossed the Thames to the west of London and, as he approached the city, morale among the defendants crumbled. At Berkhamsted they submitted to William, and on Christmas Day he was acclaimed king in Westminster Abbey. The unification of England by the house of Wessex had ensured that it fell rapidly, unlike the more lengthy processes by which the Iron Age and Romano-British kingdoms had fallen to Rome and the Anglo-Saxons respectively, but comparable to the similar invasion and monarchical coup that was to be mounted by William of Orange in 1688-69.

Above: The English earldoms before the disgrace of Godwin, 1050. At the end of Cnut's reign the kingdom was dominated by three earls, Leofric of Mercia, Godwin of Wessex (both Englishmen) and Siward of Northumbria, a Dane. By 1043, when Godwin's daughter married Edward the Confessor, the Wessex family was pre-eminent, but fell briefly from power in 1051-52, when Harold's earldom of East Anglia was given to Leofric's son Aelfgar. In 1052 the Godwin family returned and forced the king to restore their lands and titles. In 1055, on the death of Siward, Harold's brother Tostig became earl of Northumbria.

3
NORMAN ENGLAND

Left: Monumental
architecture. The nave of
Durham Cathedral, begun
in 1093, completed in 1128
and vaulted between then
and 1133, is a prime
example of the
inventiveness of English
Romanesque. The remains
of St Cuthbert were
translated into the new
cathedral in 1104.

Unlike the Danish Cnut's seizure of the throne, that by William was followed by a social revolution. William, who claimed to be the rightful successor of Edward the Confessor, may not have intended this, for Englishmen who submitted at the beginning of his reign were allowed to keep their lands and William appointed two in succession as Earl of Northumbria, but the scale of resistance to the spread and consolidation of Norman rule led to the adoption of a harsher attitude. In 1068, for example, both Edgar and Earl Gospatric of Northumbria rebelled, leading William to establish garrisons at York and Durham. The latter, however, was massacred in 1069, the revolt spread, and William responded with severity. The brutalization of the population in the 'harrying of the north' in the winter of 1069-70 was followed by a normanization of both church and land, the latter largely to the benefit of those who had helped most in the conquest. Clerical appointments (and thus the control over church lands) were denied to the English and the major-

Below: Page from the Domesday Book (1086), a land survey that revealed who owned England at that date, and thus the extent of native dispossession after the Conquest.

ity of English landlords were dispossessed, a process whose consequences were recorded by the land survey of Domesday Book (1086). Most of the new rulers of the localities were Normans, though others from northern France also benefited. Alongside a ruling dynasty that linked England and Normandy, a united aristocracy had been created, while the foundation of 'daughter' houses of Norman monasteries created new links in the Church. Latin replaced English in official documents in the 1070s.

These changes reflected the strength of the resistance to William: as with Anglo-Saxon resistance to the Danes in the late ninth and early eleventh centuries it was considerable, and there was an additional factor in the shape of foreign intervention from Denmark and Scotland. Risings in Herefordshire, Kent, the north, and the south-west (1067-68), were followed by a major crisis in 1069 involving risings in the north, the West Country and the West Midlands, and Danish and Scottish invasions. Under Hereward the Wake, the Isle of Ely resisted. Lack of co-ordination among the rebellions and the failure of sustained Scandinavian assistance were crucial to the consolidation of the new regime, but the length of time that that took means that it is inappropriate to think of the Norman Conquest as being completed in 1066. Norman authority north of the Tees did not become a reality until 1072 when William led an army north, forced Malcolm III of Scotland to do homage for Lothian, installed Waltheof, a member of the native ruling house whom he had married to a niece, as Earl of Northumbria, and built a castle at Durham. In 1075 a rebellion by disaffected Normans was combined with English and Danish action, but they were unsuccessful. Waltheof, who had rebelled, was executed, and the new bishop of Durham, a Lorrainer, was made Earl, but he was killed in a fresh rebellion in 1080 and William again had to send forces to restore order. A castle was erected at what was to become Newcastle, and effective Norman power thus reached the Tyne. A Norman was appointed bishop of Durham, but Northumberland was not normanized until the reign of Henry I.

The devastation and dislocation that these conflicts brought helped to ensure that the new order created by the Normans, a warrior people, had a military logic. This was demonstrated most clearly by the construction of numerous castles, as much signs of Norman power as the roads and forts of Roman Britain and the fortified towns of late Saxon England. Early Norman castles were generally earth-and-timber constructions, for these could be built quickly and were thus a flexible means of defence, but, as with the Romans, a process of consolidation led to more imposing and permanent structures. It is entirely appropriate that the most prominent surviving remains from Norman England are stone castles, such as the White Tower in London, and stone cathedrals, such as Durham. They were expressions of power

Left The White Tower, Tower of London, built by William I in order to dominate London.

Below: William I (1066-87) from a contemporary manuscript, with the arms of England emblazoned on his shield and surcoat and on his horse's trapper.

and control, centres for government, both political and religious.

Power is an appropriate theme at this point: the expropriations of the early Norman period constituted and reflected a change that was more sweeping than anything subsequent in English history: the only comparison is with the destruction of Catholic power and the expropriation of Catholic lands in late seventeenth-century Ireland. Castles were royal or private; they were the centres of power for royal government and of what has been termed the feudal system. Although the latter is generally attributed to the Norman Conquest, aspects of it existed in Anglo-Saxon England and might have become stronger even without the Conquest. The essential characteristics of the system were the personal relationship, cemented in an act of homage, between lord and vassal. In this relationship the lord promised support and protection in return for service, principally military, and the granting of lands, or fiefs, to vassals, again in return for, principally military, service. Anglo-Saxon grants, in contrast, contained no demand for military service, although as a consequence of their rank, ealdormen and thegns were expected to provide such service.

Norman lords held their estates by a military tenancy, obliging them to provide a number of knights for service roughly proportionate to the size of the estate, an obligation that was usually discharged by enfeoffing the required number with lands of their own in return for service. These relationships epitomized an obvious aspect of pre-'modern' society, namely the absence of a clear distinction between the sovereign power and a citizenry enjoying equal rights and status, and instead the pervasive impact both of different privileges and of relationships joining ruler and ruled which were deliberately personal rather than distant and impersonal. These relationships were to be crucial to medieval politics: it was not

Above: Castles constructed by the Normans by 1086.

Right: The seal of William II (Rufus).

shires and their courts, with only a few exceptions, remained public institutions, and that the office of sheriff, with the same few exceptions, did not become hereditary. This was a sign of the power of the Norman monarchs.

Initially designed to assist in the consolidation of Norman rule, castles rapidly lost their function of holding down the English, for the latter were turned into a conquered people remarkably fast. Although considerable assimilation took place, there is no comparison with the Roman attempt to co-opt and romanize local elites: the Normans were too land-hungry, and they had a different ethos from that of the Romans. Castles, however, were swiftly required for another function: dealing with disputes within the Norman elite. In addition, the energy and strength of Norman England were expressed in a determination to push the frontiers back, and castles played a crucial role in this process.

Rivalry within the Norman elite reflected competition between nobles, disputes between them and monarchs, and, most seriously, succession problems in the Norman dynasty. Impartibility (undivided inheritance) vied with the practice of all members of a family having a claim; and while male primogeniture (succession by the eldest male child) became the rule very quickly, it was resisted by other claimants. William I (1066-87) died as a result of injuries sustained when thrown by his horse in the French town of Mantes, which he had burnt as a result of a border conflict. William left Normandy to his oldest son Robert, who was in rebellion against him when William died, and England to the second, William II, known from his red hair as 'Rufus' (1087-1100). The latter tried to reunite the inheritance and, after some fighting, Robert pawned Normandy to William in 1096 in order to raise funds to go on the First Crusade. Politically and militarily successful, Rufus became unpopular with the Church because of his treatment of it, though he had a very high reputation in lay knightly circles. In 1092 he entered Cumbria with an army; the area had for most of the century been in the hands of an English family, but Malcolm III of Scotland had been acknowledged as overlord in 1058. Rufus created a town and built a castle at Carlisle, established a Norman ally at Kendal, and made the Solway and the Liddel the northern border of the kingdom. He was also successful against Norman rebels and the French. By leaving bishoprics vacant Rufus was able to enjoy their revenues, while a dispute with Archbishop Anselm of Canterbury, over Rufus' lack of support for ecclesiastical reform and his hostility to papal authority, led Anselm to leave the country in 1097. Rufus' death in the New Forest was probably a hunting accident.

Rufus was succeeded in England by his younger brother, Henry I (1100-35). Robert, who had taken part in the capture of Jerusalem (1099), returned to Normandy in 1100 and in 1101 invaded England, but Henry persuaded him to renounce

just that the nobility were powerful, but also that it was accepted that they should have close relations with the monarch. It was noteworthy, however, that in England, unlike France, the

his claim to the throne. Relations between the two brothers remained poor, however, and in 1105 Henry invaded Normandy; he defeated Robert at Tinchebray in 1106 and conquered Normandy, imprisoning his brother until his death in 1134. The duchy had a long land frontier and aggressive neighbours in the kings of France and counts of Anjou. Furthermore, the creation of the Anglo-Norman polity upset the political stability of northern France. Just as Cnut had concentrated on Scandinavia, so the often brutal Henry devoted most of his energies to successfully consolidating his position in northern France, by war and diplomacy. Norman power was extended by bringing the neighbouring principalities of Maine and Brittany under control, and Louis VI of France was defeated at Brémule (1119). It was important to keep England and Normandy together, because so many barons had lands on both sides of the Channel.

The costs of Henry's protracted conflicts were in large part met by England, the administration being conducted by the Exchequer, which was able to provide a regular and methodical collection of royal revenues and control of expenditure. The precocious administrative development of England was in part a result of Henry I's concentration on Normandy; means had to be found of ruling England efficiently in the absence of the king. In part it also resulted from the application of new ideas and methods, notably the abacus, used as the basis of Exchequer methods of calculation, though much of the governmental machinery of the Old English monarchy was continued. Old institutions were used for the benefit of new rulers with particular concepts of justice and government and novel problems, especially those arising from the Norman link. Both royal and ecclesiastical government therefore changed appreciably. The expansion of royal judicial activity under Henry I, and the appointment by the crown of local and itinerant justices, were signs of a more sophisticated and settled administration. Thanks to an adroit mixture of ruthlessness, patronage and consultation with the magnates, and his effective administration, Henry kept England stable, although the *Anglo-Saxon Chronicle* presents a picture of an oppressively predatory government.

Stability was jeopardized by the succession. Henry I failed in the most crucial obligation of a monarch, that of leaving an uncontested heir. He was very fertile, siring over twenty illegitimate children, but his only legitimate son, William, died in the wreck of the *White Ship* in 1120 and, despite his remarriage, there was to be no other son. Henry's hopes therefore rested on his daughter, Matilda, who in 1128 married Geoffrey Plantagenet, heir to Anjou. When Henry died in 1135, however, the throne was seized by the initially popular Stephen of Blois (1135-54), son of William I's daughter Adela. Matilda landed in 1139 and captured Stephen at the battle of Lincoln (1141). Her haughty behaviour lost her

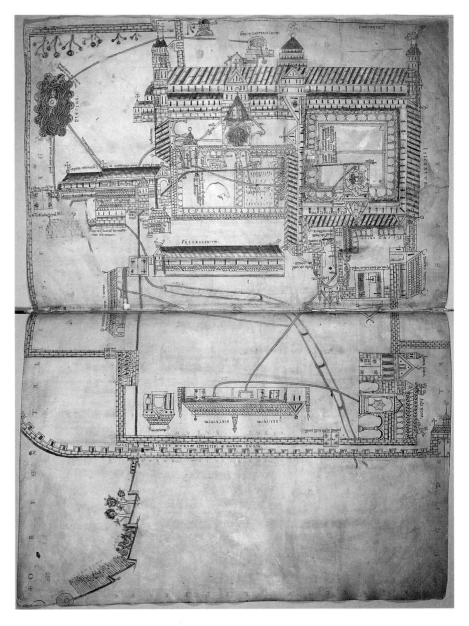

London, however; she was defeated at Winchester by Stephen's wife Matilda; and she had to exchange Stephen for her captured half-brother Robert of Gloucester (1141). Prominent nobles, such as John the Marshal in Wiltshire and Hampshire, used the civil war to consolidate their own positions and pursue their own interests. Local authority was seized by such nobles and much of Henry I's system of government collapsed. Stephen's reign acquired a reputation as a period of anarchy when 'Christ and his angels slept'. In 1144 Geoffrey completed the conquest of Normandy and in 1152 his heir Henry invaded England. The nobility on both sides wanted peace and their lands on both sides of the Channel, and in 1153 they obtained the Treaty of Westminster. Stephen was to remain king, but he was to adopt Henry as his heir. Stephen died within a year and the Angevin dynasty came to the throne in the person of Henry II (1154-89).

Norman England thus ended, as it had begun, in war. Indeed conflict had been the dominant theme of the period: the conquest of England, campaigns against Welsh and Scots, frequent

Above: The magnificence of the Church. The earliest known local map from England, this plan of Canterbury Cathedral with its monastic buildings dates from the 1150s, and is designed to show improvements made under Prior Wibert; red and green lines indicate a new water system.

Above: Redemption for the saved. The Archangel Michael brings an armful of souls to God, from a twelfth-century psalter made for a nunnery at Shaftesbury.

tary matters, while the cathedrals and churches of the period demonstrate that the same was true of expenditure on the church. In 1138, for example, Stephen's influential brother Henry of Blois, Bishop of Winchester, is reported to have begun building six castles. In some respects this consistent expenditure had a more serious impact on the lives of the people of Norman England than the individual wars of the period. The most serious, the civil wars of Stephen's reign, were traditionally regarded as devastating, though more recently, as with the Wars of the Roses, there has been a tendency to reduce earlier assessments of their destructiveness. Nevertheless, it is worth considering the psychological costs of a lengthy civil war, and the impact of an abrupt change on people who had known over three decades of civil peace under Henry I. More significantly, the wars of the period placed greater weight on the already-strong military values of society. England was not unique in this emphasis, but it was an essential feature of her society.

The other essential characteristics of society were determined by environment, technological level and socio-cultural inheritance. The Judaeo-Christian tradition, clearly enunciated in the teachings and laws of the Church, decreed monogamy and forbade polygamy, marriage with close kin, incest, homosexuality, abortion, infanticide, adultery, pederasty and bestiality. Birth was stipulated as the purpose of matrimony, and was condemned outside it. Divorce was very difficult. This moral 'agenda' was decreed and enforced with greater vigour after the disruption of the ninth- and early eleventh-century Viking invasions, and even more so after the Norman Conquest, though the effectiveness of this enforcement was probably limited until the bureaucratic developments of the twelfth century.

The Norman Conquest led to a reassertion of episcopal authority, a further expansion of the parochial (parish) system at the expense of the older minster system, monastic revival, and the creation of a new monastic structure firmly linked to developments in northern France. New institutional developments were related to the imposition of a 'foreign' emphasis, but they also reflected a widespread movement for church reform that characterized the late eleventh century, and was supported by Archbishops Lanfranc and Anselm of Canterbury (1070-1109). Lanfranc established the primacy of Canterbury over York and the authority of the archbishops over the bishops. The diocesan system was reorganized, with some sees transferred to more major centres, for example from Dorchester-on-Thames to Lincoln, and new bishoprics founded at Ely and Carlisle. New monastic orders spread, especially the Cistercians, who by 1154 had established about 40 monasteries, including Rievaulx, Fountains, Tintern and Rufford. The reform impulse led to attempts to enforce clerical celibacy and to end the clerical dynasties that had been important among the parochial clergy. Foreign prelates

hostilities with other rulers in France and, most seriously, after the death of William the Conqueror, civil war within the Norman elite, most crucially the ruling dynasty. It was scarcely surprising that military obligation should have played such a prominent role in the social structure, that fealty, loyalty and protection should have been so crucial to political links; or that so much effort should have been expended on constructing and maintaining castles. Not all castles had massive stone keeps, although these have survived better than the initially far more numerous mottes and ringworks, which relied on earthworks. All, however, exemplify the resources, in terms of money, skill and labour, taken from a relatively poor, low-productivity agrarian economy and devoted to war and mili-

sought to discipline the mainly English lesser clergy. Lay ownership of churches declined. By 1200 the parish system, as it was substantially to continue in rural England into the modern period, had been created through a vast increase in the numbers of local churches. Most surviving medieval parish churches have an eleventh- or twelfth-century core. The Romanesque style of architecture also spread to England, bringing large churches characterized by thick walls, long vaulted naves, and massive columns and arches, as for example at Durham, Ely and Peterborough. Romanesque architecture probably arrived in England in the 1050s, for Edward the Confessor used Norman architects for Westminster Abbey, but it became much more important after the Conquest. Cultural links after 1066 were very much with France. The Conquest had brought in a French-speaking elite and it was not until the late fourteenth century that English became an acceptable language in upper-class circles.

Society was not only Christian but also male-dominated, hierarchical, deferential and patriarchal, while respect for age and authority, religious and secular, legal and law-enforcing, was crucial. Patterns of birth and death reflected the dominant role of the seasons. Society was reverential of and referential to the past. Inegalitarian social practices and institutions were taken for granted, and were also central to 'politics', which was an activity restricted to the social elite. This was a society of people with differing privileges, not common citizenship, but the basic distinction was between the sexes; women were subordinated to and expected to defer to men, and wives were represented by their husbands in court. Women, nevertheless, played a vital role in the economy. Households were economic units to which women contributed greatly; not least by making clothes and processing food. In both Anglo-Saxon and Norman England, women enjoyed some rights. In the later Anglo-Saxon period there is evidence of their inheriting, holding and bequeathing lands, while married women could control separate property. Aside from in the 'enclave' world of the nunnery, individual women could gain prominence, and Henry II's wife, Eleanor of Aquitaine, was to display considerable independence. Whatever the superior status and rights of men, relationships within marriage reflected both strength of personality and affection, a pattern that was also true of parent-child relations. And yet personality and affection operated within a context of differential power and authority. The most prominent woman in early eleventh-century England was Matilda (1102-67). Married to the Emperor Henry V in 1114, a sign of the high international standing of the Anglo-Norman kingdom and in order to fulfil the diplomatic ambitions of her father Henry I, she was widowed in 1125 and accepted as heir to Henry I, but in 1128 was obliged unwillingly to marry a fourteen-year-old. An economy of inherited wealth and an elite

Above: Damnation, a twelfth-century view of the mouth of hell from the Winchester Psalter. The inscription, in Old French, reads: 'Here is hell and the angel who closes the gate.'

Left: The twelfth-century sanctuary ring on the North Door of Durham Cathedral is a leading example of Romanesque metalwork, skilfully suggesting flesh and hair.

Above: Medieval agriculture. This lively marginal scene from the Luttrell Psalter shows the patient labourer scattering seed and his dog scaring away one predatory bird, while another gorges itself on the sack behind him.

politics of dynasty ensured that many women were treated like chattels or political counters. A society organized for military service had little independent role for women.

Inheritance was so important to the social, and thus political, system in large part because of the nature of the economic system. Land, and labour on it, were central, although the value gained as a result of most labour was limited, and the bulk of the working population was therefore able to provide only limited demand. Agriculture, by far the largest economic sector, suffered from limited knowledge and technology in, for example, power sources and the selective breeding of crops and animals. There was a shortage of fertiliser, and fields were therefore left fallow (uncultivated) for a year on a two-, three- or four-year cycle, in order to maintain soil fertility. This was a characteristic feature of the open field system, in which unhedged arable fields were divided into narrow strips and communal supervision of cultivation was important. Though sometimes seen as the standard form of medieval English agriculture, it was in fact typical of the Midlands and was largely absent from upland areas, the southern counties of Norfolk, Suffolk, Essex, Kent, Devon and Cornwall, and the north-west. In these regions pasture was predominant, though there was also some arable farming. Medieval livestock were smaller than their Roman predecessors, and meat and milk yields were lower. Most labour was manual, and it was often arduous and monotonous. Communications were relatively primitive, both for goods and for people. Long-distance bulk transport was only economic by water, but rivers were affected by freezing and drought, while sea travel was at the mercy of wind and waves. Horses were used for power and as pack animals for transport, as well as for service and pleasure. The financial instruments available for most economic activity were restricted, and the

limited nature of the training, let alone education, of most of the population further constrained economic potential.

The localized nature of the agrarian economy was very pronounced. Soil types and drainage affected agricultural activity to a greater extent than in modern Britain, where their effects can be countered by fertilisers and agricultural engineering. Thus Britain was divided into a large number of local economies. These can be summarized geologically, for example as chalk or clay; or by relief, upland or lowland; or by climate; but the variations were far more numerous, for example between regions with short- and long-wool sheep. Different rural economies entailed varied field and settlement patterns, most simply the nucleated villages of arable lowlands as against the dispersed farmsteads of pastoral uplands, with obvious consequences, in terms of contrasting social organization and personal and communal experience, which lasted for centuries. The fields in dairying parishes were enclosed with hedges early, while many sheep-corn parishes kept their common fields until the nineteenth century. Different local and regional economies also led to varying rates of wealth and economic expansion; parishes given over to sheep and corn prospered differently to dairying parishes. Thus in the thirteenth century, wool exports brought prosperity to the sheep-rearing areas of eastern England, just as in the 1730s grain exports had a similar impact in Norfolk, while the heavier clay soils of the Midlands were less profitable.

There were major fluctuations in climate, which can be assessed by a number of methods including the study of Oxygen 18 isotopes from the Greenland icecap. These indicate that after a period when it became colder (*c.* 350-450), temperatures rose and were higher than those of Britain in the 1970s, by about one degree cen

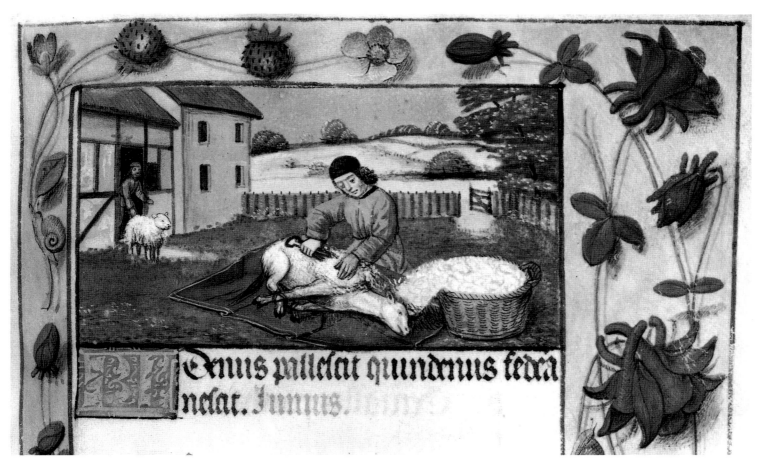

Cenus pallelat quindenus feda nclat. Junus.

tigrade in the summer, until *c*. 1180. Even small climatic changes have major environmental effects, and these included a higher tree line and the growth of crops such as vines and of forests farther north than either in the late medieval period or in the 1970s. The retreat of the icecaps led to a rise in sea level in the Anglo-Saxon period. After *c*. 1300 there was a deterioration leading to colder conditions, which persisted until a nineteenth-century rise in temperatures.

It is unclear whether global warming caused by man's impact on the environment is now in process, with warmer temperatures leading to changes in flora, fauna and agricultural conditions.

The technological basis of medieval economic life was not unvarying. Windmills, for example, were introduced in the 1170s and spread particularly fast in east England in the 1180s. There was a switch from oxen to the faster and more adaptable horses for ploughing, although this was not com-

Above: England's wealth: sheep shearing in a fifteenth-century manuscript. Wool was the leading export until the fourteenth century, although thereafter woollen cloth rose in importance.

Below. Human strength was crucial in the fourteenth-century blacksmith's shop.

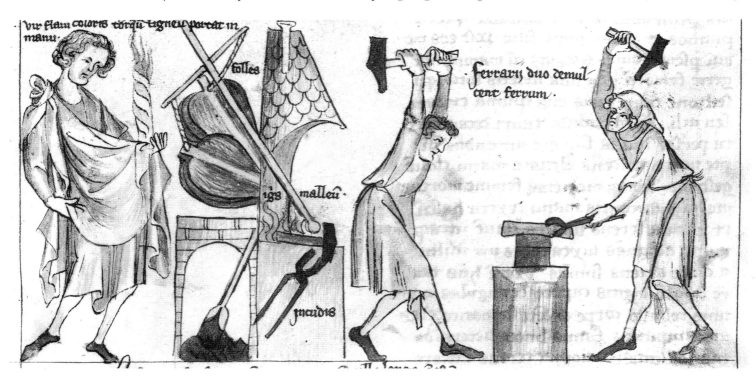

Right: The late-medieval
landscape. This is a slightly
later copy of a map drawn
*c.*1407 of Inclesmoor,
south-east of Goole in
Yorkshire, where there was
a legal dispute over rights
of pasture and peat-cutting.
The map also shows the
rivers Trent and Don.

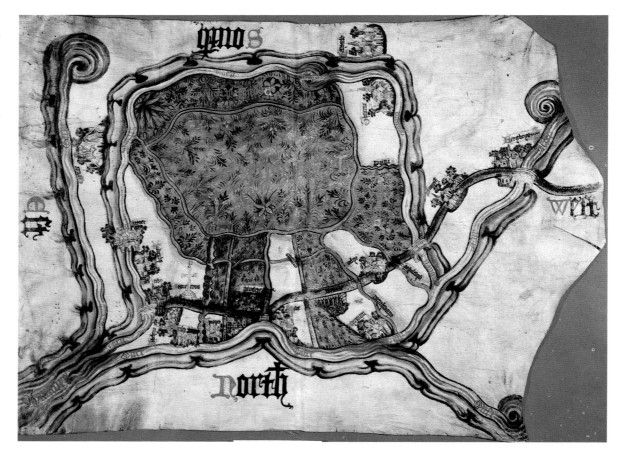

pleted until the fifteenth century. Large-scale field cultivation of legumes, which enriched the soil and provided fodder, began in the early thirteenth century, vetches being first recorded in 1268. Natural thus gave way to produced fodder. Nevertheless, the economic situation outlined above remained substantially unchanged until the last 250 years. It would, however, be misleading to imply that this prevented major changes in demographic (population), social and economic circumstances. The population expanded considerably from Domesday to the end of the thirteenth century, at least doubling to over five million, and the number and importance of towns also increased; on the eve of the Black Death, the population of London was about 100,000. Society became more complex as the distribution of wealth broadened; monetary transactions, the volume of the currency, trade, both domestic and foreign, specialization in occupations and social mobility all increased; industry spread into some rural areas; and literacy increased. Before 1201 there were only 15 markets recorded in Suffolk, but over the following century 47 new markets were founded there, while there were 67 grants of market rights in Essex between 1200 and 1350. Chattel slavery became extinct in the early twelfth century as a result of the ready availability of labour, church pressure and the power of lords over their serfs (villeins) – peasants who owed their lords often heavy labour services, as well as other obligations such as the use of the lord's mill. Given the limited scope for increasing the productivity of cultivated land, rising population entailed an ex-

pansion in the acreage of cultivated land, much woodland being cleared in areas such as the Lake District. It also led, however, to soil deterioration, falling yields and pressure on the living standards of the agricultural labour force, especially if they had little or no land. Lowland England showed signs of overcrowding in the early fourteenth century, and this was possibly responsible for a rise in the age of marriage.

The increasing role of money in the economy throughout the British Isles, and thus in revenue and taxation, helped to ensure that socio-economic shifts had direct governmental and political consequences. The feudal system established by William I was based on land, but the burdens of vassals were very speedily commuted into cash. This reflected a number of factors, including the subdivision of knights' fees, so that by the early twelfth century fractions of knights were owed as military service, fractions that were fulfilled by cash payments. In addition some lords preferred to fulfil their military obligations by employing household knights, and expecting their tenants to provide money rather than military service. The initial relationship created by the allocation of land slackened with time and the impact of hereditary property rights, and altered from that of lord and man to landlord and tenant, a cause of growing tension that probably helped to increase litigation during the reign of Henry II. Aristocratic society was never static. By 1200 what has been termed bastard feudalism, and more commonly associated with the later medieval period, was already in evidence in magnate retinues: instead of all dependents being landed tenants, some were in receipt of robes and probably fees. Far from being static or changing only slowly and with reluctance, medieval society showed a dynamic response to altering economic and political circumstances. By 1130 money rents were very common on royal manors and other large estates in England. Over the following 150 years the amount and proportion of governmental revenues coming from taxation increased substantially. This was to help in a political transformation in which the essentially personal links between monarch and greater nobles, and the consequent politics of patronage and protection, of the eleventh century (both Anglo-Saxon and Norman) became combined with a more coherent sense of national political identity, in which issues related to taxation played a major role. Thus the men who represented 'the community of the realm', principally the greater nobles, were by the late thirteenth century also able to express their views in Parliament, a new sphere of political pretension and activity and one that reflected the stress on national financial demands and national grievances that was so important in the thirteenth century.

Economic and institutional changes were vital to this development, but so also was the crucial legacy of Norman England: war, stemming from continuous confrontation with a neighbouring state. The Viking attacks on England, although serious, and in turn fatal to all the native dynasties (to Wessex in 1016, though it re-emerged with Edward the Confessor), were also episodic. The Welsh and the Scots were only able to impinge on frontier areas, although in 1018, after the battle of Carham (one of the more underrated battles of the period), Northumbria was obliged to abandon its claims to Lothian, while at about the same time the Scots also acquired the kingdom of Strathclyde, which they had reduced to client status in the ninth century. After 1066, however, England was part of a state that spanned the Channel; one that found itself obliged to ward off the ambitions of other expanding states, most significantly the kingdom of France. The

continuous military effort that this entailed was to be a central theme in the three centuries that followed the death of Stephen in 1154. Indeed, from the Roman conquest in the first century onwards, a united England was often to be politically associated with part of the Continent: as under the Romans (78-409), Cnut and his sons (1016-42), the medieval rulers (1066-1453) and the Hanoverians (1714-1837). The nature of this relationship was far from constant, but the resultant political strains were most apparent in the medieval period.

Above: Making vestments; the material is being cut into a robe ornamented with gold and jewels.

Left: War was a continuing theme throughout the Norman and Angevin period; battle scene from a fourteenth-century manuscript.

4
MEDIEVAL EMPIRES: ENGLAND

1154-1453

Left: This map of Britain by Matthew Paris, mid-thirteenth century monk at St Albans, was drawn to accompany his chronicles. Rivers play a major role, Hadrian's and the Antonine walls are marked, but northern Scotland is largely unknown territory.

Between 1154 and 1453 England was involved in the quest for empire, both in Britain and in France, although this was not a term that contemporaries used, as to them Empire meant the German empire. This quest was due largely to the ambitions of her rulers, who saw themselves not simply as kings of England but as rulers of or claimants to the wider inheritance of Henry II (1154-89), and, in time, to the French throne. Unlike his Norman predecessors, Henry II's succession in England was not a signal for conspiracy and conflict: the war for succession had already been fought during Stephen's reign. Henry's most important step was his retrieval of Cumbria and Northumbria from Malcolm IV of Scotland, for the fluid Anglo-Scottish frontier reflected the respective strength of the kingdoms and it had been pushed south during Stephen's reign, despite the English victory at the battle of the Standard (1138). Until the mid-twelfth century it had been unclear whether what is now northern England would be part of England or of Scotland, but Henry II settled the matter in 1157.

Below: The French empire of Henry II. He inherited the English kingdom (which then excluded the Welsh principalities) and Normandy from his mother Matilda; Anjou, Maine and Touraine from his father Geoffrey of Anjou; and acquired vast areas of central and south-western France through his wife Eleanor of Aquitaine.

Right: Henry II (1154-89), the most powerful of England's medieval kings and one of Europe's leading monarchs.

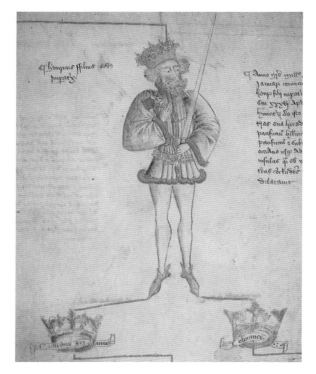

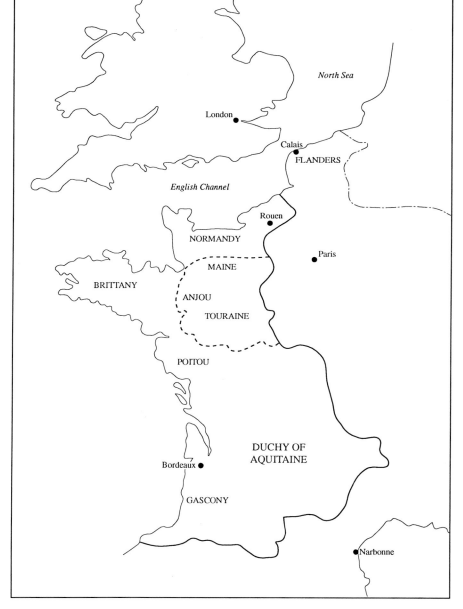

The situation in France was less happy. In 1152 Henry had married Eleanor of Aquitaine, the imperious divorced wife of Louis VII, who brought control of the duchy of Aquitaine, comprising most of south-west France. Combined with the Norman and Angevin (Anjou) inheritances, this made him the most powerful ruler in France, more so than his suzerain (feudal lord for his French territories), the King of France, and in his first twelve years Henry used this power to resolve inheritance disputes in his favour, gaining control of Brittany and more of southern France. The enmity of the French, however, ensured that when Henry's family divided over the inheritance (for like William the Conqueror, Henry II had several sons), the French kings were willing to intervene.

Such foreign intervention was a problem in Henry II's continental empire, but not in Britain. There, it was Henry's power that was dynamic. The campaigns of 1157, 1163 and 1165 made little impact on Wales, but were a sign that the situa-

tion had changed since Stephen's reign. Anglo-Norman colonization was not confined within England's far-from-fixed borders and, following initiatives by some of his nobles, especially Richard de Clare 'Strongbow', who were creating powerful lordships for themselves, Henry II intervened in Ireland in 1171, in order to establish his rights in accordance with the papal bull of 1155 from the English pope, Adrian IV. Like Wales, and in contrast to Scotland and England, Ireland was far from unified, and this provided opportunities for aristocratic and royal ambitions. A new order was established with a lordship, based on Dublin, under royal control, and English administrative practices were introduced. The extent to which this control was to be disrupted by Scottish invasion in 1315 was an indication of the value to earlier English rulers of Ireland of lack of foreign intervention. It was far more important, practicable and profitable for the ruthless Philip Augustus, King of France 1180-1223, to undermine the Angevin empire in France than in the British Isles, though later French kings were to find the latter policy a way to weaken first the English effort in France, and finally English foreign policy more generally.

Henry II is best remembered for his quarrel with Thomas Becket, Archbishop of Canterbury, which led to Becket's murder in 1170. Like a later Lord Chancellor, Sir Thomas More, who also fell out fatally with a powerful and demanding king (in his case Henry VIII), Becket was initially a friend of the monarch's. He made a stand on the rights of clerics to trial in church courts; also at stake was freedom of appeal and access to the Pope, at a time when the Papal Curia (government), under a succession of lawyer popes, was becoming effectively the legal centre of Christendom and thus a prime source of papal authority and money. Becket fled the country in 1164, when Henry turned the resources of royal judicial power against him. As with the rifts in his own family, Henry had to consider the views of a foreign power, in this case the papacy, which helped to lead him towards compromise. Returning in 1170, however, Becket was unwilling to

abide by the spirit of compromise that was necessary both if his return was to be a success and, more generally, for successful royal-papal and church-state relations. Henry's outraged explosion, 'Will no one rid me of this turbulent priest?', was taken at face value by four of his knights, who killed the Archbishop in his cathedral. Becket was canonized, and his shrine at Canterbury became a major centre of pilgrimage, but his death changed little: the balance of compromise had not shifted greatly, though restrictions on appeals to Rome were lifted and the basic immunity of criminous clerics from lay jurisdiction was confirmed.

No such upsets affected the processes of administrative development that were so important in Henry's reign, both in finance and in justice. The standardized common law, which replaced pre-Norman regional customs, gained in strength. English common law helped to consolidate England as a remarkably homogeneous state by European standards, and in the thirteenth century played a role in fostering a sense of com-

Above: The murder of Thomas Becket, graphically illustrated in a late twelfth-century Latin psalter.

Left: The Great Seal of Henry II; with its image of the king enthroned with his orb and sword, it is in a direct line of descent from Roman imperial art. Charters were authenticated by seal; those sealed with the Great Seal carried additional force.

Right: Crusader, plus
faithful horse, from the
twelfth-century
Westminster Psalter. The
international history of
medieval English
Christianity was not only
one of conflict with the
Papacy. Richard I was a
key participant in the
Third Crusade, while the
future Edward I and 300
English knights joined the
Crusade of the French king
Louis IX (St Louis) in
1270, and in 1271-72 went
on to Palestine. The
medieval knightly orders of
Hospitallers and Templars
were both established in
England.

Below: The Great Seal of
Richard I. This was lost in
a shipwreck off Cyprus, but
recovered when the body of
the king's seal-bearer was
washed ashore. It was lost
again on Richard's return
from the Crusades and he
created a new one,
requiring that charters be
resealed with it on payment
of an appropriate fee.

mon Englishness. The expansion of government activity required increasing numbers of professional administrators, a group that had first emerged clearly in the reign of Henry I. These *curiales* were mostly 'new men' who were resented by better-born nobles. The enforcement of justice and the collection of royal revenues improved and the processes of government became more effective and regular. This was shown by the introduction of regular record-keeping: the Exchequer Pipe Rolls continually from early in Henry II's reign, the Close and Patent Rolls of the Chancery from just after 1200. The development of justice was a royal initiative; land actions were begun by royal writs, law and order enforced by royal justices itinerant. Procedure was regularized through the king's actions.

The processes of government were less dependent on the personal intervention of the monarch than had been the case under the Normans, however, which was just as well as Henry II spent the greater part of his reign on the Continent. On the other hand, the crown became more dependent on financial windfalls as its landed income declined, while the improvements in the administration of justice were balanced by a striking arbitrariness on the part of the crown. Tenants-in-chief were very much at the king's will, while the greater coercive power of government made it a formidable instrument of tyranny. This was one reason for the popularity in some quarters of Becket, who had stood up to royal power, and for the immense resentment royal government aroused under John. Bureaucratic principles of

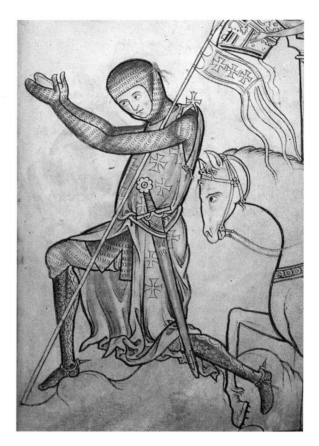

impartial government were slow to develop. In 1207-8 John wrote: 'It is no more than just that we should do better by those who are with us than by those who are against us'. The views and interests of the monarch were also crucial to government procedure. The medieval period was to witness changing patterns of royal administration, with the emphasis being either on household government or on government through Exchequer and Chancery. Under John, Henry III and Edward I the household, initially the Chamber and then the Wardrobe, was very dominant; whereas under Edward III there was far greater Exchequer control. Such variations remained the pattern during the Tudor period, and indeed medieval English monarchy prefigured Tudor government in many respects, including the scale of royal patronage and of office-holding under the crown.

Three of Henry's five legitimate sons predeceased him, and he was succeeded by his third son, Richard I (1189-99). Richard had joined his brothers in 1173-74 in their French-supported rebellion against Henry II, and thereafter had acquired considerable military experience in suppressing rebellions in the duchy of Aquitaine, which he had inherited. As king he spent an even greater proportion of his reign abroad than Henry had done. A key participant in the Third Crusade, he captured Acre and defeated Saladin at the battle of Arsuf (1191), though he narrowly failed to reach Jerusalem. Imprisoned in Germany on his way back (1192-94), his absence was exploited by his younger brother John and, more seriously, by Philip Augustus of France. Richard was ransomed for 150,000 marks, a huge sum, and a considerable tribute to English wealth and

1215 John was forced to accept the terms of what was to be later called Magna Carta in order to end what was, for him, an unsuccessful conflict. This charter of liberties was a condemnation of John's use of feudal, judicial and other governmental powers, for it defined and limited royal rights. Magna Carta was in effect an enormous list of everything that was wrong with government as John applied it. It covered practically everything, hence later calls for its confirmation. Baronial liberties were protected and freemen were provided with some guarantees against arbitrary royal actions. The crown alone would not be able to determine its rights. Constraining monarchs to

Left: King John (1199-1216) from a contemporary manuscript; not a man who improved with adversity.

Below: Magna Carta, an indictment of John's government and a demand for a better future.

government that the money was raised. He spent most of the rest of his reign in France recovering what had been lost during his absence, a process that led to his death in a siege.

Having no legitimate children, Richard was succeeded by his brother John. John's position was weakened by his tactless handling of his French vassals, which was exacerbated by accurate rumours that he had been responsible for the death in 1203 of his nephew Arthur, Duke of Brittany, the son of his older brother Geoffrey, who had predeceased Henry II. The determination and military success of Philip Augustus led to John losing much of his father's vast continental possessions, including Normandy and Anjou, in 1203-4. Naturally avaricious and suspicious, John was not a man who improved with adversity; he was tough and nasty, lacked the skills of man-management, and could not soften the impact of intrusive and aggressive government. His efforts to raise funds to help in the reconquest of lost lands and his exploitation of the royal position aroused opposition, while a dispute over an election to the archbishopric of Canterbury led to a quarrel with a very determined adversary, Pope Innocent III. In 1208 Innocent laid England under an interdict; all church services were suspended and the following year John was excommunicated.

John was able to buy his peace with Innocent by making England a fief of the papacy (1213), but his other enemies were harder to deal with. His attempt to recover his continental inheritance ended in failure when his allies were defeated at Bouvines (1214). This helped to encourage his domestic opponents to rise in rebellion, and in

accept limitations was always, however, a problematic course of action, for the effectiveness of such a settlement depended on royal willingness to change attitudes and policy, or on the creation of a body able to force the monarch to do so. John's unwillingness to implement the agreement led his opponents to offer the throne to Philip Augustus' son, Louis. England drifted into a serious civil war and John died in 1216, shortly after the quicksands and tide of the Wash had claimed a valuable part of his baggage train.

John's son, Henry III (1216-72), was a more acceptable monarch: as a child of nine he was no threat. Helped by victory in war, especially the battle of Lincoln and Hubert de Burgh's naval victory off Dover, both in 1217, Henry's supporters drove Louis to abandon the struggle (Treaty of Lambeth, 1217). Henry did not gain effective power until 1232, but neither during his minority nor subsequently was it possible to defeat the French on the Continent and regain the lands lost by John. The disastrous 1242 Poitevin campaign damaged the king's reputation and finances, and in the Treaty of Paris (1259) Henry finally accepted losses that left him only Gascony. During Henry's minority the idea developed of restricting a ruler through written regulations and insisting that he seek the advice of the nobility. 'Great Councils' were summoned to win baronial consent and thus co-operation; Magna Carta was frequently reissued.

Henry's unpopularity was due to his granting of favour to friends and advisors who were not members of the English elite and many of whom were French; and to the fact that his government entailed as much financial pressure as the king could exert, and that there was much misrule and corruption by both royal and baronial officials. Like his father, Henry proved unable to sustain acceptable relations with his leading subjects

and, by the Provisions of Oxford (1258) and of Westminster (1259), they sought to take power out of his hands, to enforce what they regarded as good kingship. War broke out in 1264 and many of the barons, under the king's brother-in-law, Simon de Montfort, Earl of Leicester, defeated Henry at Lewes. However, they were to lose decisively at Evesham in 1265, not least because quite a number of the barons stayed loyal, while others were alienated by Montfort. Royal authority was restored, though Henry took pains to adopt a more careful attitude.

His son and successor, Edward I (1272-1307), was a warrior king: impressive as ruler, general, administrator and legislator, a dominating personality and determined monarch, firm in the defence of his rights, strong and peremptory in the maintenance of his dignity. The victor of Evesham, he was on his way back from crusade, in which he had had some success, when he heard of his father's death. Edward inherited an effective and prosperous state. He did not return to England until 1274, an indication of the ability of government to continue without the king's personal supervision. English wealth was expressed in good silver coinage, with major recoinages in 1247-48 and 1278-79. The substantial yields of royal revenues, especially judicial eyres (circuit courts conducted in each shire by itinerant royal judges), were visible in Henry's work at Westminster Abbey and at palaces such as Clarendon; while the wealth of the country was

Left: Harlech was one of the royal castles built by Edward I to control Snowdonia. It was built in 1283-87 on a concentric pattern, with mutually supportive defences and a fortified track down to the sea. Its isolated garrison, reduced to 21 men, surrendered to Owen Glendower in 1404, but was regained by the English in 1408 and was held by the Lancastrians in the Wars of the Roses until 1468. As with Offa's Dyke, it represented a formidable display of administrative as well as military strength.

indicated by such works as the new cathedral of Salisbury, completed, except for the spire, in 1220-60.

Edward had more judgment, strength of will and, crucially, military ability, than his father. After establishing himself in Gascony (what was left of Aquitaine) and England, he devoted his first years as king to Wales. Llywelyn the Great (d. 1240) and his grandson, Llywelyn ap Gruffudd, rulers of Gwynedd, the principality that controlled north-west Wales, had brought the other Welsh native principalities under their authority, and taken advantage of disunity in England under both John and Henry III to push back the frontier of Anglo-Norman advance. By the Treaty of Montgomery (1267), Henry III was forced to acknowledge Llywelyn's acquisitions and his new title of Prince of Wales. Edward was determined to reverse these losses and in 1277 invaded Wales in person, forcing Llywelyn by the Treaty of Conway (1277) to do homage and to surrender his gains. Edward received help from south Wales, much of which had been under English rule since the Norman period. A sub-

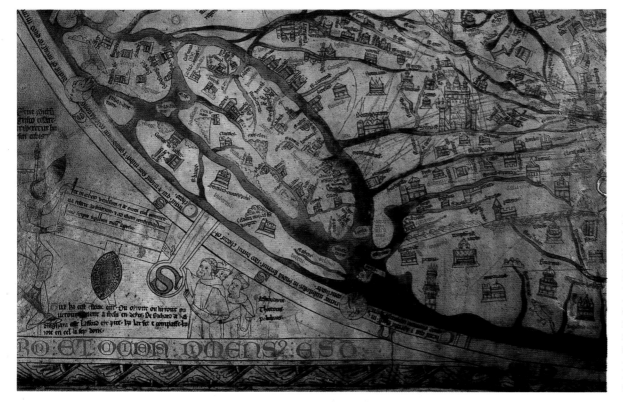

Left: Britain is shown on the edge of the map in the Hereford world map drawn by Richard of Holdingham, probably at Lincoln in the 1280s. Outside the map, Augustus Caesar is shown ordering three surveyors to measure the world. On the map, Scotland is shown as an island, with New (novo) Castle nearby, and Ireland is divided in two by the River Boyne.

Right: Scottish success obliged the English to construct new fortifications, including Dunstanburgh Castle in northern England. In 1314, the year of Bannockburn, part of the moat at Dunstanburgh was dug and the great gatehouse was under construction. In 1315 Thomas, Earl of Lancaster, was given a licence to crenellate, and after his execution in 1322 the largely complete castle remained in royal hands. Important improvements, including a new entrance, were made by John of Gaunt as Lieutenant of the Scottish Marshes. Dunstanburgh was a focal point of struggle in the Wars of the Roses; it was taken by Warwick the Kingmaker in September 1461, December 1462 and 1464 and retaken by the Lancastrians in October 1462 and the spring of 1463. The castle features in the legend of Sir Guy the Seeker, who was shown an enchanted sleeping princess in a secret chamber. Told by the guardian giant that he had the choice between a jewelled sword and an ivory horn to wake her, he blew the horn: the wrong choice. He fell senseless outside the walls, and spent the remainder of his days forlornly wandering round Dunstanburgh, haunted by the vision of what he had lost.

sequent Welsh rebellion in 1282 was crushed, and Llywelyn killed. English rule was then consolidated by the construction of a series of expensive and powerful castles, among which Beaumaris, Caernarvon, Conway, Flint, Harlech and Rhuddlan were prominent, while English common law and the shire system were introduced and the principality of Wales was eventually allocated an essentially honorific, rather than independent, position for the heirs to the English throne, the future Edward II being created Prince of Wales in 1301. Although there were to be further revolts in Wales during the reign of Edward I, they were less serious than that of 1282. Wales was to prove a more solid gain than Scotland or Ireland, though the scale of Owen Glendower's rising in 1400-8 was an indication of the extent of disaffection and the survival of separatist feeling, as well as a reminder of the potential relationship between English control over other regions in the British Isles and rebellion within England; Henry IV's position was challenged on a number of occasions.

Edward I had less success with Scotland which, by the end of the thirteenth century, had a long history as an independent kingdom. Though the kings had only limited authority over much of their kingdom, especially Galloway, the Highlands and the Isles, the kingdom of Scotland, under the able line of Canmore, was a political presence far stronger than the principalities of Wales; Scotland was more united than Wales or Ireland. Thus the movement of Norman nobles into Scotland in the twelfth century, families such as Bruce, Hay, Lindsay and Menzies, was not a piecemeal conquest of the more vulnerable lands, as in Wales, but an immigration reflecting the sponsorship of the kings of Scotland. It was related to the introduction of Norman administrative methods by David I (1124-53), who had spent his youth at the court of Henry I and held English lands, and by his successors. This normanization, which also affected the church, was

not, however, accompanied by the social and cultural revolution that mass expropriation had brought to England after the Norman Conquest. The subsequent strength of the Scottish monarchy indicates that such a revolution was not a necessary condition of the development of the English state, and raises the question as to how the Anglo-Saxon state would have developed without invasion.

The thirteenth-century Scottish kingdom was certainly strong. The Norman military machine of knights and castles, improved administrative mechanisms, especially the use of sheriffs, the skill of the rulers, and the economic expansion of the period, served as the basis for an extension of royal authority. In 1192 the papacy granted William the Lion a bull placing the Scottish church under the Holy See: there was to be no English ecclesiastical imperialism. This strengthened the authority of the monarchs. The sea still served as the basis of economic and thus political links, giving the Norwegians an empire that ranged far into the Atlantic. However, just as the Vikings in Ireland had been defeated at Clontarf (1014), so Haakon IV of Norway was defeated by Alexander III of Scotland at Largs (1263); by the Treaty of Perth (1266) Norway ceded the Western Isles and the Isle of Man to Alexander.

Under Alexander, brother-in-law of Edward I, Canmore power reached its zenith but, as so often, dynastic chance was to bring weakness and strife. Alexander died in 1286, to be succeeded by a young grand-daughter, Margaret, the Maid of Norway. Edward I saw this as an opportunity to increase his family's power, and in 1289 secured the Treaty of Salisbury by which the marriage of Margaret and the future Edward II was agreed. The rights and laws of Scotland were to be preserved but, in essence, the union of the crowns that was eventually to happen in 1603 seemed likely in 1289. Had this taken place, it is interesting to consider how far the two countries could have remained united and, if so, how far a process of convergence, political, administrative and cultural, would have occurred.

Margaret died en route for Scotland in 1290, however, leaving a number of claimants to the throne. Edward I was asked to adjudicate and in 1291 had his overlordship over the crown of Scotland recognized by the claimants, before eventually declaring John Balliol king. Balliol swore fealty and did homage to Edward; English hegemony in the British Isles seemed established. Edward's subsequent policy, however, not least his encouragement of appeals by Scots to English courts, was, unacceptable to many Scots and, with tension rising due to Scottish links with Philip IV of France, who had seized Gascony in 1294, Edward invaded Scotland (1296). He personally led the successful assault on Berwick, in which several thousand Scots were put to the sword. After a successful campaign in which the Scots were defeated at Dunbar, Balliol surrendered the kingdom to Edward. Edward's triumph was shortlived, as in 1297 William Wallace rebelled and defeated the English at Stirling. He then revealed the danger of a hostile Scotland by ravaging Northumbria. Edward I was then in Flanders, fighting the French and their allies: yet again continental commitments were weakening the position of the English crown within Britain.

A truce with France enabled Edward I to march north in 1298. Attacking Wallace at Falkirk, he found the Scottish pikemen massed in tightly packed schiltroms to defy the English cavalry, but they were broken by Edward's archers. Further campaigns accomplished territorial gains, but Edward's forces were over-stretched and resistance was not crushed, though Wallace was captured and executed in 1305. The following year Robert Bruce rebelled, and in 1307 Edward I died at Burgh-on-Sands on his way to campaign against Bruce. Edward II (1307-27) had inherited none of his father's military ability or ambition, and the less intense pace of English military pressure helped Bruce (Robert I), to consolidate his position in Scotland. In 1314 Edinburgh fell to

Bruce and Stirling promised to surrender if not relieved. Poorly led by Edward, the English relieving force was defeated at Bannockburn by the Scottish army, pikemen on well-chosen ground routing cavalry. Edward fled and, after the surrender of Stirling, the English position was challenged both in Ireland, which was invaded by Robert I's brother Edward Bruce in 1315, and in northern England. In 1318 Berwick fell and in 1319 the Scots ravaged Yorkshire. English counter-attacks were unsuccessful and in 1328, by the Treaty of Northampton, Scottish independence was recognized. This was not the end of the Scottish Wars of Independence. The treaty was highly unpopular in England, even in the northern shires which had suffered most from Scottish attacks, and it was always likely that the war would resume. In 1332 Edward Balliol claimed the throne and declared himself Edward III's liegeman. David II drove Balliol out, but in the following year English archers under Edward III defeated the Scots at Halidon Hill and captured Berwick; and in 1334 Edward III restored Balliol and received Lothian from him. The weak Balliol was driven out, however, and the English invaded Scotland again in 1335, 1336 and 1341, holding, for a while, much of the country, but Edward III had to divert most of his resources to war with France. David, urged on by his French allies, was able to invade England in 1346, but he was defeated at Neville's Cross, Durham, taken prisoner and held captive until 1357. Edward III invaded Scotland again in 1356, but peace was made in 1357.

England was far stronger than Scotland, and it is worth speculating whether she could have conquered her but for the diversion of her strength to war with France, a conflict whose scale is suggested by the term 'The Hundred Years War'. War arose with Scotland in 1296 largely because of the quarrel from 1293 between Edward I and Philip IV of France, in which the Scots became involved. Had there not been that additional complication, Edward might have run Balliol on a looser rein, and the Scots might have acted

Left: A battle scene from Matthew Paris's *Chronica Majora.* Paris was a monk at St Albans, where there was a strong tradition of writing history. In 1236 he succeeded Roger of Wendover as the historiographer of the house and continued the *Chronica Majora* to 1259, when he died. He ranged widely for his subject matter, covering political developments, natural phenomena including floods and famines, and novelties, such as the first buffaloes to arrive in England. Paris complained about the abuses of Henry III's court, his foreign favourites and the promotion of foreigners in the Church, and was a keen defender of the interests of his monastery. He also wrote an abridgement, the *Historia Minor.*

Above: The Holy Family's Flight to Egypt, from the south choir aisle of Canterbury Cathedral, twelfth-thirteenth century. One of the great products of medieval culture, stained glass was closely connected with the Gothic cathedral, playing a symbolic and didactic as well as a decorative role. Much English glass was destroyed following the Reformation.

more cautiously. Again in the 1330s Scotland mattered largely because, like the Low Countries, it was an area in which Edward III and Philip VI were competing. David II was an exile under Philip's protection in 1334-41. In addition, war with France did not preclude attacks on Scotland, as in 1346 and 1356. The vulnerability of the centres of Scottish power and economy to English invasion is notable in any account of English attacks. In 1335 Edward III found no difficulty in occupying Glasgow and Perth, and in 1336 north-east Scotland; in 1356 Henry of Lancaster occupied Perth, Elgin and Inverness. The Scots avoided battle and concentrated on harrying the English force and denying them supplies, a policy that thwarted Edward's invasion in 1356.

Had the English been able to maintain and support a permanent military presence in lowland Scotland, then the Scottish kingdom might have been so weakened and divided as to cease to be a powerful challenge. Divisions among the Scottish nobility, which greatly helped the English, might have been exploited to spread the power of the king of England, who would have been able to mount a more effective claim to the crown of Scotland, either for himself or for a protégé. The episodic military commitment dictated by Scotland's secondary role in English military policy from the late 1330s, however, exacerbated the natural logistical problems of campaigning there, and ensured that fixed positions were given insufficient support. This left the Scots with the military initiative, which was fatal to the English cause. On the other hand, it would have been staggeringly expensive to maintain enough garri-

sons and, as Scotland itself would not have been rich enough to be made to fund its own occupation, the cost would have fallen on England. Successful war in France, by contrast, went at least some way towards being self-financing.

Defeat in Scotland was matched by failure in Ireland. Edward Bruce invaded Ireland in 1315 and it has been argued that Robert I wished it conquered as a prelude, with the hope of a Welsh alliance, to a pan-Celtic invasion of England. The Anglo-Irish were defeated by the Scots, who campaigned with great savagery, until Edward Bruce was crushed and killed at Faughart (1318), one of the more important battles of the Middle Ages; the scheme for a Scottish conquest of Ireland had been wrecked. Nevertheless, English lordship in Ireland had been gravely weakened and, despite major expeditions from England in the 1360s, 1370s and 1390s, the situation continued to deteriorate. By the following century, direct English control was limited to the Pale, the area around Dublin, while the semi-autonomous Anglo-Irish lords and the independent Gaelic chieftains controlled most of the island.

This was to be one of the most important political legacies of the Middle Ages. Britain was not united politically before the religious divisions stemming from the Reformation in the sixteenth century, and the subsequent strengthening of national consciousnesses made any such process far less easy. With hindsight it is possible to emphasize the difficulty of any such task. The English relied in Scotland not on colonization but on collaboration, but it proved impossible to sustain the necessary level. The centre of English power was in the south of England, far distant from Scotland and Ireland. War in both countries posed formidable logistical difficulties for any invader; the Romans had not managed to conquer Scotland. It had already developed an effective monarchy and acquired 'modern' military techniques.

And yet the extraordinary vitality of the Normans who, through conquest, created kingdoms in southern Italy as well as England, and the fluidity of boundaries on the Continent, are reminders of the possibilities that existed. There were definite opportunities in the medieval period for enlarging the kingdom of England through marriage or conquest, and thus creating the basis of a British state, a British aristocratic elite and a British consciousness. The very fluidity of political circumstances and the element of chance that characterized the international politics of the period, a situation exacerbated by the central role of dynastic chance, the births, marriages, skill and deaths of monarchs, would necessarily have challenged any such achievement. It is unclear that any British unity could have survived the conspiracies and civil conflict of the fifteenth century. The break-up of the Union of Kalmar, joining Sweden, Norway and Denmark (1397-1523), is instructive, but so also is the unification of Spain, at least at the dynastic level, a process in which both war and marriage played a role.

If the division of the British Isles was one of the crucial political legacies of the medieval period, another was the loss, with the exception of Calais, of the continental territories of the kings of England. After the reigns of John and Henry III relatively little remained of the legacy of Henry II, but Edward I was determined to protect Gascony from the consequences of French overlordship. His ability to do so was lessened by the domestic strains produced by his policies, especially his heavy financial demands. These affected the response to the extensive reform of law and administration that he carried through by a series of statutes in 1275-90. Edward's relations with the nobility were very tense in the 1290s, and the issues of taxation and financial grievances came to play a major role. The clergy and the merchants were also alienated. There was a political crisis in 1297, with many of the nobility resisting very high taxation to pay for war and deeply unpopular demands for military service.

The situation was exacerbated under Edward's successor Edward II (1307-27), who had to face major difficulties at the very beginning of his reign, though he made them worse by his own political incompetence. Edward's inability to deal with the Scots in 1307-14 stemmed largely from his quarrels with his barons, notably over his Gascon lover, the arrogant Piers Gaveston. Edward I had banished Gaveston but his son recalled him, made him Earl of Cornwall, and gave him considerable wealth and a prominent role in the royal coronation. Edward's favour for Gaveston led to a political crisis; Edward was forced to accept Ordinances (1311) limiting royal power, and in 1312 Gaveston was murdered by nobles opposed to Edward, a murder Edward never forgave. Thomas, Earl of Lancaster, then dominated the government, until Edward was able to defeat him at Boroughbridge (1322). The Ordinances were repealed, but Edward remained distrusted and unpopular, not least because of his favour for the Despensers, father and son. Unlike an earlier homosexual monarch, William II, or indeed William III who had homosexual tendencies, Edward II was not a military king, still less a successful warrior, and he failed to conform to contemporary expectations of kingship. Lacking dignity, Edward also had unroyal tastes, such as ditching and boating. Aristocratic society depended on a widespread distribution of patronage, the crucial component of good royal lordship. The monopolization of both patronage and the king by favourites, such as Gaveston, led to aristocratic discontent, which in Edward's last years was exploited by his wife Isabella, daughter of Philip IV, 'the Fair', of France. With her lover Roger Mortimer, she overthrew and captured Edward (1326). He was deposed in favour of his son and brutally murdered in Berkeley Castle (1327). He was the first king to be murdered since Edward had been killed at Corfe in 978 (assuming that William II died acidentally). Within 160 years another three (Richard II 1400, Henry VI

1471, and Edward V 1483) had also been murdered, a testimony to the political and governmental instability of the period. The foreign and civil conflicts of Edward II's reign led to more than political instability: war taxation pressed on an overpopulated economy, hitting living standards; the north was ravaged by Scottish attacks; and, thanks to bad weather, the harvests failed in 1315, 1316 and 1322, probably causing many deaths by progressive undernourishment as well as by actual starvation.

Isabella and Mortimer ruled for the first years of the reign of Edward III (1327-77), but when Parliament met in Nottingham in 1330, Edward and his friends entered the castle through an underground passage and seized Mortimer. He was hanged and Isabella was confined in Castle Rising. Edward III possessed the ability and determination to restore royal authority in England from the depths to which it had plunged in 1327, to avenge his father's humiliations, and to reassert the position of his dynasty in France. He was also notably successful in his dealings with the barons; apart from his mistress late in his reign, he had no favourites, and he brought many of the leading barons into the royal circle as Knights of the Order of the Garter, which he established in 1348.

The international situation was altered by the extinction of the male line of Philip IV of France. Edward's mother Isabella was Philip's daughter and, as Anglo-French relations deteriorated over Gascony, Edward decided to broaden his challenge to Philip IV's nephew, Philip VI, by claiming the French throne (1337). The first two

Left: Edward III (1327-77). Son of Edward II and Isabella of France, he only began to rule in 1330, after Isabella and her lover Roger Mortimer were overthrown. He restored royal authority and prestige after the political crises of his father's reign and adopted an assertive international position, resuming war with Scotland in 1332 and laying claim to the throne of France in 1337. His victories (Halidon Hill 1333, Sluys 1340, Crécy and Neville's Cross 1346, Poitiers 1356) and successful sieges (Berwick 1333, Calais 1347) were difficult to translate into peace on terms judged acceptable, but by the Peace of Brétigny (1360) he was recognized as ruler of Calais and Gascony. In his later years he suffered losses when war with France was renewed, faced mounting domestic political problems and criticism, not least in the Good Parliament of 1376, and eventually became senile.

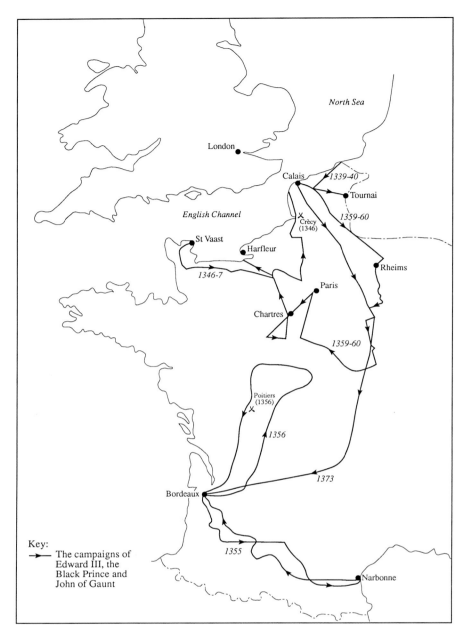

Key:
→ The campaigns of
   Edward III, the
   Black Prince and
   John of Gaunt

Above: The Hundred Years
War. The campaigns of
Edward III (1339-40,
1346-47 and 1359-60); the
Black Prince (1355 and
1356); and John of Gaunt
(1373).

Right: A marginal figure
from a fourteenth-century
pontifical, this beggar
woman suffering from
leprosy, then incurable,
carries a leper's bell to warn
the healthy of her
approach.

decades of war brought some dramatic victories.
The French fleet was crushed at Sluys (1340),
while at Crècy (1346) the French army, reliant
essentially on feudal cavalry, was routed by
English archers. As at Bannockburn, a feudal
army, centred on heavy cavalry, was spectacularly defeated by forces fighting on foot. The
English men-at-arms fought dismounted alongside the archers, producing a flexible and effective army. Ten years later Edward's eldest son,
the Black Prince, similarly routed the French at
Poitiers, capturing King John of France. This
stage of the conflict was ended by the Peace of
Brétigny (1360) by which Edward realistically renounced his claim to the French throne and to
Normandy and Anjou, but was recognized as
Duke of the whole of Aquitaine as well as ruler of
Calais, which had been captured in 1347. War
was resumed in 1369 as a result of French encouragement of opposition to Edward in Aquitaine. Edward reasserted his claim to the French
throne, but the war went badly both in Aquitaine
and at sea, and by the time of the Truce of Bruges

(1375) England held little more than Calais,
Bordeaux and Bayonne.

Even in the early years of the war, when it had
gone reasonably well, there had been serious
complaints both about its cost and about
Edward's failure to elicit sufficient support for his
policies. In 1339-41 there was a political crisis, involving opposition to war taxation and parliamentary hostility to the conduct of government.
Despite successes against France, renewed criticism of taxation demands was voiced in the Parliaments of 1343, 1344, 1346, 1348 and 1352. In
the latter half of his reign, as Edward aged and his
popular wife, Philippa of Hainault, died and was
replaced by an unpopular and expensive mistress,
Alice Perrers, tension rose. The war continued to
be expensive and was now unsuccessful. The
Black Death epidemic, probably of bubonic
plague, which killed about a third of the population between 1348 and 1351, seriously disrupted
the economy and contributed to a loss of confidence. Plague now became endemic until the
seventeenth century and held the population
down until the end of the medieval period. Given
that the Black Death was arguably the most important single event in the whole of the Middle
Ages, however, totally altering the demographic
history of the period and thus having major socio-
economic consequences, it is striking, and indicative of the nature of medieval politics, that it
had minimal direct political repercussions.

After problems about agreeing taxation at the
parliaments of 1372 and 1373, the 'Good Parliament' of 1376 witnessed a sustained attack on the
personnel and policies of the government. The
Commons, taking the initiative, elected their
first speaker and two key officials were among
those impeached (prosecuted). Parliament had
developed considerably during the reigns of the
first three Edwards. Initially it was very much an
occasion, not an institution. The Ordinances of

1311, for instance, referred to 'the baronage in Parliament', not simply Parliament; but institutional practices and pretensions were established and elaborated during the fourteenth century. Edward I's reign was very important for the development of Parliament, especially for the concept of representation, which was outlined in the writs summoning representatives of the clergy, counties and boroughs to the 1295 Parliament. They were instructed to appear with authority to give advice and consent on behalf of the communities they represented. During the reign of Edward III, the representatives of the counties (the knights of the shire) and boroughs became a fixed part of Parliament and began to meet as a separate assembly, the genesis of the House of Commons. The need to fund substantial amounts of war expenditure was crucial, as war could not pay for itself, and the king could only be independent of Parliament if war was avoided. The use of parliamentary pressure to influence the composition and objectives of government was an inevitable consequence, seen for example in 1300-1, when taxation demands were countered by requests for an enquiry into the boundaries of the area under forest jurisdiction. In one sense this simply provided a new sphere for familiar tensions. Parliament could also, however, serve as a means for eliciting support and funds for royal policies. Yet the resulting development of corporate identity and continuity also affected the freedom of political manoeuvre that monarchs enjoyed. A 1362 statute stated that Parliament must agree to all taxation of wool; the king would no longer be able to negotiate separately with urban representatives about customs duties. As the crown became less and less dependent on revenues from land and prerogative rights, and more and more dependent on grants of taxation of various types, notably customs duties and taxes on movables, so the importance of Parliament increased. Royal power was by 1300 of a totally different type to magnate power in terms of sources of wealth.

The position of the crown became more serious under Edward III's successor and grandson, Richard II (1377-99), son of the Black Prince. Poll taxes designed to fund the war led to high rates of evasion and to riots in 1379, and the process culminated in the Peasants' Revolt of 1381. This also reflected the strains in peasant society caused by the development of an active land market, agricultural production for market, and exploitation by the lords of their feudal powers, a blow to the livelihood as well as the self-esteem of peasants. Lords sought to prevent peasants exploiting the scarcity of labour resulting from the Black Death by demanding higher wages, and for a while did so very successfully. For the peasants conditions should have been improving, and to some extent were, but progress was artificially restricted. Failure in war, which led to French raids on the English coast; the disruption to the normally lucrative East Anglian cloth industry

Johannes wicleff

produced by economic problems; and a strong measure of anti-clericalism, which reflected and contributed not only to specific opposition to aspects of ecclesiastical conduct, but also to a more widespread sense of alienation, were all factors. The 1381 revolt was not an isolated episode; resistance to landlords was common and often violent.

The Peasants' Revolt was not a breakdown of authority in a frontier or distant region, but a crisis at the centre of power. The rebellion began in Essex and spread throughout southern England, being especially strong in Kent and East Anglia but also leading to disturbances in Sussex, Yorkshire, Winchester, Somerset and Cornwall. The destruction of manorial records reflected the hostility of the villeins – peasants with limited rights who were totally subject to the private jurisdiction of their lords. The Chief Justice, Sir John Cavendish, who had enforced the attempt to fix low, pre-plague labour rates by the Statute of Labourers (1351), was killed at Lakenheath. Led by Wat Tyler and a priest, John Ball, the rebels marched on and, with the help of dissatisfied Londoners, occupied London. The Tower of London was seized and royal officials, including the Lord Chancellor and the Archbishop of Canterbury, murdered. The rebels did not wish to take over the government, however, but rather to pressurize Richard II into far-reaching changes in their conditions. On 15 June Richard II met the main body of the rebels under Wat Tyler at Smithfield. Believing that he was threatening Richard, William Walworth, the Lord Mayor of London, lunged forward and killed Tyler. As fighting was about to break out, Richard averted the crisis by promising to be the rebels' leader. Once they had dispersed to their homes, however, Richard revoked the charters of freedom that had been given and punished the rebels. John Ball was tried and executed.

As he grew older, Richard came to want to rule as well as to reign, but the nobles who had dominated his minority were unwilling to yield authority and were suspicious of the favourites

Left: John Wycliff (died 1384) was a radical Oxford theologian who denied certain fundamental tenets of the Catholic faith, including transubstantiation (the doctrine that the priest's blessing turns the communion bread and wine into the body and blood of Christ); the need for priestly intercession between God and man; and papal temporal authority. Emphasizing the authority of Scripture, he advocated lay reading of the Bible, which at this time had not been translated into English, and also condemned the wealth of the monastic orders. Wycliffite ideas inspired the Lollards in England and influenced Hussite doctrine in Bohemia. There was a similar stress on grace, which was regarded as potentially undermining ecclesiastical authority. He was condemned by the Pope and the English Church but defended by John of Gaunt. In 1428 his body was disinterred, burnt and thrown into the River Swift in response to the orders of the Council of Constance.

patronized by Richard, especially Michael de la Pole, a merchant's son whom he made Lord Chancellor and Earl of Suffolk. At the 1386 Parliament Richard was pressed by a group of leading nobles, known later as the Appellants, to dismiss the Chancellor and the Treasurer and, when he refused, was threatened with deposition. A commission of nobles was appointed, with powers to reform the royal household and the realm, an unwelcome development for a monarch who stressed his prerogative as much as Richard did. Richard responded by having the commission declared illegal (1387), but his principal supporter Robert De Vere, Earl of Oxford, was routed at Radcot Bridge. The 'Merciless' Parliament (1388) condemned Richard's leading supporters for treason and they were executed.

In 1389 Richard was able to appoint a new set of ministers and in the early 1390s he ruled in a more conciliatory fashion, although tensions persisted. When the Earl of Arundel, one of the Appellants, turned up late for Queen Anne's funeral at Westminster Abbey in 1394, Richard was so furious that he struck him unconscious with an usher's baton. In 1397 Richard turned on the Appellants; a packed Parliament convicted them of treason and annulled the acts of the Merciless Parliament. The Earl of Arundel was beheaded, and Richard followed this up by extorting forced loans and blank charters from people, who were terrorized by his army of Cheshire guards. In 1399 he deprived his cousin, the exiled Henry Bolingbroke, a former Appellant, of his inheritance from his dead father, John of Gaunt, Edward III's fourth son. If such a prominent noble was not safe, who was? That May

Richard led an expedition to Ireland, but in July Bolingbroke landed at Ravenspur in Yorkshire. Richard's political incompetence had left him with an impossibly small power-base. Too few people had an interest in preserving his regime; too many had an interest in ending it. Richard returned from Ireland, was outmanoeuvred, captured and forced to abdicate. Imprisoned in Pontefract Castle, he was killed in 1400 in order to end a focus for disaffection; his supporters had already tried to murder Henry in Windsor Castle.

The brutal end of the Plantagenet line had been eased by a show of legality; Richard had resigned the crown, and Bolingbroke (Henry IV 1399-1413), was persuaded not to claim it by conquest. Parliament played a major role in the transfer of the crown. Nevertheless the removal of Richard II, like the earlier crises of his reign, was a proof of the instability produced by royal claims to exercise the prerogative as the monarch thought fit and for the benefit of those whom he wished to patronize, and the claims of some of the magnates to ensure that they were consulted. To guarantee the fidelity of their dependants, magnates required access to the benefits of court favour, for an economy of patronage was crucial to this socio-political world, a process that was accentuated by the agrarian depression of late medieval England. Many nobles were loyal but, for all, the stakes in the struggle for access to power were great, and this helped to exacerbate both disputes in Parliament and factional competition. The nature of magnate power had changed with the spread of so-called bastard feudalism, in which lords rewarded their followers and retained their services with an annual payment of money rather than with land, creating an 'affinity'. This reflected the extent to which land was now a commodity, the landlord-tenant relationship increasingly separate from that of lord and man. Land could not therefore serve so readily as the basis of a retinue, or as the source of military power. Feudal relationships became less relevant politically, as feudal control, whether of the king over his magnates as tenants-in-chief, or of the latter over their tenants, declined. Retaining offered, in the form of the affinity, the possibility of a more flexible structure of control and strength. This form of patronage and clientage was not necessarily a cause of civil conflict, but in the event of a breakdown in relations between magnates and king or in the ranks of the former, it made it easier for the magnates to sustain and mobilize their strength. Richard II's maladroit handling of the situation, his unwillingness to search for compromise in the late 1390s, ensured that the throne itself was to become a subject of contention. The problem this created was that, once one monarch had been deposed, it was impossible to prevent others from seeking to repeat the process. Edward II had been removed to make way for a government ruling on behalf of his heir, Edward III. Henry IV did not, however, have so clear a claim to the

Right: Perpendicular triumph in the chapel of King's College, Cambridge, characteristic of the style of Gothic architecture predominant in England from c.1370 until the mid 1500s. The term 'perpendicular' derives from the panel-like effect of the window design, with its pronounced vertical mullions; from the late fourteenth century this was repeated in the fan vaulting of the ceiling, as here. Henry VI, a keen patron of education, founded Eton and, in 1441, 'King's College of our Lady and St Nicholas' at Cambridge. He laid the first stone of the chapel in 1446 and in 1445-53 made frequent visits to inspect progress. His wife, Margaret of Anjou, founded Queens' College, Cambridge (1448). When Henry was deposed in 1461, King's Chapel was roofless and less than half finished. Work resumed in 1476, supported by first Edward IV and then Richard III, but was stopped after the Battle of Bosworth. It was resumed in 1508 at the expense of Henry VII, and the stonework of the chapel was completed in 1515.

throne, though his position was eased by Richard's childlessness.

The fifteenth century was to witness the continuation of two trends, war in France and domestic conflict, both of which combined to ensure that violence played a major role in the politics of the period. It was also a central feature of medieval society; incessant poverty and insecurity helped to lead to competitiveness and a high level of quarrels and violence. In the 1270s Devon had an average rate of over 36 killings per annum, and there was also a high rate of robbery. The many moated sites of the fourteenth century were probably a product of an insecure society. Neither religious teachings and sanctions nor secular administration, nor the strenuous efforts made throughout society, at all levels, to contain violence and promote conciliation, by both formal and informal means, could restrain the high crime rate; and, though the circumstances were different, it is scarcely surprising that the same was true of political violence. The problems of the rural economy following the massive fall in population during the Black Death created difficulties for most landed families until the 1470s. Rents fell, serfdom declined, many villages shrank or were abandoned, and lynchets that permitted the cultivation of steep slopes were deserted, although, as so often, there were both regional and local variations.

Nevertheless the recurrent plague that kept the population down, and the resulting scarcity of labour, brought advantage to some of the peasantry at least. Several foreign visitors commented on the wealth and prosperity of England as a whole, not just London and the court. One result of the labour shortages produced by a falling population was a new concentration in much of lowland England on pastoral farming, which required less labour. This led to a growth in wool and then in cloth exports, financing the impressive churches of East Anglian cloth centres such as Lavenham and Long Melford. Alongside London's dominance of foreign trade, these changes helped to accentuate the relative wealth of the south-east, a theme of most of British history.

Despite the economic problems of the fourteenth and fifteenth centuries, they were also an age of cultural excitement. The development of vernacular (English as opposed to French or Latin) literature led to major works such as the anonymous *Gawain and the Green Knight*, Geoffrey Chaucer's *Canterbury Tales* (c. 1387), William Langland's *Piers Plowman* (1362-92) and Thomas Malory's *Morte d'Arthur* (1469), as well as ballads, carols and mystery plays. The universities of Oxford and Cambridge, both thirteenth-century foundations, expanded with the foundation of many new colleges, while the lay education of boys developed with the establishment of elementary and grammar schools. English music became internationally more prominent, with composers such as William Cornish, John Dun-

stable and Walter Frye establishing a distinctive style. A native architectural style, the Perpendicular, seen in such soaring works as the chapel of Henry VI's foundation, King's College, Cambridge, both indicated the vitality of English culture and attracted foreign interest.

Henry IV faced a range of serious problems, of which the most urgent initially was Owen Glendower's rising in Wales, but others included French attacks on the English position in Aquitaine, the fragmentation of Ireland (where the regional power structure left little role for central power), problems with Scotland, and disaffection in England. The Percy family had supported Henry's seizure of the throne but, dissatisfied with his failure to do as they wished, they rebelled in 1403 and allied themselves with Glendower. Henry IV defeated and killed Hotspur, Sir Henry Percy, at Shrewsbury and obliged his father, the Earl of Northumberland, to disband his forces. Two years later, Northumberland, Glendower, Archbishop Scrope of York and Edmund Mortimer, Earl of March, who had a better hereditary claim to the throne than Henry IV, being des-

Above: Geoffrey Chaucer (c.1343-1400) reading his work aloud. His *Canterbury Tales* was the major work of medieval English vernacular literature. The son of a London vintner, Chaucer served as a page and was later involved in military campaigns in France and diplomatic missions, before holding official positions, including one in the Customs. His other works include *The Parlement of Foules* (1374-81), a dream-vision and *Troilus and Criseyde* (1385-90).

Right: Henry V (1413-22), a dynamic warrior king who came closest of all English monarchs to becoming ruler of France.

cended from Edward III's third son compared with Henry's descent from the fourth, rebelled but were quashed by swift action on Henry's part, and Scrope was executed. Glendower, Northumberland and March had agreed to divide England in three. The last open rebellion in England that reign was quashed when Northumberland was defeated and killed on Bramham Moor in 1408. Glendower proved a more difficult challenge, but from 1406 the English regained the initiative in Wales.

Henry IV's son and successor, the dynamic Prince Hal, Henry V (1413-22), had taken a major role in the fighting of his father's reign, in both England and Wales, and proved a warrior king. He faced an initial problem in the shape of Oldcastle's Rebellion, a conspiracy by the Lollards, an English heretical movement that had developed at the end of the fourteenth century. The Lollards' hostility to the sacraments of the Church and their stress on the sufficiency of Scripture as a rule of life, not to mention their pacifism, led to their being regarded as subversive of all authority, an opinion which Oldcastle's Rebellion seemed only to confirm. Henry V was also faced in 1415 with a conspiracy organized by the Earl of Cambridge to proclaim March king. Both were crushed easily and a crucial precondition of Henry's success in France was to be a generally peaceful and stable England. This, as much as his foreign success, was to prove the high point of Lancastrian, and indeed late medieval, England.

Henry landed on the Norman coast on 14 August 1415 and, having captured Harfleur, decided to march overland to Calais. On 25 October he beat the far larger French army which tried to stop him at Agincourt; the English longbowmen blunted the successive advances of the French cavalry with very heavy losses. The victory helped to make Henry and the war popular in England; on his second expedition in 1417, Henry conquered much of Normandy, and in 1419 its capital, Rouen. Henry was helped by serious divisions in the French camp and in 1419 he won the

Below: Part of a chart of the Atlantic coastline of Europe by Grazioso Benincasa, drawn at Venice in 1469.

alliance of the powerful Duke of Burgundy. Throughout the conflict, English successes owed much to the existence of French allies; the Hundred Years War was in part an international dimension to a series of French civil wars. The English had supporters in Normandy, Brittany, Navarre and, in the early fifteenth century, Burgundy; without these they would have done much less well. Indeed from 1204 onwards England's pressing need in her dealings with France was for an effective and dependable continental ally. Without one, little or nothing could be achieved. In 1420 Henry was betrothed to Charles VI of France's daughter Catherine, and by the Treaty of Troyes was recognized as Charles's heir and as regent during his life. Henry's aims were more ambitious than those Edward III had sought to achieve. The Dauphin, however, continued to resist, and Henry V died, possibly of dysentery, while on campaign.

Henry V's only son, Henry VI (1422-61, 1470-1), became king when only nine months old and later that year was proclaimed king of France on the death of Charles VI. His uncle, John, Duke of Bedford, who became regent, strove to maintain Henry V's impetus and to strengthen and expand Lancastrian France and had some success until the mid 1420s, but Henry VI's rival for the throne of France, his uncle Charles VII, was energized by Joan of Arc. In 1429 the English siege of Orléans was lifted by an army under Joan, and Charles was crowned at Rheims. Joan was captured and burnt as a witch in 1431, and Henry was crowned at Paris in 1430, but the balance of military advantage had crucially altered. In the shifting sands of French politics, it was vital to

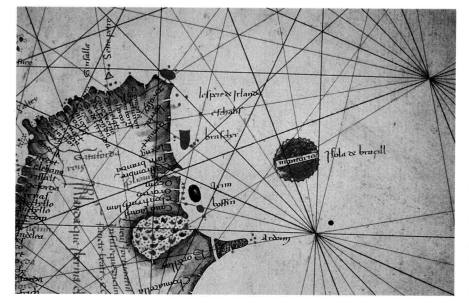

Left: The execution of Sir John Oldcastle, 1417, as illustrated by John Foxe in his *Acts and Monuments of the Church* (1563). Oldcastle was responsible for an unsuccessful Lollard conspiracy in 1414. He was captured near Welshpool in 1417, condemned by Parliament as an outlawed traitor and convicted heretic, and first hanged and then burned at the gallows at St Giles's Fields, London. Oldcastle was treated as a martyr by Protestant writers; John Bale wrote a book about the examination and death of this 'Blessed Martyr of Christ' (1544), which was used by Foxe.

appear successful. As soon as the war started going badly it became more expensive and allies began to waver. It proved impossible to negotiate peace at the Congress of Arras (1435) and the Burgundians, who had secured English control of Paris and handed Joan over, then abandoned the English. Bedford died that year, a serious blow given the need for able leadership if any of Henry V's legacy was to be retained. Paris was lost in 1436 and thereafter both negotiations with France (1439, 1444), and hopes of joining a league of French nobles against Charles VII, failed to bring any permanent advantage. Henry VI could not provide leadership. He never returned to France after his coronation and was not prepared to lead his army. The English were outmanoeuvred by the French, politically and militarily. In 1449-51 Normandy and Gascony fell swiftly to Charles VII's superior army, not least his siege artillery. An attempt under John Talbot, 1st Earl of Shrewsbury, to reverse this loss led to the recovery of most of the Bordeaux area in the winter of 1452-53, but superior French forces, and in particular artillery, smashed the Anglo-Gascon army at Castillon (1453).

France was lost. Calais was held until 1558, the claim to the French throne was only abandoned in George III's reign, and both Edward IV and Henry VIII campaigned there with some seriousness, while Henry VII besieged Boulogne unsuccessfully in 1492; but the Norman duchy, the Angevin empire and Lancastrian France, had all gone. This had major significance for fifteenth-century England, shattering the prestige of Lancastrian monarchy, but it was more important in the long term for different reasons. England had been the most important part of the royal inheritance since the reign of John, the first king since 1066, other than Stephen, to spend most of his reign in England. Yet that importance had been compromised by the continental concerns of successive monarchs. These concerns did not cease in 1453, but they had become less practicable since the recovery of French strength in the 1430s. Politically there had been a process of shrinkage, but this was a preliminary to a strengthening of national consciousness. Such a sense existed prior to the loss of France (and the Reformation); the continental involvement forwarded, rather than delayed, the development of a 'national' state, encouraging xenophobia, royal war propaganda, military service, taxation and parliament. Similarly, a pre-Reformation 'national' church might be seen as crystallizing in the context of papal claims and royal and other resistance to them. Overlapping jurisdictions, a cross-border aristocracy and England's role within the Plantagenet amalgamation of distinctive territories or 'multiple kingdom', had all, however, inhibited the political consequences of such a national consciousness, and the unpredictable nature of developments is suggested by Henry V's interest in the French throne. Thus, the defeat of the Lancastrians' attempt on that throne was of great consequence. In addition, although a loss of continental empire was not a necessary precondition for trans-oceanic expansion – Spain gained both an Italian and an American empire in 1492-1559 – nevertheless, the more insular character of England after 1453 was to be one of the keys to its subsequent domestic and international development.

5

CIVIL WAR AND THE TUDOR AGE

1453-1603

THE PERIOD 1453-1746 has a certain pattern. Until the crushing of the Northern Rebellion in 1569 it can be seen as a period of English civil war, although conflict was intermittent and there was a long period of civil peace for much of the reign of Henry VII (1485-1509) and for the early years of that of Henry VIII (1509-47). Furthermore, the conspiracies and risings of the 1530s-60s were very different from those of the late fifteenth century, in that the divisions created by the Reformation were important in the later period. Nevertheless the issues of order, especially dynastic uncertainty, and relations between the crown and 'over-mighty' subjects, were important throughout these years. The period 1637-1746 can be seen as a period of British civil war; the conflicts of these years were not isolated, and instead there was a close relationship between the situation in England and those in Scotland and Ireland. Wales was of far less consequence: it lacked an independent political life and, as far as politics is concerned, can be considered subsumed within

England, especially after the Acts of Union of 1536 and 1543. Between these two periods, 1570-1636 can be seen as an age of relative and, in some respects, increasing stability. The later conspiracies on behalf of Mary Queen of Scots, and the Essex rising of 1601, were less serious as domestic challenges than the disorders during the reign of Edward VI (1547-53) or the Northern Rebellion (1569).

If the international situation is included, the position looks less encouraging, as the war with Spain (1585-1604) threatened not only the English position in Ireland but the very independence of England. Nevertheless, the crisis of the Armada (1588) and of subsequent Spanish expeditions was surmounted. Whenever the end of the Tudor crisis is dated, it can be suggested that the early Stuart period should be seen not so much in terms of countdown to civil war but as an age of relative stability. James VI of Scotland did not have to fight for the English throne in 1603. His reign was mostly one of peace and, although the unsuccessful wars with Spain (1624-30) and France (1626-29) damaged the prestige of James's son, Charles I (1625-49), and led to domestic political difficulties, the contrast between the situation in the early 1630s and that during and after similar episodes of failure in the late medieval period was evidence of the development of the political community, certainly in England, away from a near-automatic response of confrontation and the threat of violence.

Below: The Wars of the Roses, showing the routes taken by the various armies that traversed England.

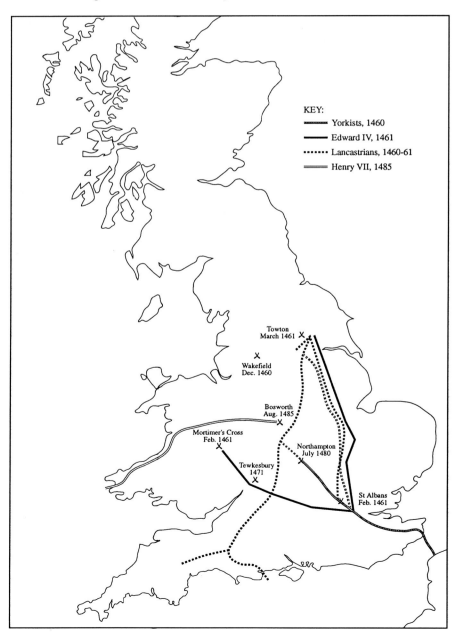

KEY:
▭▭▭▭ Yorkists, 1460
━━━━ Edward IV, 1461
• • • • • Lancastrians, 1460-61
═══ Henry VII, 1485

Towton
March 1461 ✗

✗
Wakefield
Dec. 1460

Bosworth
Aug. 1485
✗

Mortimer's Cross
Feb. 1461
✗

Northampton
July 1460
✗

Tewkesbury
1471
✗

St Albans
Feb. 1461
✗

Wars of the Roses

The disorders of the late fifteenth century were given a false coherence and a greater unity in retrospect by being called the Wars of the Roses. This was a misleading term, both literally, because the 'Lancastrian red' rose and the 'Yorkist white' were not the only identifications employed, and also because the dynastic struggle was only one theme in the violence of the period. It actually began not with the battle of St Albans (1455), when Richard Duke of York and his allies attacked nobles close to Henry VI and his wife Margaret of Anjou, but in 1450, when William, 1st Duke of Suffolk and chief minister, was murdered in the Channel, having been impeached in Parliament and banished, and a major uprising took place in Kent. Suffolk was another court favourite, monopolizing patronage and using royal backing to promote himself and his followers and to deny justice and advancement to his opponents, such as York. Cade's Rebellion reflected widespread anger at a regime seen as corrupt at home and unsuccessful abroad. Before being crushed, the rebels had defeated a royal force at Sevenoaks, occupied London and executed unpopular officials. There were also widespread disturbances in south and west England, including the killing of the Bishop of Salisbury, and widespread attacks on church property in Hampshire, Wiltshire and Dorset.

Henry VI's government therefore faced serious problems, aside from the incompetence, ineffectualness and eventual madness of the king and the better dynastic claim of the house of York to the throne, and the manipulation of royal power as an instrument of faction by Henry's followers ensured that royal government could not provide unity. Henry compromised his royal status by his partisanship in disputes between nobles, and Queen Margaret was if anything worse. Violence critically exacerbated distrust within the elite, creating blood feuds such as that between the houses of Beaufort and York, and the Neville-Percy struggle for dominance in the north. The price of failure was frequently death, the fate of Suffolk, Richard of York after the battle of Wakefield (1460) – when his head, adorned with a paper crown was publicly displayed – Henry VI's son, Edward, Prince of Wales, after the battle of Tewkesbury (1471), and many other nobles. Failure could also lead to loss of power and privilege. It was not therefore surprising that there was a recourse to arms, a determination to seize power in the kingdom. This affected both claimants to the throne and mighty nobles, such as Richard Neville, Earl of Warwick, the 'Kingmaker', though some nobles did not take part in the wars.

The fighting of the 1450s became more serious in 1460 when, after the Yorkist victory at Northampton, York claimed the throne and was acknowledged as Henry VI's heir. Henry VI had been captured, but Margaret and her son were still a centre of opposition and York set out to defeat them, only to be killed, with his second son, at Wakefield. After his defeat and death, his ambitious eldest son Edward, knowing that compromise with Margaret was impossible, claimed the throne. Margaret had followed up Wakefield by defeating Warwick at St Albans and regaining London and releasing Henry VI, but she retreated north in the face of Edward's advance. At Towton in Yorkshire (1461), the battle with the most combatants yet fought on English soil, the Lancastrians were crushed, and Edward IV (1461-83) then reigned without excessive difficulty until he fell foul of Warwick in 1469. They differed over foreign policy and over Edward's favour for the Woodvilles, relations and friends of the Queen who challenged Warwick's dominance at court. Warwick defeated Edward's army at Edgecote (1469) and gained power, only to lose it the following year and to flee to France. There he was reconciled with Margaret and committed himself to the restoration of Henry VI.

With French help, Warwick and Edward's brother George, Duke of Clarence, invaded in 1470. Edward was forced into exile and Henry VI restored, but in 1471 Edward IV invaded and defeated Warwick in thick fog at Barnet and Margaret at Tewkesbury. Warwick was killed at Barnet. The subsequent killing of Henry VI, who had been imprisoned in the Tower of London, helped to secure Edward's position. Thereafter England was more stable under Edward IV than

under his predecessor, but there were problems both from Lancastrian supporters and within the royal family. Clarence had betrayed Warwick in 1471, but was sentenced to death in 1478 for plotting against Edward and killed in the Tower, according to contemporary writers drowned in a butt of malmsey wine. The Tower was a more apt symbol of the violence of Yorkist and Tudor England than the Bastille was to be of that of eighteenth-century France.

Edward died at forty, too early to allow his young son, Edward V, to establish himself on the throne. Edward IV's surviving brother, Richard Duke of Gloucester, had his nephews declared bastards, became king as Richard III (1483-85) and sent the young princes to the Tower where they swiftly disappeared. Given the character of politics in this period – thuggery, judicial murders and eliminations – it would be surprising if they were not murdered. Richard III was a very capable man but he was widely distrusted and, having split the Yorkist establishment by seizing the throne, had only a narrow base of support and

Above: Richard III (1483-85), painted by an unknown artist. Although a competent king, Richard divided the Yorkists by seizing the throne from (and probably conniving in the murder of) his nephew Edward V, and could command little support against the invasion of Henry Tudor (Henry VII).

Above: Henry VII (1485-1509) in 1505; the cold eyes and tense fingers convey a vivid impression of a skilful and devious monarch.

deaths of the Princes in the Tower and of Clarence, however, gravely weakened the Yorkists and helped Henry VII to establish the new Tudor dynasty. Richard's body was publicly exposed after Bosworth, but the Wars of the Roses were not so easily ended. Lambert Simnel and Perkin Warbeck claimed respectively to be Clarence's son, Edward Earl of Warwick, then held in the Tower, and the younger of the two sons of Edward IV. They were supported by opponents of Henry VII until Simnel was defeated at Stoke (1487), and Warbeck was captured (1497) and hanged (1499). Yorkist plots continued, centring on the de la Pole family, and Henry VII, and, to a lesser extent, Henry VIII, remained anxious about the security of Tudor rule, but the situation was more stable than it had been in the late fifteenth century.

The Tudors

Like Charles II later, Henry VII's basic aim was to avoid having to 'go on his travels' again. To that end he manoeuvred skilfully, both at home and abroad, and improved the effectiveness of the existing governmental machinery. Henry took an active role in government, personally supervising the administration and reasserting monarchical control over the nobility. The crown's feudal rights and judicial authority were both reasserted, as was its control of the localities. Henry understood that this recovery of royal authority was essential for the re-creation of political stability. The king had not only to be respected, feared and obeyed, but also to be in a position where it was expedient for nobles to treat him thus. The peaceful country that he left Henry VIII was a testimony to Henry VII's ability and success.

Henry VIII's reign was to be most notable for the 'break from Rome', the nationalization of the English Church and the beginnings of the English Reformation, but there was little sign at his accession that the agenda of the second half of Henry's reign would be affected so greatly by ecclesiastical and religious issues. The Lollard heresy had had little lasting impact, and although hostility to the wealth and privileges of the clergy was widespread, there was also much popular devotion. There was much church building and renovation in the late fifteenth and early sixteenth centuries, for example in Suffolk and the south-west, and local shrines and particular saints, such as Brannoc whose miracles included the useful resurrection of a cow, continued to enjoy much support.

Henry VIII spent his early years devoting most of his energies to the highly competitive international relations of the period, especially war with France. Henry campaigned in person in 1513 and 1523, winning the battle of the Spurs in 1513. His leading minister Cardinal Thomas Wolsey (1513-29), the able and ambitious son of an Ipswich butcher, provided the funds for this expensive policy, but the Amicable Grant he sought to levy in 1525 led to disturbances and

was unable to trust the uncommitted. The Woodvilles rebelled unsuccessfully in 1483, as did Henry, Duke of Buckingham, who had played a crucial role in Richard's seizure of the throne. Having abandoned his new master, Buckingham was captured and executed.

Two years later, Henry Tudor, who had a weak claim to the throne through the cadet Lancastrian line, invaded with the help of French troops. The unpopular Richard was only backed by a few nobles, and crucial betrayals at the battle of Bosworth (1485) delivered victory and the throne to Henry. Henry had even less noble support than Richard: the most obvious political characteristic of the year of Bosworth was apathy. Had Richard won, he might have been able, despite his unpopularity, to consolidate his position. There would have been no 'kingmaker' and no strong Lancastrian claimant, as there had been in Edward IV's first decade. The death of the childless Richard at Bosworth, and the earlier

Henry had to abandon it. Henry's failure to have a legitimate son was, however, a question-mark against the achievement of Tudor stability, for though his wife, Catherine of Aragon, had borne him five children, only a daughter, Mary, had survived. The sole example of a female sovereign in England was Matilda, scarcely a good omen, and Henry had fallen in love with Anne Boleyn. From 1527, Henry therefore sought the annulment of his marriage to Catherine of Aragon, on the grounds that the Pope lacked the power to dispense with the biblical injunction against marrying a brother's widow, as Henry had done. Catherine, however, was the aunt of the Emperor Charles V, and the papacy proved unyielding. This led to first the fall of Wolsey and later to a break with papal jurisdiction over the English church; Henry became its 'Supreme Head' (Act of Supremacy 1534). He married Anne Boleyn, whom he described as a 'rose without a thorn', had a daughter, Elizabeth, by her and bastardized Mary by the Act of Succession (1534); and then, suspecting Anne of adultery, had her executed and declared his marriage to her void, thus bastardizing Elizabeth (1536); before marrying Jane Seymour and having a son, Edward (1537).

Meanwhile, the direction of Henry's ecclesiastical policies was creating serious problems. As a result of the royal supremacy, all religious questions became political and royal will was central to the often hesitant process of Reformation. Opponents were treated harshly and sometimes unjustly, for Henry brooked no opposition and took the customary wilfulness of monarchs very far indeed. Sir Thomas More, who had vigorously persecuted Protestants, resigned as Lord Chancellor (1532) in protest at Henry's divorce, was imprisoned for refusing to swear the oath demanded under the Succession Act, and executed for treason in 1535. From 1534 church

Left: Anne Boleyn, after Hans Holbein. Henry VIII's determination to marry Anne was the catalyst for the break with Rome.

courts were obliged to enforce parliamentary legislation. The personal and political views of the monarch took precedence over doctrinal clarity. As a young man Henry, a second son initially intended for the church, had been doctrinally conservative and had written against Luther, earning the title 'Defender of the Faith' as a result. In the 1530s his breach with the papacy, and the growing influence of Protestantism in circles close to him, led Henry to move in the direction of Lutheranism, while Anne Boleyn actively sponsored Protestants. An official English Bible was produced (1537), and every parish church was instructed to have a copy (1538).

Monasticism, one of the most visible symbols of the old ecclesiastical order, which was also an institution attacked by Protestant reformers, was

Below: The Field of the Cloth of Gold, June 1520, by an unknown artist. The meeting near Calais between Henry VIII and Francis I was a chivalric and competitive occasion for discussions that led nowhere, for in July Henry signed a treaty with Francis's rival, the Emperor Charles V. Francis beat Henry in a royal wrestling match during their meeting, while the English nobles prided themselves on not speaking French.

Right: Thomas Wolsey c.1475-1530, Henry VIII's leading adviser in the first half of his reign. Created Archbishop of York in 1514, Lord Chancellor and Cardinal in 1515, Wolsey was especially influential in foreign policy, but fell from power in 1529 due to his failure to secure Henry's divorce from Catherine of Aragon.

Below: The execution of the English Carthusians by Henry VIII in 1535 was the result of the first judicial proceedings against those who denied the royal supremacy over the Church established by the Supremacy Act of 1534. Prior Houghton of the London Charterhouse, two other Carthusian priors, John Hale, Vicar of Isleworth and a monk were punished with the full and brutal rigours of the law on treason. The Treason Act of 1534 had extended treason to cover words (not just deeds) and the denial of royal supremacy.

already established families, but its dispersal also allowed the crown to reward key supporters and make 'new men', rather as William the Conqueror had done. Sir William Herbert, who married the sister of Henry VIII's last wife, received most of the estates of Wilton Abbey. He destroyed the monastery, built a mansion and eventually became 1st Earl of Pembroke of the second creation. John Russell, who served Henry VIII as diplomat, official, admiral and general, received many of the lands of the abbey of Tavistock from Henry, and Woburn Abbey from his successor. He was created Earl of Bedford in 1550 and his successors, from 1694 Dukes, wielded political power in both Devon and Bedfordshire as a result of these grants. Thus a new political geography, which was to last in much of the country until the decline of aristocratic power in the late nineteenth century, was being created. In addition to moves by the government, the popular appeal of Protestantism was growing, though its appeal was patchy. It proved easier to destroy or change the institutions of medieval Catholicism, to expunge much of its artistic medium, such as stained glass and wall paintings in churches, than to create a new stable national ecclesiastical order or national enthusiasm for Protestantism. Illiteracy, a shortage of qualified preachers, and a reluctance to abandon the old religion, all limited the spread of Protestantism, although its impact at Henry's court and in London gave it a role beyond mere numbers.

destroyed in 1536-40. The dissolution of the monasteries was very unpopular and led to a major rising in the north, the Pilgrimage of Grace (1536-37), as well as to the Walsingham conspiracy in Norfolk (1537). The extensive monastic estates were seized by the crown, but then largely sold to pay for Henry's wars with France (1544-46) and Scotland, neither of which brought lasting success. These sales deprived the crown of what might have been a permanent accretion of wealth, and thus power. Instead ex-monastic holdings became centres of aristocratic and gentry sway. Much of the land went to

Henry's latter years were marked by abrupt and related shifts in ecclesiastical policy and factional favour, and problems over the succession. Moves

PIO AC CATHOLICO LECTORI

against Protestantism in the late 1530s, especially the restatement of Catholic doctrines in the Act of Six Articles (1539), were linked to the fall and execution in 1540 of the leading minister of that decade, Thomas Cromwell who, like Anne Boleyn, had helped the Protestants. At the end of his reign Henry moved in the opposite direction and disgraced the Howard faction, executing Henry, Earl of Surrey (1547). Surrey's cousin, Catherine, Henry's fifth wife, had already been executed for adultery (1542), Jane Seymour having died soon after the birth of Edward, while her successor, the unappealing Anne of Cleves, had been sent home (1540). Thus the Protestants were in the ascendant at the time of Henry's death.

Henry had no children by Catherine, Anne of Cleves or his sixth wife, the Protestant widow Catherine Parr, who survived him, and in 1547 was succeeded by the young Edward VI (1547-53), while royal power was wielded by Jane Seymour's brother Edward, who became Protector and Duke of Somerset. During Edward VI's reign England was open to the influence of continental Protestantism, and there was a surge of Protestant publishing. Somerset, allied with Thomas Cranmer, Archbishop of Canterbury (1533-56), introduced Protestant worship by the Book of Common Prayer (1549). Catholic religious practices and traditional rites, such as the provision of masses for the dead in wills, an indicator of confidence in the notion of purgatory, became less common. Hostility to religious change played a major role in the widespread uprisings in southern England in 1549, although opposition to landlords, particularly their enclosure (acquisition) of common land and their high rents, was also very important, especially in East Anglia. The rebellion in the south-west was primarily directed against religious change. The local gentry failed to suppress it and professional troops from outside the region had to be used. Slaughter in battle and in execution claimed a proportion of the region's population similar to that lost by the United Kingdom during the First World War. The risings were suppressed, but they were blamed in part on Somerset's opposition to enclosures and gave his principal rival, John Dudley, Duke of Northumberland, an opportunity to overthrow and, eventually execute him (1549-52).

Like Richard III, Northumberland was very able but distrusted, self-serving and patently ambitious. Again like Richard, these faults would not have mattered too much had he been successful; Edward IV, Henry VII and Henry VIII had scarcely lacked ambition and self-interest and had been unpopular with many. Like Richard, however, Northumberland's faults helped to deprive him of success. He stretched the bounds of the acceptable and, crucially, lacked the weight given by possession of the crown. It was this that he was obliged by Edward VI's poor health to remedy. Northumberland's headlong drive towards Protestantism, which led to the ex-

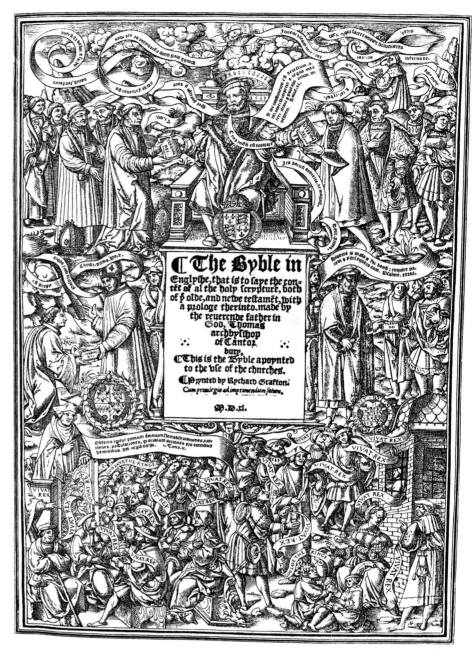

punging of the remains of Catholic doctrine and practice by the Second Prayer Book (1552), was unpopular, but the succession was the crucial issue. Edward excluded Mary and Elizabeth, claiming that they were illegitimate, and Lady Jane Grey, grand-daughter of Henry VII through his second daughter, was declared next in line. She was married to one of Northumberland's sons, and when Edward died was proclaimed queen (1553). Mary disputed this, London rallied to her and, lacking support, Northumberland fell. He and, eventually, Lady Jane were executed.

Mary (1553-58) was a convinced Catholic; she restored papal authority and Catholic practice, and married a member of the leading Catholic dynasty, her first cousin Philip II of Spain (1554), not a popular step. Opposition to the Spanish match led to Wyatt's rebellion in Kent (1554), but London refused to rise and the revolt was crushed. This helped to give further impetus to the programme of re-Catholicization. Though lay

Above: The first complete translation of the Bible to be printed in English, that by Miles Coverdale, was dedicated to Henry VIII in 1535. Coverdale was a refugee during Mary's reign.

Right: London in 1540.
Wyngaerde's *Panorama*
shows St Pauls and Old
London Bridge, with its
narrow sluices and shop-
lined roadway.

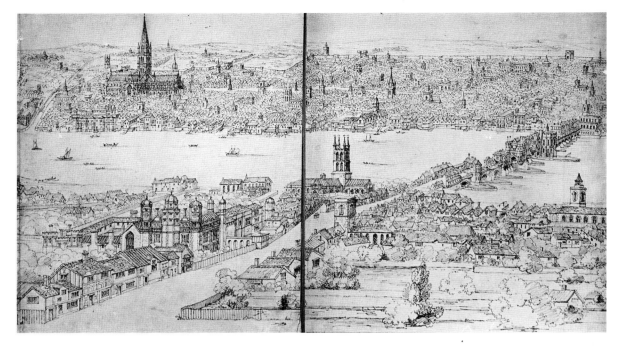

*Below: Edward VI and the
Pope* c.1548, by an
unknown artist. The dying
Henry VIII indicates his
enthroned son, the future
Edward VI, as his heir
before a group of notables
who include the Dukes of
Somerset and
Northumberland and
Archbishop Cranmer,
while the Pope languishes
below the throne.

possession of monastic estates could not be challenged, Protestantism was attacked as heresy.
Prominent Protestants, including Cranmer,
Latimer and Ridley, were burnt at the stake,
while others fled to the Continent. Protestant
exile writers resorted frequently to the vocabulary
of plague and some advocated resistance; religious turmoil helped to divide every level of
society. The Spanish marriage brought an ex-

pensive and unsuccessful war with France that led
to the fall of Calais (1558) but, more seriously,
Mary had no heir and was therefore succeeded by
her Protestant half-sister, Elizabeth I (1558-
1603). Re-Catholization had had no time to take
root. Protestantism had only limited popular support and Mary met with only slight opposition in
Parliament to her religious legislation, but the reformers' destruction of the old ways was a crucial

O Lord receiue my spirite.

Left: An illustration from Foxe's *Acts and Monuments of the Church*, popularly known as the *Book of Martyrs*, first published 1563. Foxe (1516-87), a radical Protestant, was a refugee from the Marian persecution, returned after Elizabeth's accession, and was ordained a priest in 1560. His oft-reprinted martyrology was extremely influential in propagating an image of Catholic cruelty and Protestant bravery that was to sustain a strong anti-Catholic tradition.

*Below: Elizabeth I c.*1585-90, probably painted by John Bettes. Elizabeth's lengthy reign allowed for the consolidation of a relatively conservative Protestant church settlement.

limitation on the chances of successful re-Catholicization. Yet the following century was to show, in European countries such as Bohemia, that if political circumstances were favourable Catholicism could be re-established and Protestantism driven underground.

Elizabeth's reign was most notable for its longevity. Queen for 44 years, Elizabeth was the longest reigning monarch since Edward III. This provided an opportunity for the introduction and consolidation of the Elizabethan church settlement, a Protestant system more conservative than that of Northumberland and, more crucially, for the development of a measure of political stability and the establishment of a generally acceptable Protestant succession in the shape of James VI of Scotland, great-great-grandson of Henry VII through his elder daughter. Elizabeth was the longest living English monarch hitherto; she was not to be surpassed till George II. Avoidance of marriage and the perils of childbirth were clearly helpful, but her longevity was still remarkable. Had she lived only as long as her mother or her half-brother, Elizabeth would never have become queen; if she had matched her half-sister or her grandfather she would have died before James VI's mother, the Catholic Mary Queen of Scots, unless she had had Mary executed earlier than 1587.

Elizabeth lacked the religious zeal of her half-brother and half-sister. She would have preferred a religious settlement that was closer to her father's Catholicism without Pope, monks and some superstitions, but a lack of domestic support for such an option forced her to go further, though there were limits to her Protestantism, as

Right: A contemporary caricature attacking the Marian persecution. The Protestant lambs shown bound for the slaughter are Bradford, Cranmer, Hooper, Latimer, Ridley and Rogers; the Catholic wolves are Gardiner, Bonner, Tunstall and Weston. The allegation that an unmarried clergy was prone to sin was particularly pertinent in the case of Weston, who presided over Cranmer's trial in 1554; in 1557 he was deprived of the Deanship of the Royal Chapel at Windsor and his archdeaconry of Colchester for gross immorality, although that may have been a matter of drunkenness rather than sexual conduct.

she showed in her own religious practice, and in her concern for ceremonies and clerical clothes. Elizabeth was also determined to keep royal control over the church, its bishops, doctrine and liturgy, and once the Elizabethan church settlement had been introduced, she was unwilling to heed demands for further reformation.

Elizabeth I's longevity was to see her through the suppression of the Northern Rebellion (1569), the reaction to the new church settlement and the flight to England of Mary Queen of Scots (1568); and through the subsequent Ridolfi (1571-72), Throckmorton (1582) and Babington (1586) plots on behalf of Mary. It was to see her through war with Spain, which broke out in 1585 over Elizabeth's support for the largely Protestant Dutch rebellion against her former half brother-in-law, Philip II of Spain; and through parliamentary difficulties over war finance and Puritanism, a tendency urging further Protestant reform of the church, which reflected the emergence in the 1580s of a more aggressive and self-confident Protestant culture. Elizabeth became the most experienced politician in her kingdom, keen on her prerogatives but knowing when to yield, dexterous in making concessions with-

QUEEN ELIZABETH IN PARLIAMENT

A. L. Chancellor. B. Marquises, Earles &c. C. Barons. D. Bishops. E. Iudges. F. Masters of Chancery. G. Clerks. H. Speaker of y Comons. I. Black Rod. K. Seraeant at Armes. L. Members of the Commons house. M. S. Francis Walsingham Secretary of State.

out appearing weak, a skilled manipulator of courtiers who was able to get the best out of her ministers. She did not condemn the contemporary stereotype of women as inferior to men, but instead claimed that she was an exceptional woman because chosen by God as his instrument. Elizabeth was reasonably successful in coping with divisions among her advisors, but found it difficult to control her military commanders. Her last years saw the unsuccessful attempt of her flawed favourite, Robert Devereux, Earl of Essex, to seize power (1601); serious rebellion in Ireland (1594-1603) and Spanish intervention there (1601), a long and expensive war in which Spain displayed its ability to recover from the defeat of the Armada in 1588; and serious parliamentary attacks on governmental fiscal expedients, especially the sale of monopolies. Nevertheless, there was nothing to match the crisis atmosphere of mid-century. Spanish invasion attempts were thwarted; the Ulster rebellion was defeated, Hugh O'Neill, Earl of Tyrone surrendering in 1603; Essex was executed for treason; and James VI succeeded peacefully, as James I of England, the first person to rule the whole of the British Isles. This owed more to Elizabeth than to James. She was both brave and determined and her speech to the troops assembled at Tilbury in 1588 to repel a Spanish invasion is justly famous. She stressed both her own dedication and her identification with England, and her remarks were not idle ones: four years earlier the other Protestant champion and opponent of Philip II, William of Orange, had been assassinated.

I am come amongst you . . . not for my recreation and disport, but being resolved, in the midst and heat of battle, to live or die amongst you all, and to lay down for my God and my kingdom and for my people, my honour and my blood, even in the dust. I know I have the body of a weak and feeble woman, but I have the heart and stomach of a king, and of a king of England too, and think foul scorn that Parma, or Spain, or any prince of Europe should dare to invade the borders of my realm . . .

Had the Spanish forces landed, the situation might have been less happy. The Spanish army of Flanders, led by the Duke of Parma, was the most effective army in western Europe, while the English defences were inadequate: poor fortifications, insufficient and mostly poorly trained troops, inadequate supplies. It is scarcely surprising that Providence was identified with a victory that owed much to luck and to winds favourable to the English as well as to the heroism of the navy. War with Spain fostered national consciousness, popular allegiance to Protestantism grew, and new national days of celebration recalling England's recent Protestant history became popular. Church bells were rung every 17

Right: Elizabeth I at Tilbury, 1588.

Above: English playing cards from a pack issued *c.* 1680 to commemorate the defeat of the Spanish Armada.

November to celebrate the accession of Elizabeth. Gunpowder Plot bonfires were to follow from 1605; English national culture was becoming a Protestant culture. One source of national pride were the often piratical expeditions made against Spanish America, especially the first English circumnavigation of the world, that of Francis Drake in the *Golden Hind* (1577-80). Attacks in the Caribbean were made by Drake and John Hawkins among others: Santo Domingo was sacked in 1584, Puerto Rico in 1598.

A growth in political stability was matched, however, by economic problems and more acute social tension. The population of England had remained low from the Black Death to the early sixteenth century, and there had been a widespread abandonment of settlements, but it then more than doubled from under 2.5 million to about 5 million by 1651. This was due largely to a fall in mortality, though by modern standards it was still

Left: The defeat of the Spanish Armada, showing the Spanish and English fleets at close quarters in the English Channel.

The bad harvest years of the 1590s and 1600s led to rural disturbances, including rebellions in Oxfordshire (1596) and Northamptonshire (1607) and, in the poorer areas of the country, to widespread malnutrition and some starvation. The enclosure of common land by landlords led to riots; at Osmington in Dorset in 1624 new hedges were torn down and an effigy of the landlord hanged, scarcely indicative of social subordination. Economic hardship led to social pressure on the weaker members of the community, to measures against bridal pregnancy and illegitimacy, to the insistence on a formal church wedding as the sole source of marital legitimacy, and to attempts in some parishes to prevent the poor from marrying. Churchwardens presented people to the higher church authorities for a wide variety of moral offences, including adultery and selling alcohol at the time of church services. At Wimborne Minster in the 1590s presentments included William Lucas 'for playing of a fiddle in the time of God's service'; Christopher Sylar 'for sitting by the fire in the sermon time and when we asked him if he would go to the church he said he would go when he listeth'; and 'the widow Sanders' for keeping 'a youth in her house'. Wet summers in 1595 and 1596 led to high prices and dearth in Shakespeare's hometown of Stratford. Everywhere the malnutrition of the poor reduced their resistance to ill-health and affected their lives. They ate less, and less well, than their social superiors and, as Shakespeare suggested in *King Lear* (*c.* 1605), had less access to justice:

Through tatter'd clothes small vices do appear;
Robes and furr'd gowns hide all. Plate sin with gold,
And the strong lance of justice hurtless breaks;
Arm it in rags, a pigmy's straw doth pierce it.

The poor were certainly cut off from the growing comfort that characterized the wealthier sections of the community, with their finer, sometimes sumptuous, clothes and larger and healthier dwellings. The tax assessments of the better off were unrealistically low and this helped to sustain their consumption patterns. Elizabethan England was a society that had more possessions than its predecessors; horse ownership, for example, was widespread by continental standards. Growing prosperity led to increased demand, which in turn exacerbated inflation. Printing brought books, and helped to spur rising literacy, and there was more money available for cultural and leisure activities. The Theatre, the first purpose-built public playhouse in England, was opened in London in 1576 and the Globe Theatre in 1599. The Lord Chamberlain's Men, a theatrical company in which Shakespeare had a stake, produced his plays at both theatres. The London market was sufficiently buoyant to support a number of other playwrights, including the Elizabethans Thomas Dekker, Robert Greene, Thomas Kyd and Christopher Marlowe, and the Jacobeans Francis Beaumont, John Fletcher, Ben Jonson, Philip Massinger, Thomas Middleton, William

A Soap-eater, copied from a rare print of the time of Queen Elizabeth

A Tom of Bedlam copied from an Old Drawing of the time of Edw: 6 in the possession of Fran: Douce Esq

Copied from a Drawing of the time of Henry VIIth *in the possession of Francis Douce, Esq.*

Above: Population growth in the sixteenth century and bad harvests in the 1590s and 1600s led to growing poverty and hardship and an increase in the numbers of paupers and vagrants.

very high, while a rise in fertility due to a small fall in the age of marriage was probably also important. Population growth dramatically altered the circumstances of the bulk of the population. In the late medieval period labour shortage had led to relatively high wages which, combined with comparatively low rents, offered a bearable standard of living to the bulk of the working population and their dependants. A growing population led to price inflation, which was exacerbated by the debasement and increase in volume of the coinage. Rents and food prices rose faster than wages, and this pressed hard on tenants and on those with little or no land. It led to a growth in the number of paupers and vagrants, and thus to a series of poor laws (1531, 1536, 1572, 1598, 1601). Compulsory poor rates were introduced (1572) but the situation was bleak, especially for able-bodied men unable to find work.

Left: The North Berwick coven of witches plotting against James VI (I), who in 1597 published his *Daemonologie*, attacking Reginald Scot's sceptical *Discovery of Witchcraft* (1584).

Rowley and John Webster, a group truly justifying the phrase 'an explosion of talent'. The numerous plays that were produced ranged widely in their subject matter but the vitality of contemporary London was a frequent theme, as was the wealth and social pretension of groups in society. Although the plight of the poor could be depicted, the theatre and its morality was located within a world of affluence. There were more clothes and furniture, more musical instruments and medicaments in Elizabethan England than a century earlier. The poor, however, were unable to share in this process, unless through crime, charity or as servants. If yeomen farmers did well, much of the peasantry lost status and became little different from poorly-paid wage labourers. It was, nevertheless, from political not social division that the Elizabethan system was to collapse under the Stuarts.

Left: Hardwick Hall, described by contemporaries as 'more glass than wall', illustrates the splendour of Elizabethan architecture. It was almost certainly designed by Robert Smythson, an outstanding English architect who was also largely responsible for Longleat. These are both examples of the so-called Elizabethan 'prodigy houses', built by ministers and courtiers to reflect the power and prestige of the sovereign. Ironically the Queen herself built nothing of importance.

6

Stuart and Interregnum England

1603-88

Left: Statue of James I, Bodleian Library, Oxford, on the gatehouse tower, the five storeys of which display the five architectural orders. The tower was probably designed and built by the Yorkshire mason John Akroyde, who completed the building work begun by Sir Thomas Bodley.

IN HINDSIGHT, the Stuart period has been so dominated by the Civil War that it is difficult to appreciate that the war and its course were not inevitable. The war was certainly a major struggle; more than half the total number of battles fought on English soil involving more than 5,000 men were fought in 1642-51. Out of an English male population of about 1.5 million, over 80,000 died in combat and about another 100,000 of other causes arising from the war, principally disease. Much damage was also done, buildings such as Lichfield Cathedral being badly affected. Hostilities and casualties in the related struggles in Ireland and Scotland in 1638-51 were also very severe. Bitter civil conflict was hardly without precedent, and more men may have fought at Towton (1461) than in any of the battles of the Civil War, but the sustained level of hostilities, the British scale of the conflict and the degree of popular involvement and politicization were unprecedented. In addition the war came after a long period in which most of England, especially the more prosperous south, had been peaceful; town walls had fallen into disrepair, castles into disuse. Furthermore the crisis of the mid-seventeenth century had a profound influence in shaping the values, fears and ideologies in Britain in the century and a half after the restoration of monarchy in 1660. There was urgency and fear after the Restoration, fear that the world might again be turned upside down. What was crucial then was the need to recreate the habits of thought and patterns of the past, to destroy the work of the civil war and exorcise its divisive legacy.

Though crucial in its consequences, the Civil War, like the French Revolution, was inevitable neither in its causes nor its course. There had been serious political disputes during the reign of James I and the early years of Charles I, but they had been handled peacefully. Only marginal individuals resorted to violence. A small group of Catholics put gunpowder in the cellars under Parliament, planning to blow it up when James I opened the session on 5 November 1605, and hoping that the destruction of the royal family and the Protestant elite would ignite rebellion. The attempt to warn a Catholic peer, Lord Monteagle, to be absent led, however, to the exposure of the plot. Twenty-three years later George, Duke of Buckingham, Charles I's favourite and leading advisor, was assassinated. Such events, however, were far from typical. Guy Fawkes was tortured to force him to reveal the names of his co-conspirators in the Gunpowder Plot and then executed, but that was not the fate of James I's more conventional opponents. John Felton, Buckingham's assassin, was executed, but he had no political connections.

James I (1603-25) was faced by factionalism at court, tension over religious issues and the pro-Spanish tendency of his policies, and bitter criti-

Below: The Gunpowder Plot of 1605, a Catholic conspiracy to destroy the Protestant elite, from a contemporary Dutch print.

cism of his heavy expenditure and consequent fiscal expedients. James's use and choice of favourites were unpopular. A clever man, who lacked majesty and the ability to inspire or command support but nevertheless had exalted views of his royal position and rights, James encountered problems similar to those of Elizabeth in her later years; but the Treaty of London with Spain (1604), his subsequent care to avoid war until persuaded into one with Spain in 1624, and the absence of conflict in Scotland and Ireland, increased his political freedom of manoeuvre. With the exception of the brief Addled Parliament of 1614, which neither voted money nor legislated, James ruled without Parliament between 1610 and 1621. The Addled Parliament could not have encouraged him to seek parliamentary approval. The two houses quarrelled, while the Commons were prickly about their privileges and independence, fearing that some politicians had made undertakings to manage them for the king, and reluctant to vote supply until grievances had been settled. In response to demands in 1621 that Parliament should be able to debate any subject, James tore the Protestation from the Commons Journal and dissolved Parliament. The 1624 Parliament, however, provided the basis for war with Spain, successfully linking the redress of grievances to the grant of supply and helping effectively to channel popular and political enthusiasm for the conflict.

Nonetheless the political system continued to display serious strains in Charles I's early years. His favour for Buckingham was unpopular, while the steps taken to finance unsuccessful wars with Spain and France led to parliamentary protests,

Above: James I's visit to St Paul's Cathedral, London, 26 March 1620; old St Paul's was destroyed in the Great Fire of London, 1666.

Left: The Banqueting Hall, Whitehall, by Inigo Jones, Surveyor of the King's Works 1619-22. Jones was initially known as a designer of court masques but his most significant achievement was the introduction of a classical architectural style to England, where Renaissance influence had till then been fairly superficial. The Banqueting House was intended to be the nucleus of a massive new palace at Whitehall.

Right: The ceiling of the Banqueting Hall, painted by Rubens, shows the apotheosis of James I, depicting James as the heir of Arthur and the monarch of universal peace.

Far right: Portrait of a Lady, said to be Susan, Countess of Pembroke and Montgomery by Cornelius Johnson, 1623

Below: George Villiers, Duke of Buckingham by Michiel van Miereveld, *c.*1625.

especially the Petition of Right (1628) which protested that imprisonment at royal will and taxes without parliamentary consent were illegal. The tensions of the period led to a major revival of bell ringing for the accession day of Elizabeth I, recalling times past when the monarch had been clearly identified with the successful pursuit of what were generally seen as national interests. Yet there was nothing to match the crisis of 1638-42, no parallel to the serious problems that affected France and the Austrian Habsburgs in the 1610s and early 1620s. James I and Charles I, in his early years, did not have to campaign against their own subjects as Louis XIII and Ferdinand II had to do. Not only did James succeed to the throne peacefully in 1603, but the Union of the Crowns was reasonably successful during his reign. Despite James VI and I's hopes for a 'union of love', or at least a measure of administrative and economic union between England and Scotland, the Union remained essentially personal, and Scotland was governed by the Scottish Privy Council without unwelcome innovations and in a relatively successful fashion. A closer union was regarded with suspicion in England. James's reign also saw the establishment of English colonies in North America. The Virginia Company, chartered in 1606, established a colony in the Chesapeake region, while in 1620 the *Mayflower* made a landfall at Cape Cod. Virginia and New England had an English population of 26,000 by 1640. Searching for a north-west passage to Asian wealth, Martin Frobisher explored the north-east coast of modern Canada (1576-78) and Henry Hudson entered Hudson Bay in 1610.

Left: Charles I by Daniel Mytens, 1631. Born in 1600, the second son of James VI of Scotland and I of England, Charles was a contrast to his father. Artistic, conscientious and shy, he was also arrogant. He was initially greatly influenced by James's favourite, George Villiers, Duke of Buckingham, and with him supported unsuccessful wars against France and Spain. He had considerable trouble with Parliament in 1625-29, particularly over taxation and the royal prerogative, and ruled without Parliament from then until 1640, the 'Personal Rule'. He faced difficulties over taxation, especially the extension of Ship Money to inland counties, and Archbishop Laud's ecclesiastical and anti-Puritan measures, but it was Scotland where Charles's system collapsed. The proclamation of an Anglican-type liturgy in 1637 led to the Scots rebelling; Charles was unsuccessful in the Bishops' Wars and was forced in 1640 to turn to Parliament. Failure to sustain a consensus on change led to mounting tension and, in 1642, to the outbreak of civil war.

The situation in England eased in the early 1630s. Buckingham's death, Charles I's decision in 1629 to rule without Parliament and the coming of peace all helped to reduce tension. Neutrality, while most of Europe was involved in the Thirty Years War, helped to bring a measure of prosperity. There was tension over Charles's novel financial demands, especially the extension of ship money to inland areas in 1635, but most did not follow John Hampden in refusing to pay. The toleration of Catholics at court, where the Catholic Queen, Henrietta Maria, was a prominent figure, was more serious, as was the Arminian tendency within the Church of England associated with William Laud, whom Charles made Archbishop of Canterbury (1633). Arminianism was seen as crypto-Catholic by its critics, and Charles could be harsh towards critics. Prerogative courts under royal control, especially Star Chamber and High Commission, could give out savage penalties. Nevertheless, despite differences over constitutional questions, few in England wished to overthrow Charles I. There was considerable public attachment to the role of parliaments and to the principle of taxation, but the system of government was generally believed to be divinely instituted; if Charles was a bad ruler he would be punished by God, not man, though religion was seen by some as providing justification for resistance. Rebellion and civil war were regarded by most people as akin to plagues in the body of the nation, and looked far from predictable in the mid-1630s.

The outbreak of civil war in England was a result of political crisis in 1641-42 stemming from risings in Scotland (1638) and Ireland (1641). In Scotland the absentee Charles's support for episcopacy and liturgical change, and his tactless and autocratic handling of Scottish interests and patronage, led to a presbyterian and national response which produced a National Covenant (1638) opposed to all ecclesiastical innovations. Episcopacy was abolished and when Charles responded in the Bishops' Wars (1639-40), he was defeated. As with the last military commitment, the wars with Spain and France of the 1620s, the Bishops' Wars weakened Charles, both by undermining his finances and because he was unsuccessful. They also altered the relationship between Crown and Parliament in England. Charles's 'Personal Rule' was no longer viable. Rulers of England lacked the resources to fight wars unless they turned to Parliament. To raise funds, Charles summoned the Short Parliament in April 1640, but it refused to vote them until grievances had been redressed and was speedily dissolved. The Treaty of Ripon (October 1640) ending the Bishops' Wars, however, left the Scots in occupation of the north of England and in receipt of a daily payment by Charles until a

Below: Visscher's Map of London, 1618, showing the medieval city churches, with London Bridge even more solidly built up than in 1540.

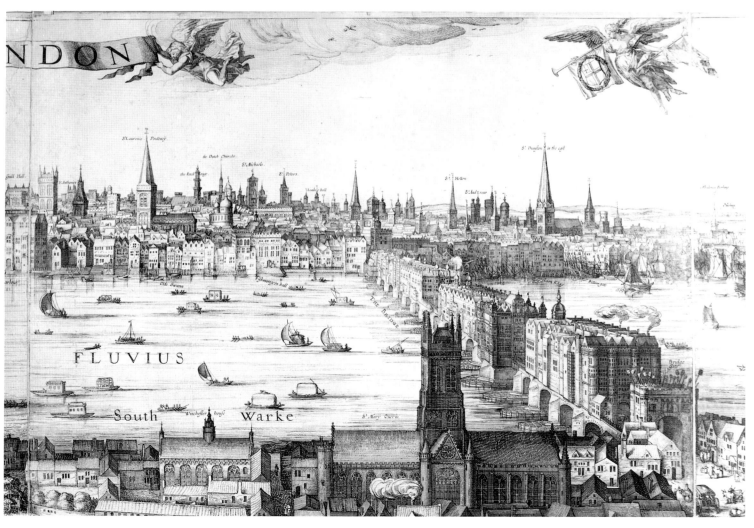

Great was surnam'd GREGORIE of Rome. Our LITTLE by GREGORIE comes short Home.

And so you will till Head from body part.

O Mr Burton, I am sick at Heart.

Raw-meats, o Bishop bredd sharp Cruditice
Eates from the Pillory? other Crueltics
As Prisoniments, by your high Inquisition
That makes your Vomits have no intermision.

My disease bredd by to much Plenitude
Of Power, Riches: The rude multitude
Did aye invy, and curbing of the zeale
Of lamps, now shyning in the Common Weale.

prepared for war, Charles left London in order to raise forces, a crucial move, as the history of civil conflict up to and including 1745 was to show that control of the resources and legitimating institutions of the capital was to be vital.

In 1642 most people sought peace and local neutrality pacts were negotiated, but determined minorities on both sides polarized the nation. Although it is dangerous to adopt a crude socio-economic or geographical determinism in explaining the divisions between the two sides, and it is clear that each had support in every region and social group, it is also true that parliamentary support was strongest in the south and east, in many of the large towns, especially London and Bristol, and in industrial areas, while that for Charles I was most pronounced in the north, Wales and the west. His supporters feared religious, social and political change. The sweeping parliamentary powers and the reformation of the Church demanded by Parliament in the Nineteen Propositions of June 1642 seemed excessive to many moderates.

Left: Caricature attacking Archbishop William Laud.

Below: This equestrian statue of Charles I, cast in 1633 by Hubert le Sueur, stands at Charing Cross in London.

final settlement could be negotiated. Charles was therefore forced to turn to Parliament again, and this 'Long Parliament', which met in November 1640, was to survive, albeit with many interruptions and changes of membership, until 1660, longer than Charles.

Initially Parliament was united in the move for the redress of grievances. Charles's ministers were punished, scarcely a novel move in such circumstances, with Thomas, Earl of Strafford, the autocratic Lord Deputy of Ireland, being attainted and executed for planning to bring Charles's Irish army to England, and Laud being imprisoned (he was executed in 1645). Restrictions on the Crown's power were more important. A Triennial Act decreed that Parliament was to meet at least every three years. Other acts banned the dissolution of the Long Parliament without its own consent, abolished Star Chamber, High Commission and Ship Money and limited the Crown's financial power. Although these changes raised serious points, they were accomplished without causing the division that religious issues created at the end of 1641. The retention of episcopacy, traditional order and discipline in the Church proved very divisive, while the need to raise forces to deal with a major Catholic rising in Ireland led to a rift over how they were to be controlled and to an escalating crisis. Charles resorted to violence, invading Parliament on 4 January 1642 in order to seize his most virulent opponents, including John Pym, but they had already fled by water to the City of London, a stronghold of hostility to Charles. As both sides

Fighting began at Manchester in July 1642 and Charles, who lacked any military experience, raised his standard at Nottingham the following month. He advanced on London, narrowly winning the battle of Edgehill (October), but was checked at Turnham Green just to the west of London in November 1642. Charles failed to press home an advantage in what were disadvantageous circumstances and retreated to establish his headquarters at Oxford; his best chance to win the war had passed. In 1643 the Royalists made gains in much of England, particularly the West Country where Bristol fell, but Charles's truce with the Irish rebels, which freed the royal forces in Ireland, was more than counteracted by the Solemn League and Covenant between the Scots and the Parliamentarians. The Scots accordingly entered England the following January and, at Marston Moor near York on 2 July 1644, they and a parliamentary army under Sir Thomas Fairfax and Oliver Cromwell crushed the Royalists under Prince Rupert

and the Duke of Newcastle. The north had been lost for Charles I.

The following year the parliamentary forces were reorganized with the creation of the New Model Army, a national army with a unified command under Fairfax, Cromwell as commander of the cavalry, and chaplains who were mostly religious radicals. In 1645 this force defeated the royalist field armies, with the victory at Naseby (14 June) being especially decisive. The superior discipline of the parliamentary cavalry played a major role. By the end of the year the Royalists were reduced to isolated strongholds, and in May 1646 Charles I gave himself up to the Scots.

Parliamentary victory was due to a number of factors, including the backing of the wealthiest parts of the country, the support of the Scots, London, the major ports and the navy, and the religious zeal of some of its followers. Cromwell saw himself as God's chosen instrument destined to overthrow religious and political tyranny, a potent belief. On the other hand, the Parliamentarians also suffered from lacklustre and unsuccessful commanders, such as Essex, Manchester and Waller, the leading generals in 1642-43; aroused hostility by high taxation; and initially had far less effective cavalry than the Royalists. As with the collapse of royal power in 1639-40, the defeat of Charles I owed much to the Scots, and it is not surprising that they played such a major role in the politics of the late 1640s, nor that England only became really stable when a government acceptable to her was installed in Scotland in the early 1650s. The Union of the Crowns ensured that the political fate of the two countries could not be separated. The Cromwellian conquests of Scotland and Ireland were the consequence, and they prefigured the Restoration of Stuart monarchy throughout the British Isles in ensuring the end of any successful attempt by Scotland and Ireland to chart a different trajectory to that of England.

As so often, victory led to disunity. Parliament, the army and the Scots were all disunited. There were crucial divisions over church government, especially the establishment of a Presbyterian system, and over negotiations with Charles, who was handed over to Parliament by the Scots when they left England in 1647. Radical social and political changes were advocated by the Levellers, who had considerable support in the army, and the army, disaffected by the attitude of Parliament and the failure to pay its arrears of pay, increasingly took a political role. Charles was seized by the army in 1647, but he rejected Cromwell's proposed settlement. Cromwell, disenchanted with both the Presbyterians in Parliament and the Levellers, whose mutiny in the army he had crushed, played the crucial role in ending the Second Civil War (1648). This arose from royalist risings and a Scottish invasion on behalf of Charles I, who had agreed in return to introduce a Presbyterian system. The risings were put down and at Preston Cromwell crushed

Below: Sir Thomas Fairfax (1612-71). He acquired his knowledge of war on the Continent, 1629-32, and was knighted by Charles I for his service during the First Bishops' War. He played a major role as a parliamentary leader in the North (1642-44) and was appointed Commander-in-Chief of the New Model Army (1645). Victorious at Naseby and Langport (1645), he also suppressed the Levellers (1649), but resigned rather than attack Scotland (1650) and was instrumental in the Restoration of Charles II.

The Pourtraicture of his Excellency Sr Thomas Farfax Generall of all the English forces for the Service of ye two houses of Parliament.

Guil: Faithorne Sculp:

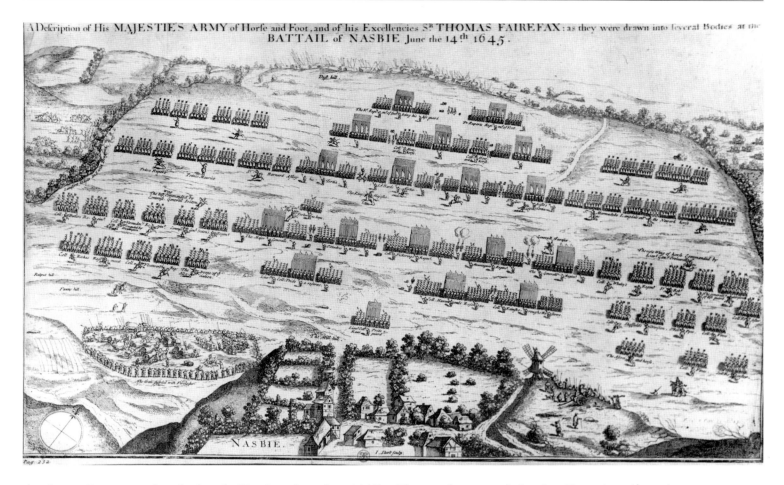

A Defcription of His MAJESTIE'S ARMY of Horfe and Foot, and of his Excellencies Sᴿ THOMAS FAIREFAX: as they were drawn into feveral Bodies at the BATTAIL of NASBIE June the 14ᵗʰ 1645.

the Scots. Determined to deal with Charles, the army purged Parliament (Pride's purge, 6 December 1648). Those who were left, the 'Rump', appointed a court to try Charles for treason

Above: A contemporary plan of the battle of Naseby, 1645, seen from the parliamentarian side. Charles I had only 3600 cavalry and 4000 foot; Fairfax 14,000 men. The royalist general Prince Rupert swept the parliamentary left from the field but then attacked the baggage train, while Cromwell on the parliamentarian right defeated the royalist cavalry and then turned on the royalist infantry in the centre, which fell to his superior forces.

Left: Royalist soldiers who fought for Charles I at the siege of Chester (1645-46); detail from a church window.

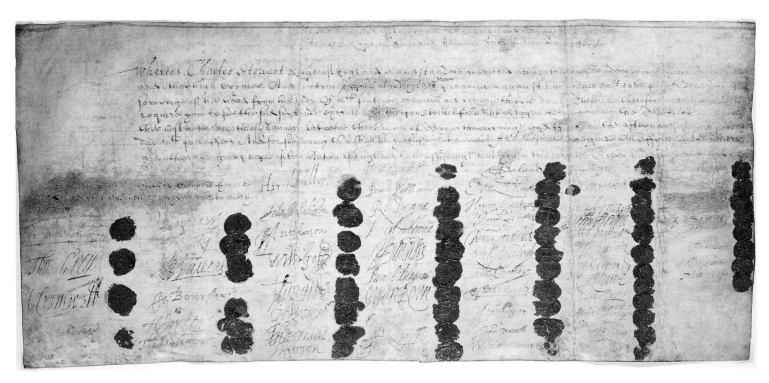

against the people. Charles refused to plead, arguing that subjects had no right to try the king and that he stood for the liberties of the people. He was found guilty and executed on 30 January 1649 at the centre of royal power, outside the Banqueting Hall in Whitehall which Inigo Jones had built for James I only thirty years before.

Republican England

The formal trial and public execution of Charles I were markedly dissimilar to the killing of medieval kings. England was declared a republic and the House of Lords abolished. The republican regime in England was faced with very different governments in Scotland and Ireland, however, and could not feel safe until these had been overthrown. In a tremendous display of military power that contrasted with the indecisiveness of much conflict on the Continent, the republican forces conquered both Scotland, a success that had eluded English monarchs, and Ireland, as well as the remaining English royalist bases in the Channel Islands, the Isles of Scilly and the Isle of Man. Cromwell crossed to Ireland in 1649 and conquered most of the east and south, a task that was completed with the overrunning of the whole island by mid-1653. Cromwell's campaign, especially the capture of Drogheda and Wexford, has since become proverbial for cruelty, and as such plays a major role in the anglophobic Irish public myth. In fact, many Irish fought the Royalists in what was an Irish civil war as much as an English invasion; massacres during conflicts in Ireland were far from new, the Catholic uprising of 1641 in particular beginning with a widespread slaughter of Protestants; and at both Drogheda and Wexford there were no attacks on women or children. Conquest, however, as a result largely of famine, plague and emigration, led to the loss

of about 40 per cent of the Irish population, and was followed by widespread expropriation of Catholic land, as the Anglo-Irish Catholics lost power and status. The Gaelic schools in which bards were trained were closed, a blow to the native cultural tradition, and the island was subjected to the Westminster Parliament.

Scottish quiescence was crucial to the early stages of the conquest of Ireland, but in 1650 Charles I's eldest son, the future Charles II, came to terms with the Scots. Cromwell invaded, but could not breach the Scottish fortified lines east and south of Edinburgh and had to retreat to Dunbar. Surrounded there by a Scottish force twice its size, Cromwell's army launched a surprise flank attack and routed the Scots (1650). Having conquered southern Scotland, Cromwell next year used his command of the sea to outflank the Scots at Stirling and occupy Perth, but Charles then marched south into England, hoping to ignite a royalist rebellion. Precautions by the government prevented this and the pursuing Cromwell surrounded and overwhelmed Charles at Worcester. Hiding in an oak tree and supporters' houses, Charles was able to flee to France but the royalist cause had been crushed. By the summer of 1652 all Scotland had fallen.

The strength, vitality and determination of the Commonwealth government was further displayed by its aggressive policy towards foreign powers. Commercial rivalry with the Dutch and suspicion of their political intentions led to the First Anglo-Dutch War (1652-54). The strength of the Commonwealth navy and the skill of its admirals, especially Robert Blake, led to success at sea, although the war was very expensive. Military strength and success, and war on the Continent, helped to win the republic international recognition. Unlike Reformation England, it was clear that the republic would not have to fear foreign intervention; its principal challenges lay at home.

There were indeed serious divisions within the republican camp. Clashes over religious issues were related to disputes over the position of the army and the nature of the constitution. Having changed the latter, and used force to achieve this, it was difficult to prevent further desire for change and recourse to force. Evidence of social and religious radicalism, however small scale its support might be, was deeply disturbing to the majority, including many supporters of the Commonwealth. A variety of sects, groupings and tendencies, including Muggletonians, Diggers, Quakers and Ranters, supported a variety of radical changes, including the communalization of waste land and abolition of the Church and of lawyers, proclaimed the superiority of personal revelation over scripture, and argued that the second coming of Christ was imminent.

Disputes led Cromwell, now head of the army, to close the purged parliament in April 1653. A new, overwhelmingly military, Council of State was appointed to administer the country, together with a nominated 'Parliament', better known as the Barebone's Parliament after a radical member, Praise-God Barebone. The electoral system was altered to replace rotten boroughs by more county seats and separate representation for expanding industrial towns, such as Bradford, Leeds and Manchester. This Parliament was the first to have representatives from Scotland and Ireland, mostly Englishmen serving there. Most members were not from the traditional ruling elite, but were minor gentry. They were if anything, however, less representative than the usual parliamentarians, as they were not elected by any process but chosen by the Council of Officers. Divorced from the bulk of the population, both elite and otherwise, the regime was taking no steps to end these divisions.

Barebone's Parliament was divided between moderates and radicals, the latter wishing, for example, to abolish tithes and the right of patrons to appoint clergy to livings, a property right and a source of gentry influence, and this led to the collapse of the Parliament in December 1653, creating a vacuum that Cromwell, as Commander-in-Chief, was obliged to fill. He did so by becoming Lord Protector. For a man born into the Huntingdonshire gentry, who had had no tenants and who had worked for a living, this was possibly the most dramatic example of social mobility in British history, although it was a side-effect of the most sweeping political revolution in that history. Cromwell told MPs in 1657 that he had taken on his position 'out of a desire to prevent mischief and evil, which I did see was imminent upon the nation'. Cromwell ruled until his death in 1658, even if he did not reign, but he faced difficulties with the Parliaments that were called, and in the localities the decision in 1655 to

Below: Cromwell taking Drogheda by storm, 10 September 1649. His superb train of siege artillery enabled him to fire 200 cannonballs at Drogheda in one day. Cromwell's Irish campaign became proverbial for cruelty and is still remembered with bitterness in Ireland. At Drogheda the garrison of about 2500 was slaughtered, the few who received quarter being sent to work the Barbados sugar plantations, but women, children and unarmed men were not killed.

Oliver Cromwell, by Robert Walker, c. 1649.

entrust authority to major-generals instructed to preserve security and create a godly and efficient kingdom was unpopular. Cromwell's willingness to sacrifice constitutional and institutional continuity and his distrust of outward forms were not generally welcomed; nor were the religious 're-forms' of republican England, such as the introduction of civil marriage, attacks on the churching of women after childbirth, changes in baptism practices, the readmission of the Jews (expelled by Edward I in 1290), and the toleration of a range of sects and practices that were anathema to many. Political, social and religious conservatism remained strong and was strengthened by the experience of the 1650s. War with Spain (1655-59) led to the capture of Jamaica, but its expense caused a financial crisis.

Cromwell died on the anniversary of his great victories of Dunbar and Worcester, but he was not an Alexander cut short in his prime; the unpopularity and divisions of the regime were readily apparent. Cromwell had neither led the latter-day children of Israel to the promised land, as he had sought to do, nor created a stable government that would maintain and further his achievements. His successor as Protector, his son Richard, was unable to command authority, but in his last months Oliver's leadership had also been faltering.

Parliamentary, army and financial problems crippled Richard's Protectorate. Deposed in 1659 as a result of a military coup, he was followed by a restoration of the Rump Parliament and the Commonwealth, but the Parliament was dismissed by the army (October 1659) and, with anarchy apparently imminent and the army divided, the commander in Scotland, George Monck, marched south, restored order and a moderate Parliament, and thus paved the way for the return of monarchy (1660).

Restored Monarchy

The Restoration Settlement brought Charles II (1660-85) to the thrones of England, Ireland and Scotland. He was an appropriate figure to preside over the reconciliation and, still more, stabilization required after the 1640s and 1650s. Able and determined on his rights, Charles was nevertheless flexible, and his essentially modest ambition was the preservation of his position, rather than the creation of a strong monarchy. He lacked the autocratic manner of his second cousin, Louis XIV of France, who assumed personal power in 1661. If there was to be a royalist reaction, it would not be led by the king. Charles's charm was also a definite asset and, if he was not trusted by all and was seen as a tyrant and a rake by some, he was able to avoid the reputations and fates of his father, Charles I, and his brother James II.

Apart from those who had signed Charles I's death warrant, there was pardon for all Parliamentarians and Cromwellians. Royal powers were to be fewer than they had been in 1640 but greater than in late 1641, let alone later in the 1640s. Charles II was given a reasonable income and control over the army, but the prerogative taxation and jurisdictional institutions of the 1630s, such as Star Chamber, were not restored. Proposals advanced in the 1650s for the reform of Parliament, the law and the universities, were certainly not welcome in the conservative atmosphere of the 1660s. The monarch might again

reign by divine right, and a very different right from the providentialism claimed by Cromwell, but he was to rule thanks to Parliament. The loss of prerogative powers and the need for parliamentary taxation ensured that Charles would also rule through Parliament. This was demonstrated in 1661-62, when Charles's hopes of a broadly-based established Church incorporating as many Protestants as possible, with toleration for the rest, were rejected by the 'Cavalier Parliament' (1661-79). The Corporation Act (1661) obliged town officials to accept an Anglicanism that clearly differentiated itself from nonconformity, while the Test Acts (1673, 1678) excluded Catholics from office and Parliament. Presbyterian clergy were ejected from their parishes, and worship with five or more people was forbidden unless according to Anglican rites. The nonconformist preacher John Bunyan was convicted of preaching without licence to unlawful assemblies and began writing *The Pilgrim's Progress* in prison. Fear as well as revenge conditioned the Restoration Settlement. A sense of precariousness, especially fears about republican conspiracies, led to Treason and Militia Acts.

Charles II was unhappy with the religious settlement and with attempts to restrict his freedom of manoeuvre, and this became more serious as a result of his Catholic leanings. Charles was the ruler on whom the fictional King Bolloximian

Above: Sir George Booth (1622-84) by Peter Lely, c.1655. Active in the parliamentary cause during the English Civil War, Booth was an MP in the Long Parliament and in Cromwell's Parliaments of 1654 and 1656. He was involved in the plot for a rebellion on behalf of Charles II in August 1659, but government vigilance ensured that only Cheshire rose. Defeated at Winnington Bridge by General Lambert, Booth was arrested disguised as a woman when seeking a shave. The restored Charles made him Lord Delamere.

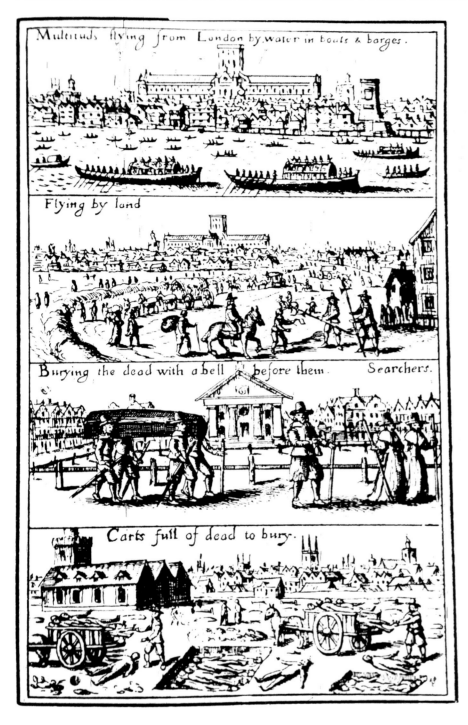

Multituds flying from London by water in bouts & barges.

Flying by land

Burying the dead with a bell before them. Searchers.

Carts full of dead to bury.

Above: Scenes showing the devastation caused in London by the Great Plague, 1665. Between seventy and a hundred thousand people died in England.

England, and the two monarchs were to unite in attacking the Dutch, the leading Protestant power. This was a real Popish Plot, and suspicion about Charles's intentions helped to bedevil the rest of his reign. It also ensured that his successor, his Catholic brother James II (1685-88), came to the throne in an atmosphere in which suspicion about Catholics had been both heightened and crucially linked to Louis XIV, whose moves against Protestants in France, culminating in the revocation of the Edict of Nantes (1685), were an apparent warning that Catholic rulers could not be trusted and would always be bitterly anti-Protestant.

The Third Anglo-Dutch War (1672-74) was also unsuccessful and led to the fall of Charles's ministry, the Cabal. Such political storms could be mastered by the adept Charles, always ready to sacrifice ministers to secure his own position, but the crisis touched off in 1678 by rumours of a Popish Plot attacked him at his weakest points. The succession was a major problem for Charles; the father of fourteen bastards, he had no legitimate children by his marriage to the somewhat unappealing Portuguese princess Catherine of Braganza (who had brought Bombay and Tangier as her dowry). Thus his brother James was his heir. The Popish Plot stemmed from the claim by the adventurer, Titus Oates, of evidence for a Catholic plot to assassinate Charles and replace him by James. The murder of Sir Edmund Berry Godfrey, the magistrate who took the evidence, and the discovery of suspicious letters in the possession of James's former private secretary, Edward Coleman, inflamed suspicions and led to politics by orchestrated paranoia, a series of show-trials in which Catholics were convicted and then executed. The revelation by political rivals that Charles II's leading minister, Lord Treasurer Danby, had been negotiating with Louis XIV fanned the flames. The Popish Plot became the Exclusion Crisis (1678-81), an attempt to use Parliament to exclude James from the succession and to weaken Charles's government. Its leading advocate, Anthony, Earl of Shaftesbury, created what has been seen as the first English political party, the 'Whigs' (an abusive term, referring to Scottish Presbyterian rebels, originally used by their opponents). The Whigs produced a mass of propaganda; the first unlicensed newspaper made clear its didactic nature in its title, 'The Weekly Pacquet of Advice from Rome . . . in the process of which the Papists' arguments are answered, their fallacies detected, their cruelties registered, their treasons and seditious principles observed . . .' Many of the characteristic features and devices of the eighteenth-century press, including a paranoid mentality, rigid convictions and a humorous style, rapidly developed.

Anti-Catholicism could help create a crisis, but the Whigs' position was weakened by the determination of most to avoid rebellion and a repetition of the chaos of the Civil War; the strength of Charles's position in the House of

of *Sodom: or, the Quintessence of Debauchery* was modelled:

Thus in the zenith of my lust I reign;
I eat to survive and survive to eat again
. . . And with my prick I'll govern all the land.

Vice and corruption at court were bad enough but a Catholic as ruler was totally unacceptable, an apparent threat, in a culture that knew little of religious toleration, to national independence, church and society.

Failure in the Second Anglo-Dutch War (1665-67), including a humiliating attack on the English fleet in the Medway (1667), was followed by the secret Treaty of Dover with the most powerful Catholic monarch, Louis XIV (1670). Charles promised to declare his conversion to Catholicism and to restore the religion to

Prospect of a Popish Successor: Display'd by Hell-bred Cruelty: Popish Villainy: Strange Divinity: intended Slavery: Old Englands Misery: &c—

Left: Anti-Catholic caricature produced during the Exclusion Crisis of 1678-81 by Stephen College, who was executed on a dubious treason charge in 1681. It blames Catholics for the Great Fire, denounces High Church Anglican clerics as crypto-Papists and promises divine support for Exclusion, the attempt to exclude the Catholic James from the succession.

Lords and the king's right to summon and dissolve Parliament as he thought fit, both of which blocked Exclusion in a legal fashion; the lack of a generally agreed alternative to James; and Charles's fixed determination. With Scotland and Ireland securely under control, Charles II did not face a crisis comparable to that of 1638-41, and he avoided foolish moves such as his father's attempt to arrest the Five Members.

Whig failure was followed by a royalist reaction that was eased by Charles's negotiation of a subsidy from Louis XIV (1681), which enabled him to do without Parliament for the rest of his reign. Whig office holders were purged and Whig leaders fled or were compromised in the Rye House Plot (1683), an alleged conspiracy to assassinate Charles and James. This led to executions and stimulated an attack on Whig strongholds. Corporation charters, especially that of London, were remodelled in order to increase crown influence, and Dissenters (Protestants who were not members of the Church of England, many of whom were Whigs) were persecuted.

Thanks to the reaction against the Exclusion Crisis, James II was able to succeed his brother with little difficulty (1685), and his situation was strengthened by the defeat of rebellions in Scotland and England in the same year. Charles II's

The Royall Katherine Command'd by John Earl of Mulgrave in the Second Dutch Warr.

Below left: The Royal Katherine, commanded by John, 3rd Earl of Mulgrave, in the Second Anglo-Dutch War (1665-67).

Above: Charles II (1660-85), painted in the studio of John Michael Wright, c. 1660-65.

most charismatic bastard, James, Duke of Monmouth, who had pressed a claim to be Charles's heir during the Exclusion Crisis, arguing that Charles had really married his mother, Lucy Walter, landed at Lyme Regis on 11 June 1685.

He won widespread support in Dorset and Somerset, and on the night of 5/6 July at Sedgemoor Monmouth nearly succeeded in a surprise attack on the royal army, but his force was routed with heavy casualties. Monmouth was executed and

some of his supporters transported to the colonies or hanged, after biased trials in the 'Bloody Assizes' of Chief Justice George Jeffreys.

Like Cromwell, victory gave James a conviction of divine approval and the rebellion led him to increase his army, but Parliament was unhappy about this and especially with the appointment of Catholic officers. James prorogued Parliament in November 1685 and, with less constraint, moved towards the catholicizing of the government. This was to make him increasingly unpopular. The changes necessary to establish full religious and civil equality for Catholics entailed a destruction of the privileges of the Church of England, a policy of appointing Catholics, the insistent use of prerogative action, and preparations for a packed Parliament. James took steps to develop the army into a professional institution answerable only to the king. And yet there was no revolution in Britain. Unlike in 1638-42, the Stuart monarchy was now strong enough to survive domestic challenges, and there was no breakdown of order in Scotland and Ireland.

The birth of a Prince of Wales on 10 June 1688 was a major shock to those unhappy with James's polities. 'It could not have been more public if he had been born in Charing Cross', noted Francis Atterbury, but unhappy critics spread the rumour that a baby had been smuggled in in a warming pan. James had no other surviving children from his 15-year-long second Catholic marriage but two daughters, Mary and Anne, living from his Protestant first marriage. Mary was married to James's nephew, William III of Orange, who was the leading Dutch political figure and a Protestant. A Catholic son threatened to make

James's changes permanent. Nineteen days later Archbishop Sancroft of Canterbury and six bishops were acquitted on charges of sedition, for protesting against James's order that the Declaration of Indulgence granting all Christians full equality of religious practice (a challenge to the position of the Church) be read from all pulpits.

This more volatile and threatening situation led seven politicians to invite William to intervene in order to protect Protestantism and traditional liberties. Motivated rather by a wish to keep Britain out of Louis XIV's camp, William had already decided to invade. In many respects his invasion was a gamble, dependent on whether Louis XIV decided to attack the Dutch, on the policies of other powers, the winds in the North Sea and Channel, and the response of the English fleet and army. After his initial invasion plan had been thwarted by storms, William landed at Torbay on 5 November 1688. He benefited from a collapse of will on the part of James, who had an army twice the size of William's. James had been a brave commander earlier in his life, but in 1688 he suffered from a series of debilitating nosebleeds and failed to lead his army into battle. As James's resolve failed, a vacuum of power developed. Most people did not want any breach in the hereditary succession, and William had initially pretended that he had no designs on the crown. However, as the situation developed favourably, especially when James had been driven into exile, William made it clear that he did seek the throne. This was achieved by declaring it vacant and inviting William and Mary to occupy it as joint monarchs. All Catholics were debarred from the succession.

Above: The Great Fire of London, which raged for four days from 2 September 1666, destroying St Paul's, the Guildhall, the Royal Exchange, 87 churches and about 13,200 houses. Charles II and his brother James took an active role filling buckets and encouraging the firefighters. John Evelyn, Christopher Wren and others subsequently produced plans for rebuilding the city to a more regular plan, but resources and will were lacking and Wren had to be content with designing the new St Paul's and a large number of churches.

7
ENGLAND
1689-1815

WHAT WAS TO BECOME KNOWN as the Glorious Revolution was both the last successful invasion of England and a coup in which the monarch was replaced by his nephew and son-in-law, though William's success also depended on an absence of extensive opposition, variously reflecting apathy, reluctant compliance and a measure of active enthusiasm. The change of monarchs led to war with Louis XIV, who gave James II shelter and support; and the need for parliamentary backing for the expensive struggle with the leading power in western Europe helped to give substance to the notion of parliamentary monarchy. The financial settlement obliged William to meet Parliament every year, while the Triennial Act (1694) ensured regular meetings of Parliament and, by limiting their lifespan to three years, required regular elections. William's was truly a limited monarchy.

The Glorious Revolution was to play a crucial role in the English public myth, and to be seen as the triumph of the liberal and tolerant spirit, the creation of a political world fit for Englishmen. This interpretation never made much sense from the Scottish or Irish perspective and it has recently been seriously challenged. What was for long seen as an irresistible manifestation of a general aspiration in British society for progress and liberty can now be seen, as it was by contemporaries, as a violent rupture, an ideological, political and diplomatic crisis. The cost of William's invasion was not only a civil war that brought much suffering to Scotland and Ireland, but also a foreign war that created considerable stresses within Britain.

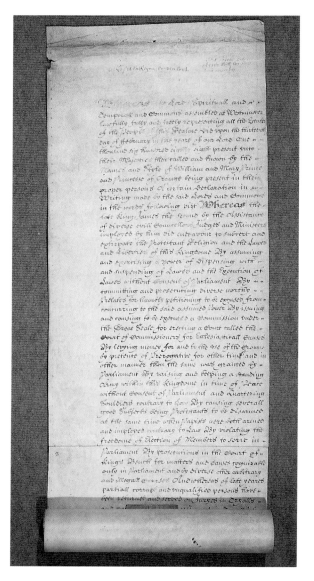

Above right: The Bill of Rights, 1689, was a decisive rejection of Stuart monarchy and paved the way for the more limited monarchy that was to follow.

Right: The Whig myth. The landing of William of Orange at Torbay, 5 November 1688, painted by James Northcote (1746-1831) and engraved by James Parker, 1801. Northcote, a protégé of Sir Joshua Reynolds, helped to form a particular image of the past from 1784 on, painting a number of historical paintings including *The Murder of the Young Princes in the Tower*, *Sir William Walworth . . . Killing Wat Tyler* and *The Revolution of 1688*. He became an academician in 1787.

Left: William III by van Wyk. The posthumous son of William II of Orange and Mary Stuart, daughter of Charles I, he married his cousin Mary, elder daughter of James II, in 1667. He gained power in the United Provinces (modern Netherlands) in 1672 and fought and negotiated against Louis XIV of France. In 1688 he invaded England in order to remove James II and to enlist English resources in the war against France; he became joint ruler with Mary and, after her death in 1694, sole ruler. He commanded the English forces at the Battle of the Boyne, 1690, and in campaigns in the Spanish Netherlands (modern Belgium).

James II was resolved to recapture England and the Glorious Revolution thus launched Jacobitism, as the cause of the exiled Stuarts came to be known from the Latin for James, *Jacobus*. Initially, James controlled most of Ireland and had support in Scotland. This situation looked back to the last period of Stuart dispossession, the English Civil Wars and Interregnum. Like Cromwell before him, however, William III was to succeed in having the Stuarts and their supporters driven from Scotland and Ireland, thus forcing them to become reliant on foreign support, which in turn was offered in accordance with a diplomatic and military agenda, timetable and constraints that rarely suited the Jacobites. James's standard was raised in Scotland in April 1689 by John Graham of Claverhouse, who was backed by the Episcopalians, the supporters of a Scottish church controlled, like that of England, by bishops. This had been the established form, but in Scotland the Glorious Revolution entailed the establishment of Presbyterianism. At the battle of Killiecrankie in July, Claverhouse's Highlanders routed their opponents with the cold steel and rush of a Highland charge, but their leader was killed and the cause collapsed under his mediocre successors. Most of the Highland chiefs swore allegiance to William in late 1691.

James II's supporters controlled most of Ireland in 1689 though Derry, fearing Catholic massacre, resisted a siege and was relieved by the English fleet. In 1690 William, who had crossed to Ireland with a force including Danish, Dutch and German troops, outflanked the outnumbered James at the Battle of the Boyne and captured Dublin. By the Treaty of Limerick (1691) the Jacobites in Ireland surrendered, many, the 'Wild Geese', going to serve James in France. Ireland was then subjected to a Protestant ascendancy; the Catholics, who had held 59% of the land in 1641, owned 22% in 1688; by 1703 this had fallen to 14%, by 1778 to 5%. Catholic officials and landowners were replaced and parliamentary legislation against Catholics was passed. Catholics were prevented from freely acquiring or bequeathing land or property and were disenfranchised and debarred from all political, military and legal offices and from Parliament. Acts forbade mixed marriages, Catholic schools and the bearing of arms by Catholics. The Catholic percentage of the population did not diminish however, because serious repression was episodic, while the Catholic clergy, wearing secular dress and secretly celebrating mass, continued their work, sustained by a strong oral culture, by the emotional link with a sense of national identity, by hedge-school teaching and by a certain amount of tacit government acceptance.

The Glorious Revolution led to English domination of the British Isles, albeit domination that was helped by and shared with important sections of the Irish and Scottish population: Irish Anglicans and Scottish Presbyterians. The alternative had been glimpsed in 1689 when James II's Parliament in Dublin had rejected much of the authority of the Westminster Parliament. This

path had, however, been blocked. Jacobitism, and the strategic threat posed by Scotland and Ireland, united those politicians in the three kingdoms who were opposed to it. The Union of 1707 between England and Scotland arose essentially from English concern about the possible hazards posed by an autonomous, if not independent, Scotland. There was some support for the measure in Scotland, but its passage through the Scottish Parliament ultimately depended on corruption and self-interest. In the early eighteenth century there was also some support in Ireland for union with England, but no Act of Union was passed until 1800. Legislation in Westminster, the result of protectionist lobbying by English interests, hindered Irish exports, while the granting of Irish lands and pensions to favoured courtiers exacerbated the problem of absentee landowners and revenue-holders, with a consequent drain of money out of the country. Long-standing religious grievances helped to increase Irish political disaffection in the 1790s.

England might clearly dominate Britain after 1691, but for the politically involved groups at least, a sense of separate identity and national privileges continued to be important in Ireland and Scotland, though not Wales. Ireland retained its Parliament until the Act of Union of 1800; Scotland had a different national church, 1689 bringing a Presbyterian establishment, and legal system. And yet the sense of separate identity was weakened, especially at the level of the elite, by the decline of Celtic languages and the growing appeal of English cultural norms and customs. Welsh, Irish and Scots all sought to benefit from links with England. Scots came to play a major

role in the expansion of empire, not least through service in the army. Protestantism, war with France and the benefits of empire helped to create a British nationhood which developed alongside the still strong sense of individual English, Scottish, Irish and Welsh indentities.

The nature of British society in the period 1689-1815 has been a matter of some controversy. It is possible to stress modernity, to see a rising middle class and an Age of Reason, a polite and commercial people, aristocratic ease and elegance, urban bustle and balance, a land of stately homes and urban squares, Castle Howard, Blenheim, Bath, the West End of London, and the New Town of Edinburgh. Brick buildings with large windows were built in a regular 'classical' style on new boulevards, squares and circles. Parks, theatres, assembly rooms, subscription libraries, race-courses, and other leisure facilities were opened in many towns.

Different images and views can also, however, be advanced. Serious disease played a major role in what was a hostile environment. The plague epidemic of 1665-66, which killed over 70,000, was the last in England: mutations in the rat and flea population were more important in preventing a repetition than clumsy and erratic public health measures and alterations in human habitat owing to construction with brick, stone and tile. There were still, however, other major killers, including a whole host of illnesses and accidents that can generally be tackled successfully in modern Europe. Measles epidemics killed many young children in, for example, 1705-6, 1716 and 1718-19. In the last, child burials accounted for 61 per cent of total deaths in Bewdley, while a high

Left: The Bank of England, founded in 1694, was crucial to the establishment of a system of public finance, guaranteed by Parliament, that enabled the state to borrow substantial sums and to service the subsequent national debt at a low rate of interest. This was essential to fund the wars with France.

rate of child mortality there in 1676 may have been due to infant diarrhoea. Smallpox, typhus, typhoid and influenza were serious problems. The year could be divided by the prevalence of different diseases: smallpox in spring and summer, dysentery in spring and autumn. In late 1750 over 100 people were recorded as having died in Kidderminster of 'malignant sore throat with ulcers'. Primitive sanitation and poor nutrition exacerbated the situation. The limited nature of the housing stock led to the sharing of beds, which was partly responsible for the high incidence of respiratory infections. Problems of food shortage and cost ensured that the bulk of the population lacked a balanced diet even when they had enough food. Illiteracy was widespread, more pronounced among women than men and in rural than in urban areas. In rural Dorset in the 1790s 56% of newly weds were illiterate.

Hogarth depicted the vigorous if not seamy side of life in London, a thriving metropolis where organized crime, prostitution and squalor were ever-present, veneral disease and destitution much feared. The criminal code decreed the death penalty, or transportation to virtual slave labour in British colonies, for minor crimes; the game laws laid down harsh penalties for poaching and permitted the use of spring guns by landlords.

Left: Inside the Rotunda at Ranelagh, Chelsea, London. The Ranelagh pleasure gardens became fashionable in the 1740s and 1750s as a place to see and be seen, set and spot fashions, find spouses or whores. Horace Walpole noted; 'The company is universal: from his Grace of Grafton down to children out of the Foundling Hospital'. Marylebone and Vauxhall were other fashionable gardens.

Right: The Georgian townscape as typified by Bath, showing the Circus, begun by John Wood in 1754 and finished in 1764, and the Royal Crescent by John Wood the Younger, 1767-75. William Pitt the Elder paid £1200 for 7 The Circus in 1753 and retained it until 1770.

Under the Transportation Act of 1718, passed in order to deal with the rise of crime in perfunctorily-policed London, 50,000 convicts were sent to America by 1775 for seven or fourteen years or life; after the loss of America the possibility of transportation to Africa was considered and, finally, a convict settlement was established in Australia.

A feeling of crisis and insecurity helps to explain the fact that, in so far as there was an aristocratic and establishment cultural and political hegemony, it was in part bred from elite fear, rather than from any sense of confidence or complacency. Continuity was sought, not because of any easy complacency, but rather from the recognition of social fragility. Aristocratic portraits and stately homes reflected a need to assert tradition and superiority, and to project images of confidence against any potential challenge to the position of the elite. There were bitter political and religious disputes. The succession was a cause of division and instability until the crushing of Bonnie Prince Charlie at Culloden in 1746. The disestablishment of Episcopalism in Scotland after the Glorious Revolution, and the sense of 'the Church in Danger' from Dissenters and Whigs in England, fed tension. Although William III (1689-1702) and, to a greater extent,

Below: Mrs Charlotte Raikes by George Romney, 1734-1802, a leading portraitist in 1775-95. Charlotte was daughter of the Hon. Henry Finch and wife of Thomas Raikes, a merchant who became Governor of the Bank of England and was also painted by Romney.

George I (1714-27) and George II (1727-60), relied heavily on the Whigs, the continued existence of a popular and active Tory party was a challenge to the practice of Whig oligarchy, as was the existence of vigorous traditions of urban political activity. The supposed politeness of early eighteenth-century Augustan literature does not survive an attentive reading of Alexander Pope or Jonathan Swift, much of whose work is spiked with bitterness and sometimes savage satire. The impulse for order which has been seen as a dominant motif of the age should not be regarded as a simple reflection of political and social realities; rather, the commentators, writers and artists of the period stressed the need for order because they were profoundly aware of the threats to that order around them.

Likewise, religious concerns still constrained and influenced the content of much cultural activity. In 1742 Handel's oratorio *The Messiah* revealed the commercial possibilities of sacred music: it had always been popular, but now it increasingly served commercial rather than liturgical purposes, being performed at concerts rather than services. This was a volatile and varied cultural world in which politics and religion were less than placid, and in which much that might seem irrational was not marginalized. Far from being a cool age of reason, it saw the religious enthusiasm that led to the foundation of Methodism, as well as almanacs and millenarian and providential notions that were not restricted to a superstitious minority. Isaac Newton (1642-1727), from 1703 President of the Royal Society, a body established in 1660 to encourage scientific

NEWTON

Left: Sir Isaac Newton (1642-1727) painted by Sir James Thornhill in 1710, was a leading scientist who made considerable advances in astronomy, mathematics and physics. His *Philosophia Naturalis Principia Mathematica* (1687) was a seminal work in mathematics and physics and revealed his discovery of the laws of motion. Newton also made major advances in optics, summarized in his *Optics* (1704), which shows that white light is composed of rays of different colours. He had a popular as well as a scientific impact; in England a big market developed for scientific textbooks and works of popularization, including some intended for children. Francesco Algarotti's *Il Newtonianismo per le Dame* (1737), which explained light and gravitation in a series of dialogues, was translated into English in 1739. James Ferguson's *Astronomy explained on Sir Isaac Newton's Principles* (1756) achieved great success.

research, discovered calculus, universal gravitation and the laws of motion, but also searched for the date of the Second Coming and argued that comets, which he and Edmund Halley had analysed, should be seen as explaining the Deluge. Newton claimed that God acted in order to keep heavenly bodies in their place; science was not therefore to be incompatible with the divine scheme. There was a widespread interest in alchemy. The eminent chemist Peter Woulfe (c. 1727-1803), who developed an apparatus for passing gasses through liquids, also pursued alchemical investigations, fixing prayers to his apparatus.

There was a profound sense of disquiet about the very nature of society, coming not so much from radicals as from clergy, doctors and writers concerned about moral and ethical values.

Morality was a central cultural theme, and the moral satires of the painter William Hogarth (1697-1764) were a considerable success; the engravings of his series *The Harlot's Progress* sold over 1000 sets and were much imitated. The plays of Colley Cibber, George Colman, George Lillo and Oliver Goldsmith propounded a secular morality opposed to vice and indulgence. The etiquette of the period condemned dishevelment and slovenliness in clothing. Samuel Richardson's *Pamela* (1740), the first of the sentimental novels, was a very popular work on the prudence of virtue and the virtue of prudence. Few contemporaries were as convinced as later historians that theirs was an age of stability. For them stability in culture and politics was regarded perhaps as something which had existed in the past

Dr Burgises Theater

Above: The Sacheverell Riots, 1 March 1710, were provoked by the Whigs' impeachment in 1710 of the Tory bishop Dr Sachaverell. Here Daniel Burgess's Presbyterian meeting-house in Carey Street, London, is wrecked by the mob.

and was now increasingly lost, or as something which should be worked towards; it was hardly something which had been achieved in the present – except through constant vigilance.

There were obvious differences between British society and those on the Continent. These included the demographic and economic prominence of London, the capital, and the high percentage of the labour force not engaged in agriculture. Common legal rights and penalties were more true of Britain than of most continental states. The rotation of crops and use of legumes that increasingly characterized East Anglian agriculture, and the growing use of coal, were not mirrored across most of Europe. Urban mercantile interests were more politically significant than in other large European states. And yet it would be inappropriate to focus on such differences and to suggest that therefore it is unhelpful

to consider Britain in a European context. 'Progressive' features of British agriculture and industry were matched elsewhere. The agricultural techniques of East Anglia owed much to those of the province of Holland, while coal was already used for industrial processes in a number of continental regions, such as the Ruhr and the Pays de Liège. If many miles of canals were constructed in Britain in the eighteenth century, the same was true of Russia. Industrial development was not restricted to Britain, but was also the case in a number of continental regions, such as Bohemia and Silesia.

The economic picture, once the basic similarity of technological and other aspects already outlined has been discussed, is not, however, one of identifying comparisons or contrasts between Britain and the Continent, for Britain is unhelpful as a unit for analysis. The variations between, and indeed within, regions inside Britain were such that it is more pertinent, as in more recent times, to note common indicators between individual British and continental regions rather than to stress the divide of the Channel. There was no nation state as far as economic experience and trajectory were concerned. The protectionist and regulatory legislation enacted by British (and continental) governments did not create effective economic spaces.

In socio-economic terms, therefore, it is, possible to stress similarity, rather than contrast, between Britain and the Continent. This is more problematic as far as politico-constitutional aspects are concerned. The 'Glorious Revolution' led to a contemporary emphasis on specificity that has been of considerable importance since. The Whig tradition made much of the redefinition of parliamentary monarchy, in which Parliament met every year, of triennial elections, the freedom of the press and the establishment of a funded national debt. The Revolution Settlement, the term applied to the constitutional and political changes of the period 1688-1701, was seen as clearly separating Britain from the general pattern of continental development. To use a modern term, it was as if history had ended, for if history was an account of the process by which the constitution was established and defended, then the Revolution Settlement could be presented as a definitive constitutional settlement, and it could be argued that the Glorious Revolution had saved Britain from the general European move towards absolutism and, to a certain extent, Catholicism. In Strasburg in 1753 the French historian and dramatist Voltaire told William Lee, a well-connected English tourist, that he came from 'the only nation where the least shadow of liberty remains in Europe'. For fashionable intellectuals on the Continent Britain offered a model of a progressive society, one that replaced the Dutch model that had been so attractive the previous century, although there was also criticism of aspects of British society. Many eighteenth- and nineteenth-century

French and German historians and lawyers looked to Britain (by which they tended to mean England) as culturally and constitutionally superior, and thus as a model to be copied. With time, however, Britain became more important as an economic model and a source of technological innovation.

Many foreign commentators underrated the divisions in eighteenth-century British society. Politics, religion, culture and morality, none of them really separable, were occasions and sources of strife and polemic, and the same was true not only of views of recent history, most obviously the Revolution Settlement, but also of the very question of the relationship between Britain and the Continent. Alongside the notion of uniqueness as derived from and encapsulated in that Settlement, there was also a habit, especially marked in opposition circles, of seeking parallels abroad. Thus the long ministry of Sweden's Count Horn could be compared with that of Walpole, while *Fog's Weekly Journal*, a leading Tory paper, could suggest in 1732 that the *Parlement* of Paris was readier to display independence than the Westminster Parliament. This habit was accentuated from 1714 by the Hanoverian connection, for under both George I and George II the contentiousness of that connection led to a sustained political discourse about the extent to which Britain was being ruled in accordance with the foreign interests of her monarchs, and the extent to which she was being affected by those interests in other ways, especially cultural.

Britain was not the only European maritime and trans-oceanic imperial power, but her naval

Left: David Garrick (1717-79) by Thomas Gainsborough. Gainsborough painted Britain's leading actor twice, in 1766 and 1770. An actor-impresario whose career began in 1741, Garrick was closely associated with Shakespearean tragic roles, and was responsible for the Stratford Shakespeare Jubilee in 1769.

strength and colonial possessions had grown considerably since the mid-seventeenth century. Her control of the eastern seaboard of North America north of Florida had been expanded and consolidated with the gain of New York from the Dutch (1664), the French recognition of Nova Scotia, Newfoundland and Hudson's Bay as

Below: The British empire in 1714, demonstrating the growth of naval strength and colonial possessions since the mid-seventeenth century.

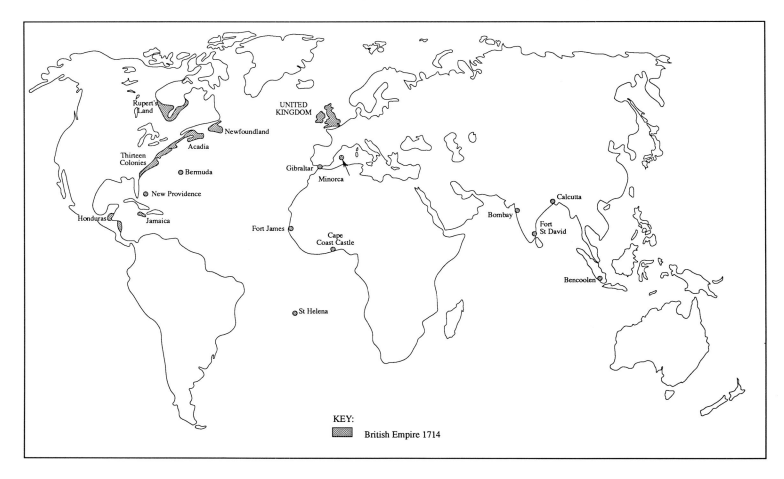

KEY:

British Empire 1714

Above: Lady with a Muff by Tilly Kettle (1735-86), a London portrait-painter who also worked in India 1770-77; she died en route for a second visit.

200,000 people emigrated from the British Isles to North America during the seventeenth century, far outnumbering the French settlers in Canada and Louisiana, and the settlements founded included Charleston (1672), Philadelphia (1682), Baltimore (1729) and Savannah (1733). The English also made a major impact in the West Indies, acquiring Bermuda (1609), St Kitts (1624), Barbados (1625), Antigua and Montserrat (1632) and Jamaica (1655) and developing a sugar economy based on slave labour brought from West Africa, where British settlements included Accra (1672). The East India Company, chartered in 1600, was the basis of British commercial activity, and later political power, in the Indian Ocean. Bombay was gained in 1661, Calcutta in 1698. Trade outside Europe became increasingly important to the British economy, and played a major role in the growth of such ports as Bristol, Glasgow, Liverpool and Whitehaven. The mercantile marine grew from 280,000 tonnes in 1695 to 609,000 in 1760, the greater number of experienced sailors providing a pool from which the navy could be manned, in part by the dreaded press gangs.

The Glorious Revolution is crucial to the Whig myth, or interpretation, of British history, central to the notion of British uniqueness. This concept can, however, be queried by comparing Britain and the Continent in the post-1688 period in both a functional and an ideological light. Functionally, the crucial relationship in both was that of central government and nobility, a term that in Britain, from a functional viewpoint, should be taken to include the more substantial landed gentry. The nobility owned and controlled much of the land and were also the

British (1713), and the foundation of colonies including Maryland (1634), Pennsylvania (1681), Carolina (1663) and Georgia (1732). Possibly

Right: The Press Gang by Thomas Rowlandson. In order to man the growing navy, an official body of officers and men was established with the power to seize, or 'impress', any able-bodied man for compulsory naval service.

Above: The Thames and City of London from Richmond House by Antonio Canaletto *c.*1747. The view across the water shows, from the left, the Savoy, the trees and white wall of the Somerset House stairs, and Christopher Wren's St Paul's. The cityscape is dominated by churches.

Left: The Thames during the Great Frost of 1739-40 by Jan Griffier the younger, a landscape painter who practised in London. Until the Thames was deepened and embanked it froze over in severe winters.

Above: Portrait of Colonel Robert Abercromby (1740-1827) by George Romney, 1788. A Scot, Abercromby served in the Seven Years War, being present at the capture of Montreal, and in the War of American Independence, where his brother James was killed. In 1788 he took his 75th regiment to India and, as Commander-in-Chief at Bombay, took part in the Third Mysore War (1790-92). He served as Commander-in-Chief in India 1793-97.

Lacking the reach of modern governments, those of the early modern period relied on other bodies and individuals to fulfil many functions that are now discharged by central government, and these reflected the interests, ideology and personnel of the social elite. Whatever the rhetoric and nature of authority, the reality of power was decentralized and, therefore, consensual. Social welfare and education was largely the responsibility of ecclesiastical institutions or of lay bodies, often with religious connections, such as the Society for Promoting Christian Knowledge, which encouraged the foundation of charity schools in the early eighteenth century. Education in England had to be paid for by the pupil's family, which was generally the case in the grammar schools, mostly sixteenth-century foundations, or by a benefactor, dead or alive. The regulation of urban commerce and manufacturing was largely left to town governments. The colonels of regiments were often responsible for raising their forces, and also for supplying them, as the administrative pretensions of the early modern state in military matters were generally unrealized. This was especially true so far as land forces were concerned, although the British navy was administratively as well as militarily impressive. Most crucially, the administration of the localities, especially the maintenance of law and order and the administration of justice, was commonly left to the local nobility, whatever the formal mechanisms and institutions of their authority.

In all these respects Britain can be seen as yet another continental state for, despite the constitutional differences, the shared reality at the local level was self-government of the localities by their notables and, at the national, a political system that was largely run by the nobility. The Romantic poet Lord Byron (1788-1824), described aristocratic electioneering in the sixteenth canto of *Don Juan* (1824):

Lord Henry was a great electioneer
Burrowing for boroughs like a rat or rabbit.
But county contests cost him rather dearer,
Because the neighbouring Scotch Earl of Giftgabbit
Had English influence, in the self-same sphere here;
His son, the Honourable Dick Dicedrabbit,
Was member for the 'other interest' (meaning
The same self-interest, with a different leaning).

The stately homes of the period were a testimony to wealth and confidence. Sir John Vanbrugh (1664-1726), the prime exponent of English baroque, displayed at Blenheim, Castle Howard and Seaton Delaval a degree of spatial enterprise similar to the architects of princely palaces on the Continent. Robert Adam (1728-92) rebuilt or redesigned many stately homes, including Harewood House, Kedleston Hall, Kenwood, Luton Hoo and Syon House, his work redolent with classical themes. Landscape gardening, inescapably linked to wealthy landed patronage, flourished and was influential abroad. The architect

local notables, enjoying social prestige and effective governmental control of the localities. Central government meant in practice, in most countries, the monarch and a small group of advisors and officials. The notion that they were capable of creating the basis of a modern state is misleading; central government, itself a questionable term because of its modern connotations and its suggestions of bureaucratic organization, lacked the mechanisms to intervene effectively and consistently in the localities. Furthermore in what was, in very large part, a pre-statistical age, the central government of any large area lacked the ability to produce coherent plans for domestic policies based on the premise of change and development. Without reliable, or any, information concerning population, revenues, economic activity or land ownership, and lacking land surveys and reliable and detailed maps, governments operated in what was, by modern standards, an information void. The contrast with the established churches of the period is instructive. Because they possessed a universal local system of government and activity, the parochial structure, and an experienced and comprehensive supervisory mechanism, the episcopal structure, the churches were able to operate far more effectively than secular government, not least in collecting information.

William Kent (1684-1748) developed and decorated parks (grounds of houses) in order to provide an appropriate setting for buildings. Lancelot 'Capability' Brown (1716-83) rejected the rigid formality associated with continental models, contriving a setting that appeared natural but was nevertheless carefully designed for effect. His landscapes of serpentine lakes, gentle hills and scattered groups of newly planted trees swiftly established a fashion, in a world where the small number of patrons and their interest in new artistic developments permitted new fashions to spread swiftly, while their wealth enabled them to realize and develop these fashions. Brown's ideas were developed further by Humphry Repton (1752-1818) in accordance with the concept of the 'picturesque', which stressed the individual character of each landscape and the need to retain it, while making improvements to remove what were judged blemishes and obstructions and to open up vistas. Landscape gardening and decoration was of direct interest to some members of the elite, for example Richard, 1st Viscount Cobham at Stowe, and his protégé William Pitt the Elder, who helped to lay out the grounds of his friends' seats and erected a temple dedicated to Pan and a garden pyramid at South Lodge, Enfield. Pride of possession characterized Pitt, who became 1st Earl of Chatham,

like other landlords. He had a public way which crossed his Somerset estate of Burton Pynsent sunk between deep hedges in order to hide it from view.

The key to stable government in Britain, as on the Continent, was to ensure that the local notables governed in accordance with the wishes of the centre, but this was largely achieved by giving them the instructions that they wanted. For the notables it was essential both that they received such instructions and that they got a fair share of governmental patronage. This system worked and its cohesion, if not harmony, was maintained not so much by a formal bureaucratic mechanism, as by the patronage and clientage networks that linked local notables to nobles wielding national influence and enjoying access to the monarch. The strength and vitality of the British aristocracy in the post-1688 world is readily apparent, not least because there was no sharp divide between them and the wealthy commoners, mostly landed, who largely dominated and comprised the House of Commons. At the local level the gentry, as Justices of the Peace, were the dominant figures. They had been entrusted with much of the business of government in the localities from the fourteenth century, and their role continued whoever directed affairs in London. Law and order depended on the JPs, and

Above: Fonthill, the architectural extravagance of William Beckford (1759-1844). Inheriting a vast fortune based on Jamaican plantations, Beckford travelled widely, wrote the fantasy *Vathek*, and was a largely inactive MP, before settling at Fonthill in 1796. The family mansion was replaced by an elaborate neo-Gothic fantasy where Beckford lived as a recluse, collecting books and works of art. Financial problems led him to sell Fonthill in 1822 and the 300-foot-high tower collapsed in 1825.

Right: The Pantheon in the gardens at Stourhead, built 1753-54. The gardens were laid out in 1741-80 by Henry Hoare, the owner of the house, and were planned as a neoclassical scene, an English realization of the classical landscapes of Roman Italy as presented in the paintings of Claude Lorrain. The Pantheon was designed by Henry Flitcroft, as was King Alfred's Tower, a folly built in 1772 at the edge of the estate. The house was completed in about 1712, also in neoclassical style, by the Scottish architect Colen Campbell, who was influenced by Palladio.

in Hanoverian Britain they were also the crucial figures in the local allocation of the Land Tax. The system cohered through patronage and personal connection, leaving copious documentation in the private correspondence of prominent politicians, such as Thomas, Duke of Newcastle, Secretary of State, 1724-54 and First Lord of the Treasury, 1754-6, 1757-62. Aside from this 'functional' similarity between Britain and the Continent, there was also an 'ideological' counterpart in the form of a shared belief in the rule of law, and of government being subject to it. The constitutional mechanisms by which this should pertain varied, but there was a common opposition to despotism.

Thus the public myth of uniqueness that played such a major role in the Whig inheritance (by the 1770s all politicians could see themselves as Whigs) can be qualified, and indeed was by domestic critics who charged, with reason, that the Whigs had abandoned their late seventeenth-century radical ideas, and denied that the British system was different and better than those across the Channel. Particular attention was focused on the way in which the 'executive' had subverted the freedom of Parliament by corruption. What was being witnessed was the re-creation of stable government by means of a new consensus, in which patronage and the avoidance of radical changes were dominant, smoothed by practices that lessened the chance of unpredictable developments: practices, in short, that neutered politics. Therefore, despite the role of a permanent and quite effective Parliament, the ministerial (Old Corps) Whigs could be seen as having created a state that bore comparison both with strong continental monarchies and with that attempted by the Stuarts, and indeed, though

paradoxically, such comparisons were to be pressed home in the 1760s and early 1770s, when George III broke with the tutelage of the Old Corps Whigs, those who had governed under Walpole and the Pelham brothers, and allegedly sought to create a stronger monarchy. Contemporaries searched for parallels in the Maupeou Revolution in France (1771) and in Gustavus III's coup in Sweden (1772), both seen as measures designed to subordinate 'intermediate institutions' to crown authority, and in Sweden a coup d'etat. Apparent differences were between Britain and the Continent was also eroded by the widespread process of public politicization on the Continent. In France this was stimulated first by the mid-century controversies centring on Jansenism and later by those arising from the Maupeou Revolution.

The principal political threats to the Protestant succession and the Whig system were seen as coming from Jacobitism, until the mid-century, and from France. James II was succeeded in 1701 by the 'warming pan baby', 'James III', and, though the latter's attempt to invade Scotland with French support in 1708 was abortive, his claim was a threat to the Hanoverian succession. The childless William III (1689-1702) had been succeeded by his sister-in-law Anne (1702-14), none of whose many children survived to adulthood. Under the Act of Succession (1701), she was to be succeeded by the German house of Hanover, descendants of James I's daughter Elizabeth. The peaceful accession of George I in 1714 was a major disappointment for James, but the consequences were not completely unhelpful, for George's enthusiastic support of the Whigs alienated the Tories, whom Anne had favoured in her last years, and helped to revive Jacobitism. This led to risings in Scotland and northern

Left: Queen Anne by Edmund Lilly, 1703. This portrait hangs at Blenheim, the palace constructed for John Churchill, created 1st Duke of Marlborough after his successful 1704 campaign against the French in Germany, and his wife, Anne's favourite, Sarah. Anne wears the collar of the Garter and holds the sceptre. Her crown, resting on a bible, and the orb are on the table beside her.

Right: George I and his family from the ceiling of the Painted Hall, Greenwich by Sir James Thornhill, who worked on the Hall from 1708 to 1727. Thornhill, who became Serjeant-Painter to the King and King's History Painter in 1720, was the first native artist to be knighted. He made a fortune by his art, purchased and rebuilt his ancestral seat at Thornhill, Dorset, and from 1722 until his death was MP for Weymouth and a firm supporter of the Walpole government. The *Gentleman's Magazine* proclaimed him 'the greatest history painter this kingdom ever produced'.

England in 1715, but they were both defeated. Tories were excluded from most senior posts in government, the armed forces, the judiciary and the church. In 1719 there was an unsuccessful Spanish invasion on behalf of the Jacobites and in 1722 the Atterbury Plot, a plan to seize London, was blocked by prompt government action, including the creation of a large army camp in Hyde Park. The 1720s and 1730s were bleak years for the Stuart cause because the leading minister, the venal but able Sir Robert Walpole (1721-42), followed policies that were less aggressive and objectionable than his predecessors and, crucially, kept Britain at peace for most of the period, thus denying the Jacobites foreign support. Walpole was unwilling to support any further improvement in the legal position of Dissenters, a measure that threatened the position of the Church of England and its Tory supporters in the localities. Walpole was certainly corrupt and his ministry a Whig monopoly of power, but he caused offence principally to those who took a close interest in politics, rather than to the wider political nation, whose position was eased by his generally successful determination to reduce taxation, especially on land.

The Walpolean system broke down, however, in his last years. The collapse of Anglo-Spanish relations over vigorous Spanish policing of what they claimed was illegal British trade with their Caribbean possessions, symbolized by the display to a committee of the House of Commons of the allegedly severed ear of a merchant captain, Robert Jenkins, led to war (1739-48), a war that Walpole had sought to avoid. He did very badly in the general election of 1741, in part as a result of support for the opposition from Frederick, Prince of Wales, who had fallen out with his

father, George II, and his father's ministers, rather as George himself had done while Prince of Wales in 1717-20. The ministry under the dynamic leadership of John, Lord Carteret, which replaced that led by Walpole, sent British troops to the Continent in 1742 in order to resist French advances.

Britain had already fought France in 1689-97 (War of the League of Augsburg or Nine Years War) and 1702-13 (War of the Spanish Succession). These wars were designed both to prevent Louis XIV's domination of western Europe and to safeguard the Protestant Succession. William III had only limited success in the 1690s, but John, Duke of Marlborough, the husband of Queen Anne's cantakerous favourite Sarah Churchill, won a series of crushing victories (Blenheim 1704, Ramillies 1706, Oudenarde 1708, Malplaquet 1709), which drove French forces out of Germany and the Low Countries. George I was able to negotiate an alliance (1716-31) with the regency government that followed Louis XIV, committing France to support the Hanoverian succession, and Walpole kept the peace with France; but his successor's abandonment of this policy led to French support for Jacobitism. In 1743 the British defeated the French at Dettingen, George II being the last British king to command in battle, but in 1744 the French responded with a planned invasion of England on behalf of the Jacobites, only to be blocked by Channel storms.

The following year 'James III's' eldest son, Charles Edward (Bonnie Prince Charlie) evaded British warships and landed in the Western Isles. He quickly overran most of Scotland, despite the reluctance of some Jacobite clans to rise for a prince who had brought no soldiers, and the hostility of the many Scots who were not Jacobites. The British force in Scotland was outmanoeuvred and then fell victim to a Highland charge at Prestonpans outside Edinburgh (21 September 1745). Crossing into England on 8 November 1745, Charles Edward took Carlisle after a brief siege and then, without any resistance, Lancaster, Preston, Manchester and Derby, which was entered on 4 December. The British armies had been outmanoeuvred and, though few English Jacobites had risen to help Charles, his opponents were affected by panic and lack of support. The Jacobite council, however, decided on 5 December to retreat, despite Charles's wish to press on. The lack of English and French support weighed most heavily with the Highland chiefs; there had been a crucial breakdown of confidence in the prince among his supporters, arising from the failure of his promises over support. The Scots considered themselves as having been tricked into a risky situation.

Had the Jacobites pressed on they might have won, capturing London and thus destroying the logistical and financial infrastructure of their opponents. By retreating they made defeat almost certain, not least because, in combination with bad weather and the British navy, the retreat led the French to abandon a planned supporting invasion of southern England. Charles evaded pursuit, retreated to Scotland successfully and, on 17 January 1746, beat a British army at Falkirk; but George II's inexorable second son, William, Duke of Cumberland, brought up a formidable army and on Culloden Moor near Inverness on 16 April 1746 his superior firepower smashed the Jacobite army. Cumberland recorded of his opponents that 'in their rage that they could not make any impression upon the battalions, they threw stones at them for at least a minute or two, before their total rout began'. He had secured the Protestant Succession established by William III.

The aftermath was harsh. The Hanoverian regime had been overthrown in Scotland, the army humiliated, and the government was determined to ensure that there was no recurrence of the '45. The Highlanders were regarded as barbarians and Cumberland's successor, the Earl of Albemarle, offered his solution for 'the bad inclination of the people in most of the northern counties and their stubborn, inveterate disposi-

John Duke of Marlborough

Left: John Churchill, 1st Duke of Marlborough, by Sir Godfrey Kneller. Marlborough was a brilliant general who played a vital role in defeating Louis XIV during the War of the Spanish Succession.

tion of mind . . . nothing could effect it but laying the whole country waste and in ashes, and removing all the inhabitants (excepting a few) out of the kingdom'. The 'pacification' of the Highlands was to be characterized first by killings, rapes and systematic devastation, and secondly by a determined attempt to alter their political, social and strategic structure. The clans were disarmed and the clan system broken up, while roads to open up the Highlands and forts to awe them were constructed. Hereditable jurisdictions were abolished; the wearing of Highland clothes prohibited. The rebellion and its suppression therefore gave cause and opportunity for the sort of radical state-directed action against inherited privilege, especially regional and aristocratic privilege, that was so rare in Britain. More longterm political changes were also important. In effect Scotland, like many dependent parts of multiple kingdoms or federal states, was losing its capacity for important independent political initiatives. This affected both the Highlands and the country as a whole. It was not a case of English pressure on an unwilling people, for political changes profited, and were in part shaped by, local politicians. Many Scots were firm opponents of the Stuarts and supporters of the Protestant Succession, and London relied on Scottish politicians, not Englishmen sent to govern Scotland.

The '45 both revealed the vulnerability, and led to the firm establishment, of the Hanoverian regime. It thus closed a long period of instability and, instead, provided the basis for a fundamental recasting of British politics in which Toryism lost its Jacobite aspect, thus facilitating the dissolution of the Whig-Tory divide over the following 17 years. Attempts to conciliate and comprehend opponents within ministerial ranks, and expectations concerning the future behaviour of the heir to the throne, first Frederick Prince of Wales, who died in 1751, and then the future George III, along with the behaviour of the latter after he came to the throne in 1760, compromised the cohesion and identity of the Tories, and brought some of them into government. In addition the relationship between England and Scotland became essentially one of the willing co-option of the powerful Scots through patronage, with no alternative Jacobite or nationalist focus of loyalty and with a diminishing emphasis on coercion.

The unification of Britain helped her in the conflict with France. The decisive struggle was the Seven Years' War (1756-63), which ended

Below: 'The Music Party' Frederick Prince of Wales and his Sisters, by Philip Mercier, 1733. Anne, Princess Royal, is at the harpsichord, Caroline plays a mandora, a form of lute, and Amelia listens with a volume of Milton in her lap. The Dutch House at Kew, in the background, was Anne's home before her marriage to William IV of Orange in 1734.

Left: George II by Thomas Hudson, 1744. The previous year George, the last English sovereign to lead his troops into battle, had acquired glory through his victory at Dettingen, but in 1744 his throne was threatened by French plans to invade on behalf of the Jacobites.

with the Thirteen Colonies on the eastern sea-board of North America and the British possessions in India secure, with Canada, Florida, and many Caribbean islands acquired, and with Britain as the leading maritime power in the world, thus fulfilling what James Thomson had seen as the national destiny in his ode 'Rule Britannia' (1740):

Rule Britannia, rule the waves:
Britons never will be slaves.

This was the achievement of the ministry of William Pitt the Elder and the Duke of Newcastle (1757-61), and of a number of able military leaders including Wolfe, Clive, Hawke and Boscawen. Robert Clive's victory at Plassey, over the vastly more numerous forces of the Indian Prince Surajah Dowla in 1757, laid the basis for the virtual control of Bengal, Bihar and Orissa by the East India Company. The French were subjugated in India in 1760-61, and Britain emerged as the most powerful European state in the Indian subcontinent. The French attempt to invade Britain on behalf of the Jacobites was crushed by the British naval victories of Lagos (off Portugal) and Quibéron Bay (1759). That year, British troops also beat the French at Minden in Germany, while Quebec was captured after a hazardous ascent of the cliffs nearby, General James Wolfe dying at the moment of glorious victory on the Plains of Abraham. The bells of victory rang out across Britain: the ringers at York Minster were paid four times between 21 August and 22 October for celebrating triumphs, beginning with

Minden and ending with Quebec. The victories were also a tribute to the national unity that had followed the defeat of Jacobitism; a Highland charge played a major role at Quebec. In 1762 British forces campaigned round the globe. They helped the Portuguese resist a Spanish invasion, fought the French in Germany, and captured Martinique from the French and Havana and Manila from the Spaniards, an extraordinary testimony to the global reach of British power and the strength of the British state.

The Destiny of Empire 1763-1815

Britain was soon to have to defend its maritime and colonial position from serious challenges: rebellion in America and Ireland, war with Revolutionary and Napoleonic France. The society that did so was changing both socially and economically. After a century of limited growth, if not stagnation, population growth rates shot up, leading to a rise in the population of England and Wales from about 6 million in 1742 to 8.2 in 1789. Real wages suffered and Britain had to import grain to feed the growing numbers, but this greater population was sustained and high growth rates continued. A decline in the death rate was less important than an increase in fertility from the 1780s to the 1820s. Agricultural improvement, the construction of canals and better roads, and the development of industry and trade, led to a growth in national wealth and a different economic structure; the percentage of the male labour force employed in industry rose

Below: The British empire after the Peace of Paris, 1763.

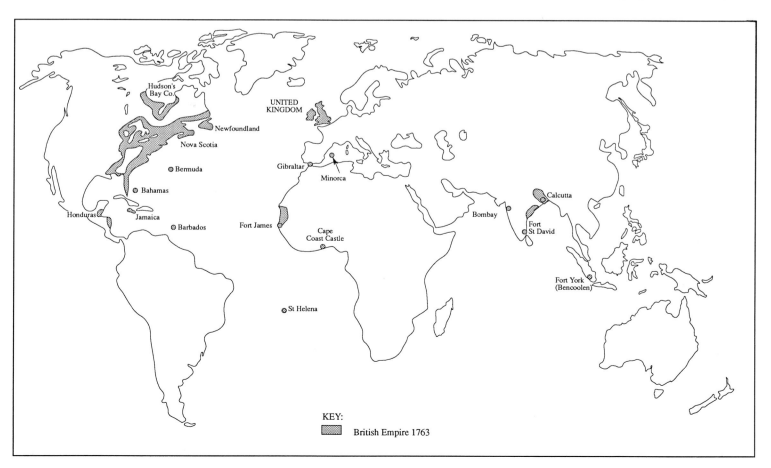

KEY:

British Empire 1763

Left: Turnpike gates at Hyde Park Corner, 1792; the construction of better roads, and more effective communications generally, contributed to a growth in national wealth in the second half of the eighteenth century.

from 19 (1700) to 30 (1800), while that in agriculture fell from 60 to 40, although agricultural productivity increased. In 1790 the Oxford Canal reached Oxford, creating the final link in a network joining the rivers Trent, Mersey and Thames. Scientific advances were made in a number of fields. William Brownrigg (1711-1800) formulated the concept of a multiplicity of chemically distinctive gases. Joseph Black (1728-99), Professor of Chemistry at Glasgow and later Edinburgh, discovered latent heat and first fixed the compound carbon dioxide. Henry Cavendish (1731-1810), a master of quantitative analysis, was in 1766 the first to define hydrogen as a distinct substance and, in 1781, the first to determine the composition of water, by exploding a mixture of hydrogen and oxygen in a sealed vessel. Joseph Priestley (1733-1804) discovered a number of gases and oxides.

The spread of fodder crops such as clover, coleseed and turnips helped to eliminate fallow and to increase the capacity of the rural economy to rear more animals, sources of the 'roast beef of old England', woollen cloth and crucial manure. The

Left: James Hargreaves' spinning jenny, invented in about 1764 and called jenny after his wife, multiplied eightfold the productive power of the spinner and largely superseded the spinning-wheel. An alarmed mob of Blackburn spinners destroyed Hargreaves' jenny and gutted his house in 1768. Hargreaves moved to Nottingham and took out a patent in 1770.

Right: The world's first iron bridge spanning a river was erected at Coalbrookdale, Shropshire, in 1776. Wrought iron had long been a valued decorative material, but the replacement during the eighteenth century of charcoal by coke smelting meant that reliable and precise cast iron became available. The Coalbrookdale bridge has a 120 foot span, carrying the road on arched ribs springing from the bases of two vertical iron uprights. The construction details were worked out by experienced iron-founders and the project as a whole was initiated by Abraham Darby, manager of the Coalbrookdale company. Unlike later examples, however, the bridge was designed by a local architect, Thomas Farnolls Pritchard, rather than by an engineer, and its lines echo those of traditional masonry building.

percentage of enclosed land increased greatly, and hedges became even more characteristic of lowland Britain. Enclosure did not necessarily raise efficiency, and there are examples of unenclosed areas that witnessed agricultural improvement. Enclosure made it easier to control the land, however; was often linked to innovation; and was frequently accompanied by a redistribution of agricultural income from tenant farmer to landlord. Progressive landowners disrupted traditional rights and expectations and the enclosure of common lands led to particular bitterness.

Even if the rate of industrialization was less impressive than used to be believed, the qualitative impact of economic change was obvious to contemporaries. The impression was of Prometheus Unbound, of extraordinary opportunities offered by technological innovation. The *Darlington Pamphlet* of 1772 reported that 'an ingenious mechanic has just invented a machine with which a girl of ten years of age may spin several threads'. John Kay's flying shuttle of 1733, which was in general use in Yorkshire by the 1780s, increased the productivity of handloom weavers. James Hargreaves' spinning jenny (c. 1764), Richard Arkwright's waterframe (1769) and Samuel Crompton's mule (1779) revolutionized textile spinning, while in 1769 James Watt patented a more energy-efficient use of steam engines. Greater ease of communication helped to unify the elite, facilitating education, socializing, and travel for business or political reasons. London newspapers were sent to the provinces in increasing numbers. Postal services improved greatly, with Royal Mail coach services starting in 1784, to the benefit of the expanding banking system as well as to the letter writer, that central character in two recent and rapidly developing literary forms, the novel and the magazine.

Many of the social features that were to be associated with economic transformation were already common. Far from Britain being a rural elysium, lacking a Boucher to depict plenty and languorous calm but all too soon to be ravaged by industrialization, the rural world had already in the fifteenth and sixteenth centuries witnessed massive disruptions of land and labour. Neither enclosure, sweeping changes in land use and rural proletarianization, nor the social and economic changes wrought by industrialization, technological change and the rise and decline of specific areas and economic activities were new; though they were to increase in scale and pace from the late eighteenth century, and never to cease to do so thereafter. This process of continual change, more than anything else, marked the birth of modern times.

Right: Thomas Newcomen's steam engine was used to pump water out of mines, improving both safety and productivity.

For those who wielded power, however, political challenges were foremost. The Whig-Tory two-party system was replaced in the 1760s by a number of essentially personal political groups, with the rivalries of political leaders and the changing preferences of George III (1760-1820) fostering instability. As much as any continental ruler who did not have to face a powerful representative institution, George was determined to reject what he saw as the politics of faction, to thwart the efforts of unacceptable politicians to force their way into office. As did other rulers, George found it most difficult to create acceptable relationships with senior politicians at his accession, when he had to persuade both those who had had a good working relationship with his predecessor, and those who had looked for a dramatic change, to adjust to his wishes. George broke with Pitt in 1761 and Newcastle in 1762 and made his favourite, John, 3rd Earl of Bute, First Lord of the Treasury in 1762, only to see the weak-willed Bute resign in 1763 in the face of bitter domestic opposition. George complained to the French ambassador in 1763 about 'the spirit of fermentation and the excessive licence which prevails in England. It is essential to neglect nothing that can check that spirit'. The ambiguity of a number of constitutional points, such as the collective responsibility of the Cabinet, and the degree to which the monarch had to choose his ministers from those who had the confidence of parliament, exacerbated the situation; as did the volatile political atmosphere in London. Dis-

satisfaction there was exploited by a squinting anti-hero John Wilkes, an entrepreneur of faction and libertine MP, who fell foul of George III as a result of bitter attacks on the king in his newspaper the *North Briton*. He was arrested in 1763 but pleaded parliamentary privilege. Not until 1770 did George find in Frederick, Lord North a minister who could control Parliament.

The discontent and divisions of the 1760s over the determination of George III to pick ministers of his own choice paled into insignificance, however, beside the collapse of the imperial relationship with America. The determination to make colonies, not represented in Parliament, pay a portion of their defence burden was crucial, although so also was the increasing democratization of American society, a millenarian rejection of British authority, concern about British policy in Canada, and the borrowing of British conspiracy theories about the supposed autocratic intentions of George III. The fact that Britain's most important colonies in the western hemisphere, those in the West Indies, did not rebel, despite the sensitivity of their elites on questions of constitutional principle, suggests that it was the increasingly serious social, economic and political crises in the American colonies that were crucial. Fighting broke out near Boston in 1775 as a result of the determination of the government of Lord North to employ force, and the willingness of sufficient Americans to do likewise. The Americans declared independence (1776) and the British were driven from the bulk

Left: George III Reviewing the Troops; this massive painting by Sir William Beechey was destroyed in the fire at Windsor Castle on 19th November 1992.

of the Thirteen Colonies but held Canada (1775 – spring 1776), before counterattacking to regain New York (1776). The British seizure of Philadelphia was matched by defeat at Saratoga (1777), and after the French entered the war on the revolutionary side (1778), the British lacked the resources necessary for America and were pushed on to the defensive in a world war. Spain joined France in 1779 and at the end of 1780 the Dutch were added to the list of Britain's enemies in what was truly a global conflict.

Though the Franco-Spanish attempt to invade England failed (1779), and the British held on to Gibraltar, India and Jamaica, defeat at Yorktown (1781) was followed by the acceptance of American independence. This split the unity of the English-speaking world. America, inhabited by an independent people of extraordinary vitality, was to be the most dynamic of the independent states in the western hemisphere, the first and foremost of the decolonized countries, the people best placed to take advantage of the potent combination of a European legacy, independence, and the opportunities for expansion and growth that were to play an increasingly important role in the new world created from 1776. America was to play a crucial role in Europe during both World Wars, helping to ensure the success of the alliances in which Britain was a partner; and also ensured that aspects of British culture, society and ideology, albeit in altered forms, were to enjoy great influence outside and after the span of British empire. The role of the English language today owes more to America than to modern Britain.

As so often in British history, defeat led to the fall of the government. Lord North's resignation in 1782 was followed by a period of marked ministerial and constitutional instability. George was forced to accept ministers whom he disliked, threatened abdication, and in 1783-84 breached several fundamental political conventions in engineering the fall of the Fox-North ministry and supporting, without a Commons majority, that of the 24 year-old William Pitt the Younger, the severe (but sometimes drunk) second son of the elder Pitt. Pitt's victory in the 1784 general election was also therefore a triumph for George and it began a period of generally stable government that lasted until Pitt's resignation in 1801. Like Walpole and North, Pitt understood the im-

portance of sound finances, and although he was interested in electoral reform, he did not push this divisive issue after it had been defeated in 1785. As so often in a monarchical state, however, continuity was threatened by the succession. George III's eldest son, later George IV, was not only opposed to the frugality, virtue and duty of his father, but also to Pitt, preferring instead the latter's opponent, Charles James Fox, who, unlike the Prince, had talent but, like him, lacked self-control. When in late 1788 an attack of porphyria led to the conviction that George III was mad, the resulting Regency Crisis nearly produced the fall of the government; fortunately for Pitt, the king recovered in early 1789.

Defeat at the hands of America had led to reform, especially in the Royal Navy, and this was to help Britain in the more serious challenge that lay ahead. She bounced back from the loss of the Thirteen Colonies, Florida and various Caribbean islands (Treaty of Versailles, 1783), to establish the first British foothold in Malaysia (Penang 1786) and the first European colony in Australia (1788), and to thwart Spanish attempts to prevent her from trading and establishing settlements on the western coast of modern Canada (Nootka Sound crisis, 1790). In contrast, the French took a long time to recover from their loss, during the Revolutionary-Napoleonic period, of maritime power and colonial possessions and pretensions, while Spain never recovered from the loss of her Latin American empire in the early nineteenth century.

Though buffeted seriously during the war with Revolutionary and then Napoleonic France (1793-1802, 1803-14, 1815), most worryingly by the Irish rising of 1798 and the threat of invasion by Napoleon from 1803, Britain survived, thanks in particular to a series of naval victories culminating in Nelson's apotheosis at Trafalgar (1805). The war against Revolutionary France had revealed, however, that the British were unable to defend the Low Countries, and subsequent expeditions there, including the 1799 landing in Holland under George III's son Frederick, Duke of York (now best remembered in a nursery rhyme for marching troops up and down hills), and the 1809 attack on Walcheren, ended in failure. Napoleon's domination of the Continent was a major challenge to British interests. He sought in the Continental System, which was inaugurated in November 1806, to bring Britain to her knees by economic means. The Berlin Decrees declared Britain blockaded, and banned trade with her. Napoleon's extra-European interests were also a threat to Britain. His invasion of Egypt in 1798 had been gravely weakened when Nelson destroyed the French fleet at the Battle of the Nile in Aboukir Bay, but thereafter Napoleon remained interested in the prospect of weakening the British in India, possibly in co-operation with Russia, and of establishing new French colonies.

The war placed a major strain on British resources, and defeats led to or exacerbated political problems. William Pitt the Younger (Prime Minister 1783-1801, 1804-6), discovered that wartime leadership was considerably more difficult than the period of reform and regeneration he had earlier helped to orchestrate, and he died, worn out, in office. The cost and economic disruption of the war pressed hard throughout society, leading to the introduction of income tax (1799), the stagnation of average real wages and widespread hardship, especially in the famine years of 1795-96 and 1799-1801. Radicals found their activities prohibited or limited, while trade unions were restricted, though not ended, by the Combination Acts of 1799 and 1800, which made combinations for improved pay or conditions illegal. Further economic difficulties arose from the war with the United States of America (1812-14) over British regulation of neutral trade. The British burnt Washington and defended Canada successfully, but were defeated outside New Orleans.

That conflict, the only war Britain fought with the United States after 1783, was only a diversion from the struggle with Napoleon. Eventual triumph in that came as part of an alliance to which Britain contributed money (£66 million in subsidies and armaments to her allies) and the Duke of Wellington's victories in the Peninsular War (1808-13) in Portugal and Spain, such as Vimeiro (1808), Talavera (1809), Salamanca

Below: Charles James Fox, looking into the mirror, sees Oliver Cromwell in armour. This caricature by James Sayers, published on 20 January 1784, suggested that Fox's opposition to the new ministry of William Pitt the Younger, which was backed by George III, was dangerous and a threat to the constitution. Cromwell was regarded very unfavourably. Fox was alleged later to have declared that Sayers' caricatures did him more harm than all the parliamentary or press attacks on him.

The Mirror of Patriotism.
C. J. FOX

(1812), and Vitoria (1813). The disciplined fire-power of the British infantry played a major part in these triumphs. Wellington never had more than 40,000 British troops under his personal command and was always outnumbered in both cavalry and artillery, but he was a fine judge of terrain; at Vimeiro, the well-positioned British lines succeeded in blunting the attacking French columns, while at Salamanca he used his lines in attack with great effect. British commitment culminated in the major roles taken at the Congress of Vienna and, under Wellington, on the battle-field of Waterloo (1815). Though British troops composed less than half of the Anglo-German-Dutch force that Wellington commanded, they played a decisive role in stopping the successive advances of French cavalry and infantry, until finally Napoleon's veteran Guard units were driven back and the Prussians could attack the French flank.

Naval power permitted Britain to dominate the European trans-oceanic world during the Revolutionary and Napoleonic wars. Danish, Dutch, French and Spanish naval power were crippled; Britain was left free to execute amphibious attacks on the now-isolated centres of other European powers, and to make gains at the expense of non-European peoples. The route to India was secured: Cape Town was captured in 1795 and then again in 1806, after it had been restored to the Dutch in 1802, the Seychelles in 1794, Réunion and Mauritius in 1810. The British position in India and Australasia was consolidated, while her gains at the Congress of Vienna included Trinidad, Tobago, St Lucia, Malta,

Cape Colony and Guyana. The Pacific became a British rather than a Spanish lake, while India served as the basis of British power and influence around the Indian Ocean.

The nature both of the British empire and of the European world altered dramatically. In 1775 the majority of British subjects outside Britain were white (though the population of the West Indian colonies was predominantly black slaves), Christian, of British, or at least European, origin, and ruled with an element of local self-government. By 1815 none of this was true. By then most of the trans-oceanic European world outside the western hemisphere was British; by 1830 this was true of the vast majority of all European possessions abroad. The situation was not to last; indeed 1830 was the date of the French occupation of Algiers, the basis of their subsequent North African empire. Nevertheless the unique imperial oceanic position that Britain occupied in the Revolutionary, Napoleonic and post-Napoleonic period was to be of crucial importance to its nineteenth-century economic and cultural development. France was to become a great imperial power again; Portugal and the Dutch were to make gains; Germany, Italy, Belgium (and the United States) to become imperial powers; but for none of these was empire as important, as central a feature of public culture, as it was for Britain by the late Victorian and Edwardian period.

The rise in British imperial power had a great influence on the British economy, on the British elite, who were provided with a new sense of role and mission and, in many cases, with careers, and

Right: The Attack on Bunker Hill with the Burning of Charles Town, 17 June 1775, by an unknown artist. The British attack on American positions was described by a British general, John Burgoyne: '. . . They met with a thousand impediments from strong fences and were much exposed. They were also extremely hurt by musketry from . . . Charles Town . . . We threw a parcel of shells and the whole was instantly in flames. Our Battery afterwards kept up an incessant fire on the Heights. It was seconded by a number of frigates, floating batteries, and one ship of the line. And now ensued one of the greatest scenes of war, that can be conceived. If we look to the right, Howe's corps ascending the Hill in the face of entrenchments . . . and in the arm of the sea, our ships and floating batteries cannonading them. In a straight line before us a large noble town in one blaze, the church steeples being made of wood, were great pyramids of fire . . .'

Left: The Battle of Waterloo, 18 June 1815, watercolour by Denis Dighton showing the attack on a British square by the French cavalry. The repeated attacks of Napoleon's army were stubbornly beaten back by the disciplined fire of the British infantry, drawn up in unbreachable squares. The fall of men and horses seemed to one British officer 'like that of grass before a mower's scythe'.

on British public culture. Service in the colonies, particularly in India, came to be prestigious, more so than anything similar in France or Germany. The sense of Britain playing a major role in resisting challenges to the European system, which had characterized opposition to Louis XIV, the Revolution and Napoleon, ebbed as empire, especially from the 1870s, set the themes of Britain's role and identity, a process that was furthered by the development of widespread emigra-

tion to certain colonies. The establishment of the British imperial position owed much to success in war, and it was not surprising that the pantheon of imperial heroes defined and depicted in the nineteenth century was largely composed of naval and military figures such as Nelson. Wellington, 'the last great Englishman' according to the Poet Laureate, Alfred, Lord Tennyson in 1852, was the only former general in British history to become Prime Minister (1828-30, 1834).

Below: The British Empire 1815, after the Congress of Vienna.

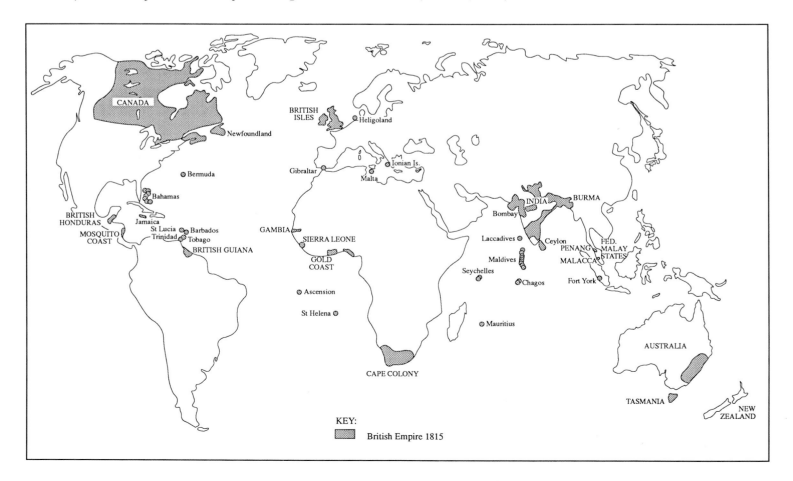

KEY:

▨ British Empire 1815

8

THE NINETEENTH CENTURY

1815-1914

Left: A May Day procession passes along Kingsway, London, 1912; the increasing organization of the labour movement was a feature of the late nineteenth and early twentieth centuries.

THE RISE OF BRITAIN to become the greatest imperial power in history was not alone responsible for the divergence which took place between her and the other European powers; the process was accentuated by economic development and the rise of nationalism. The harnessing of technological change led to the economic transformation of the country, owing to the benefits of readily available capital and labour, and the burgeoning markets of a growing home and colonial population. The Wheal Virgin steam engine of 1790, produced by the Birmingham partnership of Boulton and Watt, could do the work of 953 horses. The widespread use of coal to fuel mechanical power freed the economy from its earlier energy constraints, reducing costs and increasing the availability of heat energy. As a mobile source of energy, the steam engine permitted the concentration of industrial production in towns, but it is also appropriate to stress, alongside major changes, the gradual and evolutionary nature of the Industrial Revolution. Handloom weaving, for example, persisted on an appreciable scale in Lancashire into the 1840s: London and Birmingham were primarily cities of workshops, not factories.

The Industrial Revolution gave Britain a distinctive economy. The annual averages of coal and lignite production, in million metric tons for 1820-24, were 18 for Britain, 2 for France, Germany, Belgium and Russia combined. The comparable figures for 1855-59 were 68 and 32, and for 1880-84 159 and 108. Raw cotton consumption in thousand metric tons in 1850 was 267 for Britain and 162 for the rest of Europe, and in 1880 617 and 503. The annual production of pig-iron in million metric tons in 1820 was 0.4 for Britain and the same for the rest of Europe, in 1850 2.3 and 0.9, in 1880 7.9 and 5.4; of steel in 1880, 1.3 for Britain, 1.5 for the rest of Europe. The British population (excluding Ireland), rose from an estimated 7.4 million in 1750 to 29.7 in 1881, and much of this growing population lived in the shadow of mill, mine and factory. The 1851 census showed that, for the first time, the English urban population exceeded its rural counterpart.

The Great Exhibition of that year was a tribute to manufacturing skill and prowess, as was the evolution from the stationary to the locomotive steam-engine and the consequent railway revolution. The Stockton and Darlington Railway was opened in 1825; the Liverpool to Manchester in 1830. In the following two decades a national system developed, albeit one constructed and run by competing companies. Services from London reached Bristol in 1841, Exeter in 1844, cutting the journey time from 21 to less than 6 hours; Norwich in 1845, Plymouth in 1847 and Truro in 1859. The locomotive that began services on the Stockton and Darlington Railway attained a speed of twelve to sixteen miles an hour. When Goldsworthy Gurney's steam-jet (or blast) was applied to George Stephenson's *Rocket* locomotive in 1829, the engine reached a speed of 29 miles an hour. The railway network spread throughout Britain and was far more extensive than that of the canals which it largely consigned to decay. In 1911 there were 130 manned stations in Devon and Cornwall.

The railways brought new sounds and smells, the dramatic engineering of viaducts, tunnels and bridges – such as Brunel's across the Tamar – opened in 1859, and transported goods and people around the country. Economic patterns changed. Trains were used to move perishable goods, such as fruit, flowers and milk, to the major cities: over 15,000 tons of Cornish broccoli annually by 1900 and a special daily refrigerated van carrying Devon rabbit carcasses to London in 1939. Train travel encouraged domestic tourism

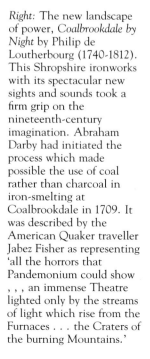

Right: The new landscape of power, *Coalbrookdale by Night* by Philip de Loutherbourg (1740-1812). This Shropshire ironworks with its spectacular new sights and sounds took a firm grip on the nineteenth-century imagination. Abraham Darby had initiated the process which made possible the use of coal rather than charcoal in iron-smelting at Coalbrookdale in 1709. It was described by the American Quaker traveller Jabez Fisher as representing 'all the horrors that Pandemonium could show , , , an immense Theatre lighted only by the streams of light which rise from the Furnaces . . . the Craters of the burning Mountains.'

Left: The use of steam power to bring coal to the surface in Staffordshire collieries.

and the development of the seaside resorts that changed much of coastal Britain, such as Newquay, Ramsgate, Bournemouth, Hove, Eastbourne, Margate, Southend, Yarmouth, Skegness, Cleethorpes, Bridlington, Scarborough, Morecambe and Blackpool.

In Britain the nineteenth century was an age of dramatic economic change, possibly most so in Bradford, whose population climbed from 16,012 in 1810 to 103,778 in 1850 as the city became the global centre of worsted production and exchange. Factory horsepower in the town rose 718 per cent in 1810-30. Mechanization brought profit, larger factories and a wave of immigrants. Innovation was continual. The mechanization of yarn spinning was followed in 1826, despite riots by hostile workers, by that of worsted weaving. By 1850 the work formerly done in Bradford by

Left: An early railway scene; a locomotive taking in water at Parkside on the Manchester and Liverpool railway. On 15 September 1830, during the opening celebrations, the train stopped at Parkside, many of the passengers left the carriages, and William Huskisson, MP for Liverpool, was killed by the Dart, another locomotive.

producing women's dress fabrics. Mechanization was crucial to uniformity; the production of low-cost standardized products. As a result brands of mass-produced goods, such as chocolate and soap, could be consumed and advertised nationally. Although factory production did not predominate until the second half of the century, industry and trade changed the face of the nation and the life of the people:

. . . many a weary hand did swelt
In torched mines and noisy factories.
(John Keats, *Isabella*, 1820).

The consequences were varied. At the great seaport of Liverpool about 30,000 sailors were ashore at any one time, leading to a major rise in prostitution: there were about 300 brothels in 1836, 538 in 1846, and in 1857 there were at least 200 regular prostitutes under the age of 12. Industrial growth, far from uniform across the country, was concentrated in the North-East, the Midlands, southern Lancashire, the West Riding of Yorkshire, South Wales and Clydeside. Once important areas, such as East Anglia and the South-West, suffered de-industrialization, in part because they lacked coal, and de-population. The wealthy businessmen of the industrial areas purchased landed estates, patronized the arts and increasingly sought political and social influence.

One of the greatest was William Armstrong (1810-1900), whose career epitomized the opportunities of the Victorian age, the intertwined forces of technology and industry. Grandson of a Northumberland yeoman farmer and son of a

Main industrial areas (1851 census)

Above: The main industrial areas, 1851.

thousands of handloom weavers, working in the countryside, was now performed by 17,642 automatic looms contained in factories and mass-

Right: The Great Exhibition, Crystal Palace 1851, view along the main avenue at the opening ceremonies. Planned by Prince Albert in 1849, it was intended as a demonstration of British achievement and a reflection of 'England's mission, duty and interest to put herself at the head of the diffusion of civilization and the attainment of Liberty.'

Newcastle corn merchant, he became a solicitor but was also an amateur scientist, with a particular interest in hydroelectrics. His development of the hydraulic crane led him to establish an engineering works at Elswick (1846). Armstrong subsequently expanded into both armaments and shipbuilding, his Elswick Ordnance Company becoming one of the largest engineering and armaments concerns in the world. The 110-ton, nearly 44-foot-long, Armstrong breech-loaders manufactured for *HMS Victoria*, which was launched in 1887, were the largest and most powerful guns in the world. Warships were also built for a host of foreign powers, including Japan, Italy, Argentina and Chile. When he died, Armstrong was employing 25,000 people.

Armstrong was at the forefront of technological application, responsible for the installation of

Left: Clifton suspension bridge, Bristol, under construction. The design submitted in 1831 by Isambard Kingdom Brunel (1806-59) was accepted as the most mathematically exact of all those tendered. Brunel was appointed engineer and the works were begun in 1836 but unfinished in his lifetime due to lack of funds. The bridge over the Avon gorge near Bristol was eventually completed according to Brunel's plans, and using chains taken from the old Hungerford suspension bridge which he had constructed over the Thames in 1841-45.

the world's first hydroelectric power station, and the mock-baronial stately home he built at Cragside was in 1880 the first house to be properly lit by light bulbs. Armstrong supplied the hydraulic equipment to raise Tower Bridge, opened in 1894 and a potent symbol of empire. He was also responsible for the hydraulic lifts that were necessary if the London Underground railway system was to expand with deep stations. A major local benefactor, who helped provide Newcastle with a better water supply and supported local education and health, Armstrong gained great wealth and became a peer in 1887. He was President of the Arts Association and a patron of contemporary British painters such as Dante Gabriel Rossetti. It was appropriate that in 1894 this greatest of the Victorian, or indeed modern British, warlords should have purchased Bamburgh Castle, the centre of Northumbrian power for much of the Anglo-Saxon period, and a powerful medieval royal fortress.

Isambard Kingdom Brunel (1806-59) was less successful than Armstrong, but shared his desire to apply technological innovations. Brunel's formidable engineering triumphs included the Clifton suspension bridge and his achievements as chief engineer on the Great Western Railway 1833-46, as well as his large iron-clad steamships, the *Great Western* (1838), *Great Britain* (1845) and *Great Eastern* (1858), which reflected his

Above: The Fighting Temeraire Tugged to her Last Berth to be Broken Up (detail), by Joseph Mallord William Turner, 1839. This famous image was understood by contemporaries as representing the passing of an old Britain.

Right: The Rickyards, Winter by George Clausen, 1902, shows the simple tools and hard physical toil of rural labour.

work at the forefront of technical innovations on, for example, screw propellers. The *Great Western* was, when launched, the largest steamship afloat and the first to sail regularly to America; the *Great Britain* was the first large ship using a screw propellor; the *Great Eastern*, the largest steamship yet built, was constructed by new methods.

Economic growth did not, however, mean that there were no fears of continental economic competition. France was much feared as an industrial rival down to the 1840s, while concern about German industrial competition was a major reason for the repeal of the Corn Laws. In the parliamentary debates of February-March 1839 on the Corn Laws, in response to the depression, almost every speaker was aware of the threat from foreign manufacturing, especially as a result of the German *Zollverein* (Customs Union). Confidence was most developed in the 1850s and 1860s, which were abnormally prosperous decades, and even then it was not unqualified.

Nevertheless, it was not simply the scale of British economic development that was of importance, but also the links that, literally, were being forged. The ending of protection for British agriculture, with the repeal of the Corn Laws (1846), and the technological changes, including steamships, barbed wire, long-distance railways and, in the 1880s, refrigerated shipholds, leading to the development of agricultural production for the European market in other temperate climes and to the ability to move products rapidly without spoilage, meant that Britain became, from the 1870s and 1880s, part of a global agrarian system. She was looking to empire, both formal and informal, rather than to Europe; grain from Germany, Poland and Russia was only bought in significant quantities in some years. Some continental agricultural products were important, most obviously fruit and vegetables, German sugar-beet and Danish bacon and dairy products, and by the end of the century Danish bacon and eggs were the staple of the British breakfast. Nevertheless, it was North American grain, Argentine beef and Australasian wool and mutton that were crucial.

In combination, these imports led to a severe and sustained domestic agricultural depression from the 1870s, which badly affected farmworkers and rural craftsmen, and led to high rates of rural depopulation until the end of the century. The spread of new technology, for example combined reaping and mowing machines, also affected the rural labour force. The total area devoted to agriculture in Britain fell by half a million acres between the 1870s and 1914. The cheap food that fed the growing workforces of the industrial north helped to cause a serious depression throughout much of the south, a regional disparity that was to be reversed the following century. Sunderland, now a city with many urban problems, was in 1850 the greatest shipbuilding town in the world, with high wages and a high rate of owner-occupied housing.

Empire was not simply a matter of power politics, military interests, elite careers, and an ideology of mission and purpose which appealed to the propertied and the proselytizing. It also had relevance and meaning throughout society, and this was reflected in the jingoistic strains of popular culture, the ballads of music hall and the

Above: Stonehaven by W F Douglas, 1870s. Despite the growth of major cities, much of the British population still lived in smaller towns.

Right: An election
caricature of 1831 shows
the Whigs – Grey (holding
up the reform bill),
Brougham, Lord John
Russell, Burdett and
O'Connell – sitting on the
lower end of the seesaw,
which is weighted down by
the crown (William IV)
and the press, most
prominently *The Times*.
The Tories are in the air –
a fat bishop grasping a
crozier, the Duke of
Cumberland, Wellington,
Peel, Wetherell and a sack
inscribed 'Charles St
Committee Purse', a
reference to the Tory
election fund. John Bull,
standing on the edge of a
pit, supports the seesaw on
his shoulders.

THE BALANCE of POWER in 1831.

images depicted on advertisements for mass-produced goods; although, on the other hand, many workers appear to have been pretty apathetic about imperialism. Empire reflected and sustained the widespread racist assertions and assumptions of the period, both of which were amply demonstrated in contemporary literature. The sieges of the Indian Mutiny and the Boer War offered drama for the entire country. Newspapers spent substantial sums on the telegraphy that brought news of imperial conflict. The Prot-

estant churches of Britain devoted their resources to missionary activity outside Europe, particularly, though not only, within the Empire, and not to proselytism on the Continent.

With the succession of Queen Victoria in 1837, the dynastic link with Hanover was broken. Nevertheless Britain's global responsibilities meant that, although she took a view of the world in which 'Europe' was simply one element, it was a very important element. The concepts of the 'Concert of Europe' and 'the Balance of

Right: Belgian
independence from the
Dutch was agreed by the
powers at a London
conference. Here the
developments are brought
home to the British public
by a domestic caricature.

THE SEPARATION or the Grey Mare-the better Horse - Did you not hear a buzzing of a Separation between them. Shak

Power' indicate how central the Continent was in the conduct of British foreign policy. Prominent Foreign Secretaries, such as George Canning, 1807, 1822-27, Prime Minister 1827, and Henry, Viscount Palmerston, Foreign Secretary 1830-41, 1846-51, Prime Minister 1855-58, 1859-65, were extremely concerned with continental international relations, for example in Iberia, Greece and the Near East. In addition, imperial issues could have a European dimension, most obviously with the 'Eastern Question'.

More generally, educated Victorians were acutely aware of what they shared with other European peoples as a result of a common culture based upon Christianity and the legacy of Greece and Rome. Gladstone published three books on Homer, while the growing number of public schools made the classics the centre of their teaching. Those who could afford to do so performed and listened to German music, read French novels and visited the art galleries of Italy. Mendelssohn and Dvorak were especially popular, and Mendelssohn's *Elijah* was written for the 1846 Birmingham Festival. The British were involved, for most of the century, in what was happening on the Continent. This was obviously true of the Napoleonic and Crimean Wars but, in addition, the Greek War of Independence and the *Risorgimento* (Italian unification) aroused enormous interest, more so than many of the minor colonial wars and acquisitions of colonial territory. The Tory *Morning Post* in 1829 referred critically to 'the spurious sentimentality so prevalent both in England and France on the subject of Greece'. The manner in which the Italian hero Garibaldi was mobbed by working-class crowds when he visited England in 1864 testified to the way in

which Victorians of all social classes were able to relate many of the events taking place on the Continent to their own struggles and aspirations. The failure to relieve General Gordon at Khartoum in 1885 caused outrage and was a major blow to the popularity of Gladstone's second government, but in 1876 Gladstone had been able to embarrass Disraeli's ministry seriously over the massacre of Bulgarians by the Turks. Continental news remained very important in the British press, although more attention was devoted to imperial questions from the 1870s.

A major difference between Britain and continental countries, especially in the mid-nineteenth century, was that Britain traded abroad far more than they did, and far more widely. Continental economies were more self-sufficient; what foreign trade they did was mainly with other European countries. Britain was dependent on foreign trade, and on the wider world outside Europe, in a way they were not. From this followed many aspects of Britain's difference from the Continent: Britain's outward-lookingness and internationalism; her interest in peace, which was believed to create the best conditions for trade, and which determined her diplomatic isolation from the Continent (except in 1854-56), to avoid being dragged into wars; and her opposition to a large and expensive army. Empire was a vital part of this dependence on the outer world, but only a part.

The British attitude towards America was ambivalent. Many Victorians wrote about it; for example Dickens, Trollope and James Bryce, all of whom were taken by its energy and drive, yet often shocked by its 'vulgar' (populist) politics. A standard means of criticizing a politician was to

Left: The Peterloo Massacre, 16 August 1819. This took place at a meeting held in St Peter's Field, Manchester, to demand parliamentary reform. About 60,000 unarmed people turned out to hear 'Orator' Henry Hunt. The magistrates ordered the Manchester Yeomanry Cavalry to seize the speakers, but the untrained cavalry also attacked the crowd. There was public outrage at what was termed, by analogy with Waterloo, the Peterloo Massacre. *The Times* deplored 'the dreadful fact that nearly a hundred of the King's unarmed subjects have been sabred by a body of cavalry in the streets of a town of which most of them were inhabitants, and in the presence of those Magistrates whose sworn duty it is to protect and preserve the life of the meanest Englishman'.

accuse him of the 'Americanization' of British politics, and Gladstone and Joseph Chamberlain both suffered accordingly. There was also much downright hostility between the two states: over the Crimean War, when the British, being very short of troops by 1855, tried to recruit American mercenaries; the American Civil War, when the British were considered too favourable to the South; and disputes about clashing imperial interests, for example involving Venezuela in the 1890s. It was not only power politics that led to hostility. There were also cultural and economic rivalries, for example over copyright law in the 1850s.

Empire was a crucial component of British nationalism, especially towards the end of the century. So also was a sense of the perfectibility, if not perfection, of the British constitution. Though political expedients, compromises and the search for short-term advantage played a major role in the details of political reform, a sense of idealism was also important, the 'moral economy' of eighteenth-century paternalism and crowd sentiment being replaced by the 'moral politics' of the nineteenth century. Moral campaigns, for example against slavery and cruelty to animals, aroused widespread support and fuelled a major expansion in the voluntary societies that were such a characteristic feature of Victorian Britain; while the numerous hymns of the period made clear the commitment to a Christian society: faith was far from being a matter of personal salvation alone.

Although domestic radicalism had initially been encouraged by the French Revolution (1789), the growing ferocity of the Revolution led, especially from 1792, to reaction, a rallying to Church, Crown and nation, with which the name of Edmund Burke will be always linked. This conservative surge helped to see Britain through years of defeat at the hands of France, but

serious economic strains and social discontent did not end with the war and were indeed exacerbated from 1815 by post-war depression and demobilization. Unemployment, which owed something to new technology and thus inspired Luddites to destroy machines in 1811-12; the unbalanced nature of industrial change and the economic problems it caused; poor harvests and agitation for political reform; all produced a volatile post-war atmosphere. This led to repressive legislation, most prominently the Six Acts of 1819 (though by the standards of modern totalitarian regimes there was no police state), and to the Peterloo Massacre in Manchester (1819), a panic charge on a reform crowd by the yeomanry which led to eleven deaths and many injuries. It inspired widespread revulsion. The radical poet Percy Bysshe Shelley (1792-1822) depicted *The Mask of Anarchy* as:

. . . Trampling to a mire of blood
The adoring multitude.

and called for a popular rising: 'Ye are many – they are few'. A small group of extremists plotted to murder the entire cabinet, but they were arrested in Cato Street in 1820. George IV (Prince Regent 1811-20, while his father was incapacitated by porphyria, King 1820-30), was very unpopular, especially when he tried in 1820 to divorce his wife, Caroline, and to remove her royal status. Her cause was taken up by public opinion and the government felt obliged to abandon its campaign against the queen, although she was successfully denied a coronation. *The Times* remarked in 1830, 'Never was there a human being less respected than this late king . . . what eye weeps for him?' Discontent was widespread in the 1810s and, to a lesser extent, the 1820s, and arson and animal-maiming frequent in rural areas, for example in Essex. The invention of friction matches in 1826 by the Stockton chemist

Right: Fashionable life; *Tom and Jerry at the Almack Ball in the West End of London* by Isaac Robert Cruikshank (1789-1856) from *Life in London* by Pierce Egan the Elder (1772-1849). *Life in London; or, The Day and Night Scenes of Jerry Hawthorn, Esq., and his elegant friend, Corinthian Tom, accompanied by Bob Logic, the Oxonian, in their Rambles and Sprees through the Metropolis* was a very successful shilling monthly with Cruikshank's illustrations, launched in 1821. George IV accepted the dedication. It provided alternate scenes of high and low life with lively dialogue, and inspired imitations, including *Real Life in London* (1821-22), as well as prints, dramatic version, decorations on handkerchiefs and teatrays, and 'Tom and Jerry' fashions. The play *Tom and Jerry; or Life in London* (1821) enjoyed great success in Britain and America. In 1828 Egan produced his *Finish to the Adventures of Tom, Jerry and Logic*: Tom breaks his neck at a steeplechase, Jerry returns to the country, marries his early sweetheart and becomes a generous landlord.

The Reformers' Attack on the Old Rotten Tree; or, the Foul Nests of the Cormorants in Danger. Pub.d E. King Chancery lane.

Left: A caricature advocating electoral reform. Reformers chop down a decayed tree which bears a number of rotten boroughs, while opponents, including Peel and Wellington, try to prop up the tree. William IV watches from 'Constitution Hill'.

Below: *The Man Wot pays the Taxes!!* The First Reform Act was no remedy for poverty.

John Walker, and their subsequent manufacture as 'strike anywhere lucifers' made arson easier.

Tensions eased during the prosperous years of the early 1820s, but in the late 1820s an industrial slump and high bread prices helped cause a revival both in popular unrest and in pressure for reform of Parliament, to make it more representative of the wealth and weight of the community. The Whig government of Lord Grey that took power after the elections of 1830 thought such reform necessary, but the House of Lords was opposed. Grey thought the situation 'too like what took place in France before the Revolution'. Commons majorities for reform and popular agitation, including riots in Bristol, Merthyr and Nottingham, led to a political crisis, and William IV (1830-37), a former naval officer, eventually felt it necessary to agree that he would make enough new peers to create a majority for reform in the Lords. This led the Lords to give way. The First Reform Act (1832) fixed a uniform right to vote in the boroughs, which brought the franchise to the 'middle class', and reorganized the distribution of seats in order to reward growing towns, such as Birmingham, Bradford and Manchester, and counties, at the expense of 'rotten boroughs', seats with a small population that were open to corruption. Voting qualifications still differed between boroughs and counties, the size of electorate still varied greatly by seat, and women were still disenfranchised, but about one fifth of all English adult males could vote after 1832.

Grey was to complain in 1837 that the Reform Act had made 'the democracy of the towns paramount to all the other interests of the state',

THE CHRONOLOGIST   N.o 9

In what better condition am I now that the Reform Bill has past! I have been obliged to Rob my Family to pay Taxs and now thay tell me I'm Trenchised, that is I suppose Lean, meagre, and to live upon Trogs.

marks fect

THE MAN *Wot pays the* TAXES!!
London J.L.Marks Long Lane

which was not what he had intended. The following year William Wordsworth (1770-1850), one of the greatest of the Romantic poets and initially a radical and a supporter of the French Revolution, revealed in his *Protest Against the Ballot* the extent of the conversion to conservatism that was to help him gain a Civil List pension (1842) and the Poet Laureateship (1843). It began:

Forth rushed, from Envy sprung and self-conceit,
A Power misnamed the SPIRIT of REFORM,
And through the astonished Island swept in storm,
Threatening to lay all Orders at her feet
That crossed her way.

Wordsworth continued by urging St George to stop the introduction of the ballot as it threatened to spawn a 'pest' worse than the dragon he had slain. Not one of Wordsworth's masterpieces, the poem underlines the hostility and fear that reform aroused in many circles. Others, however, were dissatisfied with the limited extent of reform. This led in the late 1830s to a working-class protest movement,

Below: A caricature of 10 June 1829, possibly by Robert Seymour, showing ragged and thin workers clinging to a broken shaft labelled 'Manufactures and Commerce'. They are pulled down by two larger employers and, in turn, by 'the great tax eater Church and State'. Seymour was to etch the plates for *The Pickwick Papers*.

known as Chartism, which called for universal adult male suffrage, a secret ballot and annual elections. The Six Points of the People's Charter (1838) also included equal constituencies, the abolition of property qualifications for MPs and their payment, the last two designed to ensure that the social elite lost their control of the representative system. Parliament resisted Chartist mass petitions (1839, 1842, 1848); England did not share in the disorders of 1848, the year of revolutions on the Continent, and the movement collapsed as a result of its failure, and of growing prosperity; mass support for Chartism was apparent only in times of recession. Similarly, rural protest movements against heavy rent and tithe burdens, such as the Rebecca Riots in Wales (1839-44), did not change the situation.

The pressure that economic circumstances placed on the bulk of the population is indicated by the decline in the height of army recruits in the second quarter of the century. The strains of industrialization in the early nineteenth century caused much social and political tension. Unlike cotton textiles, many other industries were slow to experience technological transformation, with the result that general living standards rose noticeably only from mid-century. The unstable credit structure exacerbated slumps. The Factory Acts regulating conditions of employment in the textile industry still left work there both long and arduous. The 1833 Act established a factory inspectorate and prevented the employment of under-9s, but 9-10 year olds could still work 9-hour days, and 11-17 year olds 12 hours. The 1844 Act cut that of under-13s to 6½ hours and of all women to 12; those of 1847 and 1850 reduced the hours of women and under-18s to 10 hours.

If the bulk of the working population faced difficult circumstances, the situation was even worse for those who were more 'marginal' to the economy. Henry Stuart, who reported on East Anglian poor relief in 1834, found three main groups of inmates in the parish workhouses, often 'abodes of misery, depravity and filth': the old and infirm, orphaned and illegitimate children, and unmarried pregnant women, the last a group that was generally treated harshly, far more so than the men responsible. The Poor Law Amendment Act (1834) introduced national guidelines, but the workhouse system that it created was not generous to its inmates. In Wimborne, workhouse beds had to be shared, meat was only provided once a week, there were no vegetables other than potatoes until 1849, men and women were segregated, and unmarried mothers had to wear distinctive clothes. Social assumptions and conventions pressed harder on women than on men. Women, not men, were blamed for the spread of venereal disease. Under the Contagious Diseases Acts (1864, 1866, 1869), passed because of concern about the health of the armed forces, women suspected of being prostitutes (but not men who also might have spread disease) were subjected to physical examination and detention,

Manufactures & Commerce support the Workmen they the Merchants & Masters who are the chief tax payers & thereby support The great tax eater Church-and-State.

MANUFACTURES &

COMMERCE

STATE OF THE NATION

FATHER THAMES INTRODUCING HIS OFFSPRING TO THE FAIR CITY OF LONDON.

Left: Father Thames Introducing His Offspring To The Fair City of London, Punch, 3 July 1858. A filthy Thames, polluted by factories, sewerage and steamships, presents diphtheria, scrofula and cholera to an appalled female figure representing the city, in a facetious design for a fresco for the new Houses of Parliament.

if infected, in garrison towns and ports. After an extended campaign, in which women acquired, experience of acting as political leaders in the Ladies National Association, the Acts were repealed in 1886. Charity could temper hardship, but it often entailed deference if not subordination for its recipients. Andrew Reed's charity established in 1813 for the education of orphans led to the foundation of schools at first Clapton and then Watford (girls and boys were, as was usual, educated separately). Subscribers to the charity were awarded votes, and widows had to lobby them to gain entry for their offspring.

Hell is a city much like London –
A populous and a smoky city;

Shelley's statement in *Peter Bell the Third* (1819) seemed increasingly appropriate. Fast-expanding towns became crowded and polluted, a breeding ground for disease, and working conditions were often unhealthy and hazardous. Mortality rates remained high, although smallpox declined, thanks in part to vaccination. Cholera, a bacterial infection largely transmitted by water affected by the excreta of victims, struck first in 1831. By 1866 about 140,000 people had died of cholera. Disease struck most at the poor living in urban squalor, but also threatened the rich. The Prince of Wales nearly died of typhoid, another water-borne infection, in 1871. Dysentery, diarrhoea and enteric fever were significant problems, and frequently fatal. The death or illness of breadwinners wrecked family economies, produc-

ing or exacerbating poverty and related social problems. Neither these nor political discontents, however, led, to revolution in 1848. There was no equivalent to the attempted insurrection by the Young Ireland nationalist movement. Instead, 1848 saw the Public Health Act, which created a General Board of Health and an administrative structure to improve sanitation, especially water supply. The new Act enabled the creation of local Boards of Health; the one constituted in Leicester in 1849 was instrumental in the creation of a sewer system and in tackling slaughter-houses and smoke pollution.

The contrast with the violent nature of political development on the Continent led to a measure of complacency. Having suffered from defeat and colonial rebellion in 1791-1835, Britain's colonial and maritime rivals were absorbed in domestic strife and continental power politics over the following four decades. Meanwhile, as reform legislation was passed within Britain, so British imperial power spread throughout the world, and the two processes were fused, as first self-government and later dominion status were granted to the 'white colonies'. New Zealand achieved self-government in 1852, Newfoundland, New South Wales, Victoria, Tasmania and South Australia in 1855, Queensland in 1859; the dominion of Canada was created in 1867. It is scarcely surprising that an optimistic conception of British history was the dominant account in academic and popular circles. A progressive move towards liberty was discerned, a

Above: Work *by Ford Madox Brown, 1863, a painting dignifying work, the first version of which was commissioned in 1856 for 400 guineas. Brown taught at the Working Men's College in 1857 and its Christian socialist principal, FD Maurice, appears in the picture alongside Thomas Carlyle, whose* Past and Present *(1843) stressed the disadvantages of unemployment. The navvies were based on those Brown saw working in Hampstead. Other figures represent the leisured and middle classes, the unemployed and vagrants.*

seamless web that stretched back to Magna Carta in 1215 and the constitutional struggles of the barons in medieval England, and forward to the nineteenth-century extensions of the franchise. These were seen as arising naturally from the country's development. This public myth, the Whig interpretation of history, offered a comforting and glorious account that seemed appropriate for a state which ruled much of the globe, which was exporting its constitutional arrangements to other parts of the world, and which could watch the convulsions on the Continent as evidence of the political backwardness of its societies and the superiority of Britain. The leading British role in the abolition of the slave trade and the emancipation of the slaves also led to self-righteousness and a degree of moral complacency, not least about the position of the poor in Britain. In addition the nineteenth century was very much a period of Evangelicalism, which was by no means confined to the middle class, and this further encouraged a sense of national distinctiveness and mission.

There was confidence in the present, faith in the future. In 1857 William Bell Scott stated 'that the latest is best . . . not to believe in the 19th century, one might as well disbelieve that a child grows into a man . . . without that Faith in Time what anchor have we in any secular speculation'. His painting *Industry on the Tyne: Iron and*

Coal (1861) sought to capture, as he stated, 'everything of the common labour life and applied science of the day', including workers at Robert Stephenson's Newcastle engineering works, one of the largest manufacturers of railway engines in the world, an Armstrong gun, the steam of modern communications, and telegraph wires.

The Britain of Queen Victoria (1837-1901) had a sense of national uniqueness, nationalistic self-confidence and a xenophobic contempt for foreigners, especially Catholics. Nationalism played a major role in the contemporary sense of distance from the Continent, not simply because of a British rejection of foreigners and foreignness, and the loss of the cosmopolitanism that had characterized much of the eighteenth-century elite; but also because of the development of a sense of national identity, politically, economically, culturally, and ethnically, in the continental states of the period. The reign of Victoria was the age of the unification of Germany (1871) and Italy (1870). Political reform on the Continent ensured that by 1865 many European states had more extensive franchises than those of Britain. Whether they had a 'democratic' facet or not, continental states increasingly seemed better able to challenge British interests. British governments worried about the plans and actions of their continental counterparts. Invasion by France, possibly via a planned Channel tunnel, was feared in 1847-48, 1851-52 and 1859-60, while Russian moves in the Balkans led Britain to go to war with her in the Crimea (1854-56). This was the last war that Britain fought with a European power until the First World War in 1914, an unprecedented length of time. The war was characterized by administrative incompetence, heavy manpower losses and a series of military misjudgments, most famously the Charge of the Light Brigade into the face of Russian artillery at Balaclava in 1854, an action as outmoded and unsuccessful as the attempt to defend rotten boroughs in 1832. An imperial power that could conquer much of the world lacked the military strength, crucially a large European army, to compete effectively in European power politics. Nevertheless the war also indicated Britain's continued ability to project her power around the world, naval attacks being mounted on Russian coasts as far as Kamchatka, and in this she was assisted by technological advances. The warships sent to the Baltic in 1854 were all fitted with steam engines, and also benefited from Brunel's work on gun-carriages.

Britain was still clearly the leading imperial power at the end of the century. She ruled a quarter of the world's population and a fifth of the land surface. Between 1860 and 1914 Britain owned approximately one-third of the world's shipping tonnage and by 1898 about sixty per cent of the telegraph cables, a crucial aspect of imperial government and defence planning. In 1890-1914 she launched about two-thirds of the world's ships and carried about half of its marine trade. In his poem *Cargoes*, published 1903, John Masefield was able to present the three ages of marine trade through a 'quinquireme of Nineveh', a 'stately Spanish galleon', and lastly, a 'dirty British coaster' carrying a cargo of British exports. Investment abroad ensured that overseas income as a percentage of UK gross domestic product rose from 2 in 1872 to 7 in 1913. These were also years of still-spreading territorial control. Britain gained the most important share of the two leading colonial carve-ups of the period, the scramble for Africa and the seizure of hitherto unclaimed island groups. She became the leading power in southern and east Africa, successfully invading Egypt in 1882; defeating the Mahdists of Sudan at Omdurman (1898), a battle in which the young Winston Churchill served; gaining what was to become Botswana, British Somali-

Left: Industry of the Tyne: Iron and Coal by William Bell Scott, 1861. Painted for Sir Walter Trevelyan, Wallington Hall, Northumberland, this is not in fact an accurate account of the Newcastle quayside, but an assemblage of Tyneside industry. The workmen are employees of Robert Stephenson's engineering works, one of the largest manufacturers of railway engines in the world. The 100-pound, 7-inch breech-loading gun and shell in the foreground were produced in Armstrong's ordnance factory. The conical chimney underneath the High Level Bridge (completed in 1849) belonged to a Gateshead glass-works. There were no telegraph wires running along the quayside then. The pit-boy holding a Davy Lamp and a whip for driving ponies and the loaded keel are references to coalmining. The newspaper carries an advertisement for a panorama of Garibaldi's victories in Italy.

land, Kenya, Uganda, Zambia, Malawi and Zimbabwe; and eventually defeating the Afrikaner republics of southern Africa, the Orange Free State and Transvaal, in the Boer War of 1899-1902. The war proved far more difficult than had been anticipated, but the ability of Britain to spend £250 million and deploy 400,000 troops was a testimony to the strength of both her economic and imperial systems, while her unchallenged control of the South African ports allowed her to bring her strength to bear. Many contemporaries were deeply worried by Britain's performance, however, and the war was followed by a budgetary crisis.

British strength spread throughout the oceans of the world. Between 1850 and 1914 her list of island possessions was enlarged by the Andaman, Nicobar, Gilbert and Ellice, Kuria Muria, South Orkney, South Shetland and Cook islands, Malden, Starbuck, Caroline, Pitcairn, Christmas, Phoenix, Washington, Fanning and Jarvis islands, Fiji, Rotuna, the Solomons, Tonga, Socotra, and South Georgia. British naval power was supported by the largest and most wide-ranging number of bases in the world, a testimony to the global reach of the British state. In 1898 these included Wellington, Fiji, Sydney, Melbourne, Adelaide, Albany, Cape York (Australia), Labuan (North Borneo), Singapore, Hong Kong, Weihaiwei (China), Calcutta, Bombay, Trincomalee, Colombo, the Seychelles, Mauritius, Zanzibar, Mombasa, Aden, Cape Town, St Helena, Ascension, Lagos, Malta, Gibraltar, Halifax (Nova Scotia), Bermuda, Jamaica, Antigua, St Lucia, Trinidad, the Falklands and Esquimalt (British Columbia). The peacetime army grew in size to 195,000 men in 1898, and this force was supported by a substantial body of native troops in the Indian army, the basis for a powerful expansion of British power in southern Asia in the Victorian period. Sind was conquered in 1843, Baluchistan and Kashmir became British vassals in 1843 and 1846 respectively, the Punjab was annexed in 1849, and by 1886 all Burma had followed. The Indian Mutiny of 1857-58 was a severe shock and the Afghan tribes resisted several invasions successfully, but the British governed India with considerable success in co-operation with the landlords and native princes. British explorers, particularly James Bruce, David Livingstone, Mungo Park and John Speke, explored much of Africa. Others explored Australia and Canada, while the Royal Navy charted the oceans of the world.

Yet the process of late Victorian expansion took place in a context of European competition that was far more serious, and gave rise to more concern, than the position in 1815-70, worrying as that had been at times. The British economy remained very strong and new industries, such as engineering and automobiles, developed. The pace of scientific advance and technological change was unremitting, and British scientists led in a number of fields. Michael Faraday (1791-1867), the son of a Surrey blacksmith, discovered electromagnetic induction in 1831, making the continuous generation of electricity a possibility. The development of commercial generators later in the century led to the growing use of electricity. New distribution and retail methods, particularly the foundation of department and chain

Below: Florence Nightingale (1820-1910) in the Military Hospital at Scutari. Nightingale, superintendent of nurses in British hospitals in the Crimean War, vastly improved conditions and laid the basis of modern nursing.

Left: Naval strength; the Naval Review at Spithead, 1856.

stores, helped to create national products. The international context was less comforting. This was due to the greater economic strength of the major continental powers, their determination to make colonial gains in pursuit of their own place in the sun, and the relative decline in British power. These factors combined and interacted to produce a strong sense of disquiet in British governmental circles.

The growth of German economic power posed the starkest contrast with the situation earlier in the century. The annual average output of coal and lignite in million metric tons in 1870-74 was 123 for Britain, 41 for Germany; by 1910-14 the figures were 274 to 247. For pig-iron the annual figures changed from 7.9 and 2.7 in 1880 to 10.2 and 14.8 in 1910; for steel from 3.6 and 2.2 (1890) to 6.5 and 13.7 (1910). The number of kilometres

Below: The British empire in 1914, reflecting the huge geographical range of late Victorian expansion.

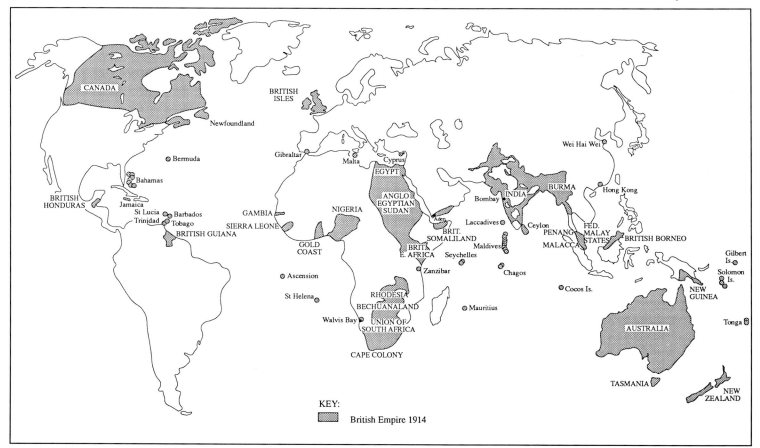

KEY:

British Empire 1914

Above: Windsor Castle in Modern Times by Sir Edwin Landseer (1802-73). Queen Victoria and Prince Albert as an idealized family; Albert has just been shooting and the gardens of Windsor Castle are visible through the open window. Landseer was Victoria's favourite painter, and a specialist in animal paintings.

of railway rose in Britain from 2,411 (1840) to 28,846 (1880) and 38,114 (1914); in Germany the comparable figures were 469, 33,838 and 63,378. In 1900 the German population was 56.4 million, that of Britain, excluding Ireland, 37, and including her, 41.5. In the Edwardian period Britain's second most important export market, after India, was Germany.

The tremendous growth in German power posed a challenge to Britain, in whose governing circles there had been widespread support for German unification and a failure to appreciate its possible consequences. France and Russia were also developing as major economic powers, while American strength was ever more apparent in the New World and, increasingly, the Pacific. Given the importance of imperial considerations in governmental, political, and popular thinking, it is not surprising that British relations with and concern about the continental powers registered not in disputes arising from European issues, but in differences and clashes centring on distant, but no longer obscure, points on the globe, ranging from Fashoda in the forests of the Upper Nile to the islands of the western Pacific. French and German expansion in Africa led Britain to take counter measures: in West Africa, the occupa-

tion of the interior of the Gambia in 1887-88, the declaration of the protectorate of Sierra Leone in 1896, the establishment of the protectorates of Northern and Southern Nigeria in 1900, the annexation of Asante in 1901. German moves in East Africa led to the establishment of British power in Uganda in the 1890s. Suspicion of Russian designs on the Ottoman Empire and French schemes in North Africa led the British to move into Egypt; concern about French ambitions led to the conquest of Mandalay (1885) and the annexation of Upper Burma; while Russia's advance across Asia led to attempts to strengthen and move forward the 'north-west frontier' of British India and the development of British influence in southern Persia.

Specific clashes of colonial influence interacted with a more general sense of imperial insecurity. In 1884 there was concern about British naval weakness and the increase in the French navy; in 1889 public pressure and the need to give credibility to Mediterranean policies obliged the government to pass the Naval Defence Act, which sought a two-power standard, superiority over the next two largest naval powers combined. Expenditure of £21,500,000 over five years was authorized. The importance of naval dominance was taken for granted. In the preface to his *History of the Foreign Policy of Great Britain* (1895), Captain Montagu Burrows RN, Professor of Modern History at Oxford, wrote that: 'this fortress-isle of Britain, safely intrenched [sic] by stormy seas, confronting the broadest face of the Continent, and, later on, almost surrounding it with her fleets, was and was not a part of Europe according as she willed'.

The myth of national self-sufficiency peaked in these years and naval strength was a prerequisite of such an ideal. By the turn of the century it was Germany, with its great economic strength and its search for a place in the sun, that was the principal threat. British resources and political will were tested in a major naval race between the two powers, in which the British launched HMS *Dreadnought*, the first of a new class of battleships, in 1906. A projected German invasion was central to *The Riddle of the Sands* (1903), a novel by Erskine Childers which was first planned in 1897, a year in which the Germans were indeed discussing such a project. Military discussions with France following the Anglo-French entente of 1904 were to play a major role in leading Britain towards the First World War.

The state that was taking part in this growing confrontation with imperial Germany was different from that of the early years of Victoria's reign. Britain had become more urban and more industrial. Her population was more literate and educated and was linked by modern communications and a national press. Changes in the press were symptomatic of the modernization of the country. One of the many ways in which Victorian London was at the centre of British life and that of the British Empire was in the provision of news. Through its press, which lay claim to the title of the 'fourth estate' of the realm,

Left: Field Marshal Robert Lord Napier (1810-90), who served in the Sikh wars (1849), the Indian Mutiny (1857-58), China (1860) and Ethiopia (1868). Napier was a child of empire, born in Colombo, his second name, Cornelis, commemorating the Javanese fort where his father was fatally wounded in 1810. Commissioned into the Bengal Engineers, Napier was also responsible for canals, roads and public buildings in the Punjab, 1849-56. He was severely wounded in the relief of Lucknow, 1857, and served as Commander-in-Chief in India, 1870-76. His state funeral was the most imposing since that of Wellington.

London created the image and idiom of Empire, and shaped its opinions. Aside from this political function, the press also played a central economic, social and cultural role, setting and spreading fashions, whether through company statements or theatrical criticism. In what was increasingly a commercial society, the press played a pivotal role, inspiring emulation, setting the tone, fulfilling crucial needs for an anonymous

Left: A contemporary artist's impression of the suppression of the Indian Mutiny; captured sepoys are about to be blown from cannon by the Bengal Horse Artillery.

Above: The 'breaking up' at Dotheboys Hall by 'Phiz' from the novel Nicholas Nickleby by Charles Dickens, published in monthly parts 1838-39. Nicholas, sent to teach at Dotheboys Hall in Yorkshire, is horrified by the headmaster Wackford Squeers who, knowing their uncaring parents will not intervene, mistreats and starves the pupils and doses them with brimstone and treacle. Nicholas rebels and thrashes Squeers unconscious.

launched in 1855, led the way and by 1888 had a circulation of 300,000. The penny press was in turn squeezed by the halfpenny press, the first halfpenny evening paper, *The Echo*, appearing in 1868, while halfpenny morning papers became important in the 1890s with *The Morning Leader* (1892) and the *Daily Mail* (1896), which was to become extremely successful with its bold and simple style. *The Echo* peaked at a circulation of 200,000 in 1870. The papers that best served popular tastes were the Sunday papers, *Lloyd's Weekly News, The News of the World* and *Reynolds's Newspaper. Lloyd's*, the first British paper with a circulation of over 100,000, was selling over 600,000 by 1879, over 900,000 by 1893 and in 1896 rose to over a million. The Sunday papers relied on shock and titillation, drawing extensively on police court reporting.

In comparison, an eighteenth-century London newspaper was considered a great success if it sold 10,000 copies a week (most influential papers then were weeklies) and 2000 weekly was a reasonable sale. Thus an enormous expansion had taken place, one that matched the vitality of an imperial capital, swollen by immigration and increasingly influential as an opinion-setter within the country, not least because of the communications revolution produced by the railway and better roads. The development of the railways allowed London newspapers to increase their dominance of the national newspaper scene. Thanks to them these papers could arrive on provincial doorsteps within hours of publication. Railways also led to the massive development of commuting in London.

The press gave Charles Dickens (1812-70) early employment. His subsequent novels reflected many of the concerns of mid-Victorian society. Dickens himself was a supporter of reform in fields such as capital punishment, housing and prostitution. *Bleak House* (1852-53) was an indictment of the coldness of law and church, the delays of the former and the smugness of the righteous Reverend Chadband; *Little Dorrit* (1855-57) an attack on imprisonment for debt, business fraud and the deadening bureaucracy of the Circumlocution Office. Dickens's friend and fellow-novelist Wilkie Collins (1824-89) was criticized by the poet Algernon Swinburne for sacrificing his talent for the sake of a mission. His novels dealt with issues such as divorce, vivisection and the impact of heredity and environment, the last a major concern to a society influenced by the evolutionary teachings of Charles Darwin and thus increasingly concerned with living standards.

mass-readership. The press was itself affected by change, by the energizing and disturbing forces of commercialization and new technology. It was to be legal reform and technological development that freed the Victorian press for major development. Newspapers had become expensive in the eighteenth century, in large part due to successive rises in Stamp Duty. In the mid-nineteenth century these so-called 'taxes on knowledge' were abolished: the Advertisement Duties in 1853, the Newspaper Stamp Duty in 1855 and the Paper Duties in 1861. This opened up the possibility of a cheap press, and that opportunity was exploited by means of a technology centred on new printing presses and the continuous rolls or 'webs' of paper that fed them. A steam press was first used, by *The Times*, in 1814; web rotary presses were introduced in Britain from the late 1860s; mechanical typesetting was introduced towards the end of the century.

New technology was expensive, but the mass readership opened up by the lower prices that could be charged after the repeal of the newspaper taxes justified the cost. The consequence was more titles and lower prices. The number of daily morning papers published in London rose from 8 in 1856 to 21 in 1900, of evenings from 7 to 11, while there was a tremendous expansion in the suburban press. The repeal permitted the appearance of penny dailies. *The Daily Telegraph*,

Such concern led to a determination to reform, i.e. change, popular pastimes. Leisure was to be made useful; drink was to be replaced by sport. Organized sport expanded, in part a response to the clearer definition of leisure time in an industrial and urban society, to the reduction in working hours, and to the increase in average real earnings in the last quarter of the century. Profes-

Reform was the leading divisive issue; reform of the protectionist system and reform of the franchise. Peel's repeal of the Corn Laws (1846) split the Tories, and was followed by the repeal of the Navigation Acts (1849). Free trade became a central theme of British policy. Reform was linked to the growth of middle-class culture and consciousness in the great northern cities such as Newcastle and Leeds; the civic gospel, expressed architecturally in their great Town Halls, Manchester's opened in 1877. Their newspapers played a major role in orchestrating opinion in favour of reform. The Anti-Corn-Law League was a symbol of middle-class aggression, while the mismanagement of the Crimean War helped to boost middle-class values of efficiency in politics at the expense of the aristocracy. This was linked to the movement of Whiggism toward Liberalism in the 1850s and 1860s as, in acquiring middle-class support, the Whigs became a party fitted for the reformist middle class. Reform was central to their appeal.

More active local government was an important source and instrument of reform with, for example, the public health movement from the 1840s, the laying out of public parks, especially following the Recreation Grounds Act (1859) and the Public Health Act (1875), and the building of libraries for workers, though much was funded by charity or public subscription. A professional police force replaced the yeomanry and the sometimes incompetent constables and provided a much more effective check on working-class immorality: a powerful weapon of middle-

sional football developed, while there was also a boom in middle class sports, such as golf and lawn tennis, whose rules were systematized in 1874. By 1895 the *Daily News* covered racing, yachting, rowing, lacrosse, football, hockey, angling, billiards, athletics, cycling and chess. Less respectable traditional sports and pastimes, such as cockfighting, ratting and morris-dancing, lost popularity or were suppressed.

Left: Sir Robert Peel 1788-1850. As Home Secretary he established the Metropolitan Police in 1829, hence their nicknames of 'peelers' and 'bobbies', the latter still in occasional use.

THE MINISTERIAL SPLIT.

Palmerston. "I'LL JUST FRIGHTEN THEM A LITTLE."

Left: Henry, 3rd Viscount Palmerston (1784-1865), Foreign Secretary 1830-41, 1846-51, Home Secretary 1852-5, Prime Minister 1855-58, 1859-65. This *Punch* cartoon refers to Palmerston's resignation on 16 December 1853 in protest against Lord John Russell's proposals for a reform bill. Palmerston returned to office after ten days on the understanding that the proposals were still open to discussion.

Above: Expanding and changing cities; *Newcastle upon Tyne from Windmill Hills, Gateshead* by Myles Birket Foster, c. 1871-72, shows formerly prominent buildings, the castle keep and the cathedral, now joined by factory chimneys and the railway bridge.

class cultural dominance. Peel's Metropolitan Police Act (1829) created a uniformed and paid force for London. This process was extended by acts of 1835 and 1839, and the County and Borough Police Act (1856) made the formation of paid forces obligatory. The new police largely replaced individuals as prosecutors in cases of criminal justice in England and Wales. The Hanoverian legal code was transformed. In the 1830s-50s the death penalty was abolished for most crimes, as was the transportation of convicts to colonial dumping grounds. Instead, prisons were built and reformatory regimes developed. Knowledge about prison conditions and other such social issues was spread by the Condition of England movement, which was linked to the cult of novels that was so strong from the 1840s on. There was a great expansion of reading, and the expanding middle-class also patronized a major upsurge in art, poetry and the performance and production of music. Cities such as Glasgow, Liverpool and Manchester founded major art collections, musical institutions, such as the Hallé Orchestra (1857), and educational bodies. Civic universities were created. Mason Science College, which eventually became part of the University of Birmingham established in 1900, was founded in 1880 by Sir Josiah Martin, a self-educated manufacturer. He spent part of his fortune on local orphans as well as on his new foundation, which was designed to be especially useful

for local industries. Men such as Martin set the tone for much of urban Victorian Britain. Their views and wealth stimulated the process of improvement, civic and moral, that was so central to the movement for reform.

Middle-class interests increasingly set the legislative agenda. The Second Reform Act, passed by a minority Tory government (1867), nearly doubled the existing electorate and, by offering household suffrage, gave the right to vote to about 60 per cent of adult males in boroughs. The Liberal victory in the following general election (1868) led to the first government of William Gladstone (1868-74), who pushed through a whole series of reforms, including the disestablishment of the Irish Church, and the introduction of open competition in the Civil Service (1870) and of the secret ballot (1872). The 1870 Education Act divided the country into school districts and stipulated a certain level of educational provision, although its provisions were resisted. In Enfield, tenacious efforts by the Church of England to protect voluntary education and resist the introduction of public Board Schools, ignoring the implications of rapid population growth, left 500 children unschooled 25 years after the Act. The end of long-established distinctions, variations and privileges played a major role in the reform process. The Endowed Schools Commission established in that year redistributed endowments and reformed governing bodies. The Church of England underwent a similar change. Gladstone was a formidable and multi-faceted individual, a classical scholar and theological controversialist, a hewer of trees and a rescuer of prostitutes. A Tory President of the Board of Trade and Colonial Secretary in the 1840s, he became the leading Liberal politician of the age, committed to reform at home and a moral stance abroad. His political skills bridged the worlds of Parliament and of public meetings; under his leadership, Liberalism became a movement enjoying mass support.

The Tories or, as they were now called, Conservatives, came to power in 1874 under Benjamin Disraeli, an opportunist and skilful political tactician who was also an acute thinker, able to create a political culture and focus of popular support around the themes of national identity and pride and social cohesion, an alternative to Liberal moral certainty. Legislation on factories (1874), public health, artisans' dwellings, and pure food and drugs (1875) systematized and extended the regulation of important aspects of public health and social welfare. The Factory Act (1874) limited work hours for women and children in the textile industry. The Prison Act (1877) established state control. These, however, were less important for Disraeli than his active foreign policy, which involved the purchase of shares in the Suez Canal (1875), the creation of the title of Empress of India (1876), the acquisition of Cyprus (1878), and wars with the Afghans and Zulus. Economic difficulties and political problems, skilfully exploited by Gladstone in his electioneering Midlothian campaigns (1879-80), led to Conservative defeat in the 1880 election. Imperial and Irish problems affected Gladstone's second government (1880-85), however, notably the First Boer War (1880-81) in South Africa, the occupation of Egypt (1882-83), the massacre at Khartoum (1885), the Coercion Act, designed to restore order in Ireland (1881), and the murder of Lord Frederick Cavendish, the Chief Secretary for Ireland, in Phoenix Park, Dublin, by the Invincibles, an Irish secret society (1882). In 1884 the Third Reform Act extended to the counties the household franchise granted to the boroughs in 1867; over two-thirds of the adult males in the counties received the vote.

The process of reform, both political and social, continued with the Redistribution of Seats Act (1885), the Local Government Act (1888), creating directly-elected county councils and county boroughs, and the Workmens' Compensation Act (1897), obliging employers to provide compensation for industrial accidents. A welfare state was developing, while state intervention in education helped in the decline of illiteracy. The political situation was complicated, however, by the longstanding malaise over the Irish question. Fenian terrorism in Ireland, England and Canada led to casualties, and there was both pressure for land reform and agitation for home rule for Ireland (the creation of an Irish parliament). Propo-

Left: 'New Crowns for Old Ones!', Punch, April 1876. Benjamin Disraeli (1804-81) offers Victoria the new imperial crown of India.

sals for home rule were defeated in 1886 and 1893 at Westminster, where they helped to divide politicians. Conservatives led the resistance, but the defeat of the First Home Rule Bill in 1886 was due to the defection of 'Liberal Unionists' from Gladstone's third government.

The political hegemony of the Liberals was destroyed that year as the Conservatives, under

Below: William Ewart Gladstone (1809-98) on the stump. These Reminiscences of the Last Midlothian Campaign, 1892, were drawn by Campbell Veitch in the Sketch.

Above: Victorian sentimentality and pathos. The tomb of Ellen Jane and Marianne Robinson, in Lichfield Cathedral: 'Their affectionate mother in fond remembrance of their heaven loved innocence consigns their resemblances to this sanctuary in humble gratitude for the glorious assurance that of such is the Kingdom of God'.

the 3rd Marquess of Salisbury, won the general election. Although the Liberals won the 1892 election, the Conservatives dominated the period 1886-1905, with Salisbury (Prime Minister 1885-86, 1886-92, 1895-1902) and his successor and nephew, Arthur Balfour (1902-5), following a cautious policy on domestic reform. Salisbury, owner of Hatfield House, one of the palaces the British domesticate as 'stately homes', derived most of his disposable income from urban property, including London slums. There was growing pressure for more radical political and social policies. Joseph Chamberlain's 'Un-authorized' Liberal Programme of 1885 called for land reform, and was followed in 1891 by the Newcastle programme, which also called for the reform or abolition of the House of Lords. The social order could be harsh as well as inegalitarian; that year Tom Masters, a 13-year-old Northamptonshire farm labourer, was whipped by his employer for insolence.

Pressures from within the Liberal party were soon supplemented by the development of more explicitly working class movements, both political and industrial. The development of trade unions reflected the growing industrialization and unification of the economy, the growth of larger concerns employing more people and, by the end of the century, a new and more adversarial and combative working-class consciousness. The Trades Union Congress, a federation of trade unions, was established in 1868; unionism spread from the skilled craft section to semi-skilled and unskilled workers; and there were major strikes in the London gasworks and docks in 1888-89. Keir Hardie, Secretary of the Scottish Miners' Federation, founded the Scottish Labour Party (1888) and the Independent Labour Party (1893). The latter pressed for an eight-hour day and 'collective ownership of means of production, distribution and exchange'. Six years later the Trades Union Congress advocated an independent

working-class political organization, which led in 1900 to the formation of the Labour Representation Committee, the basis of the Labour Party.

These developments reflected a situation of sustained doubt, if not a crisis of confidence, in late Victorian society. This society did not seem beneficent to the growing numbers who were becoming both emancipated and politicized, and many commentators were also concerned about the relative weakness of Britain, economically and politically, compared to the leading continental states. British industries no longer benefited from cheaper raw materials, energy and labour, and foreign competition was responsible for closures, including in 1901 the Tudhoe ironworks, which employed 1500 men. There was less confidence that British institutions and practices were best. In the 1890s and early 1900s there was much interest in the German educational system, and much envy of its 'practical' orientation. Salisbury was not alone in being pessimistic about the future of the empire. These varied strands of disquiet were to lead to fresh pressure for reform and new political divisions in the period up to the First World War. The British could take pride in the spread of empire and the triumphalism of Queen Victoria's Gold and Diamond Jubilees in 1887 and 1897, but the divisions of the first half of the century, which had diminished or disappeared in its prosperous third quarter, were re-emerging, taking on new forms and being accentuated by new sources of tension. Economic change brought significant levels of social disruption. In Cornwall, for example, serious falls in the prices of copper and tin in the late 1860s and 1870s, in part due to growing world competition, led to a decline in the number of mines and heavy emigration. The Cornish diaspora amounted to about 210,000 in 1891, roughly 42% of all the Cornish-born population. About 45% of these were living in England and Wales, but the rest were spread over much of the world.

There was persistent and justified concern about the 'state of the nation'. Infant mortality rates were high; in the north-eastern mining communities half the total deaths occurred before the age of six and a high proportion in the five to fifteen age group. Many families lived in only one room. Gastro-intestinal disorders linked to inadequate water and sewerage systems were responsible, for example, for Bradford's very high infant mortality rate, and poor urban sanitation, housing and nutrition were blamed for the physical weakness of much of the population. The army found this a serious problem at the time of the Boer War and the First World War; the Metropolitan Police thought their London recruits physically weak; and defeats at the hands of the visiting New Zealand All Blacks rugby team in 1905 led to discussion about a supposed physical and moral decline arising from the country's urban and industrial nature. There was also concern at the apparent extent of atheism among the urban working classes.

'We are all Socialists nowadays', declared Sir William Harcourt in a speech at the Mansion House in 1895. He was referring to the creation of public utilities, 'gas and water socialism', and to the concern for social welfare which was such an obvious feature of late-Victorian values and which played a role in the amelioration of living conditions, especially the decline of epidemic disease. The supply of clean water was begun or improved and London at last acquired a sewerage system appropriate for the capital of a modern empire. Typhus had virtually disappeared by the 1890s, typhoid was brought under partial control, and death rates from tuberculosis and scarlet fever declined. Improved diet, thanks in part to a significant fall in food prices, played an important role in the decline in mortality rates, while medical advances, not least the replacement of the 'miasma' theory of disease by that of 'germs', helped, though mortality contrasts between registration districts persisted. There was a noticeable, though not invariable, relationship between life expectancy and population density, crowded cities, such as Liverpool, having very much higher mortality rates. Public health problems, however, also existed in small towns and rural areas. Reports on the situation in Bruton in Somerset in the 1870s and 1880s graphically described insufficient and defective toilet arrangements, inadequate sewerage disposal and a lack of clean water. A reluctance to spend money, however, ensured, that, as in mid-century London, plans to improve the situation

were delayed; although the sewerage system was finally improved, Bruton did not construct a water supply system in the Victorian period. Social welfare was linked to the growing institutionalization of society, leading to the construction of schools, workhouses and asylums. The Wiltshire asylum was opened in Devizes in 1851,

Above: The backyard of a London slum, 1878, with outside privy, clothes drying in the polluted air, smoking factory chimneys and gas-holder.

Left: Crowded accommodation in London, with railway lines on viaducts, by Gustave Doré *c.*1870.

Above: The Immigrants' Ship by John Dollman, 1884. Both emigration and immigration greatly altered English society in the Victorian period. Large numbers of emigrants went to Australia, Canada and New Zealand; in the 1850s the Australian population rose to nearly 1.2 million.

Right: Party political poster 1909.

replacing private madhouses run for profit. By 1914 a basic network of infant and child welfare centres had been created, health-visiting was expanding, and educational authorities had been made responsible for the medical inspection of schoolchildren. Far from unconstrained capitalism, this was increasingly a regulated society.

Nevertheless there were serious policy differences, reflecting fundamental disagreements over Ireland, trade union relations and the nature of the British political system. Ireland was the most threatening issue; the determination of the Ulster Protestants to resist home rule took Britain to the brink of civil war in 1914. The formation of the Ulster Unionist Council (1905) and the Ulster Volunteer Force (1913) revealed the unwillingness of the Ulster Protestants to subordinate their sense of identity to Irish nationalism. They were assisted by the Conservatives, from 1912 the 'Conservative and Unionist Party', who resisted the Home Rule Bill introduced in 1912.

The Conservatives meanwhile were suffering from successive defeats at the hands of the Liberals, who were allied with the new Labour party. Victors in the landslide 1906 election, the Liberals remained in power until a coalition government was formed in 1915. Particularly under the dynamic Lloyd George, they were determined to undermine the power and possessions of the old landed elite, and keen to woo Labour and the trade unions. In 1906 the Liberals passed a Trade Disputes Act which gave unions immunity from actions for damages as a result of

Left: The Pinch of Poverty, Thomas Kennington, 1889. Poverty was often far harsher in its consequences than this genteel scene with its charming flower seller and romantically pale mother.

strike action, and thus overturned the attempts of the courts, through the Taff Vale case (1901), to bring the unions within the law. The Mines Regulations Act (1908) limited the number of hours that miners could spend underground. Lloyd George, Chancellor of the Exchequer 1908-15, wished to move the Liberals to the left, and pushed through a People's Budget introducing new taxes for the wealthy. The opposition of the Conservative-dominated House of Lords to this led to the Parliament Act (1911) which removed their right to veto Commons' legislation. That year Lloyd George also defused the first general railway strike.

1910-12 saw a number of major strikes as well as the continued growth of the Labour Party and of trade union membership, and a vociferous suffragette movement (demanding the vote for women). The militant tactics of the Women's Social and Political Union were designed to force public attention, and Labour officially endorsed

women's suffrage in 1913. The situation seemed increasingly volatile. Labour won 29 seats in the general election of 1906 and 40 in that of 1910, though it was not until 1922 that it emerged as the second largest party. Aside from the apparent imminence of conflict in Ulster, strikes also brought widespread violence in Britain with rioting, for example, in Cardiff and Llanelli in 1911. These took place against a recent history of often bitter labour relations, for example in North Wales where in 1900-3 the workers in Lord Penrhyn's huge slate quarries engaged in an ultimately destructive struggle with their employer. In 1914, however, the Liberal party displayed few signs of decline at the hands of Labour, while over 75% of the working population were not members of trade unions, and divisions within the work force, between skilled and unskilled, Protestants and Irish immigrants, and different regional economies, remained important. Much of the working class was, as in the Black Country, prepared

Right: Labour problems in a Glamorgan colliery, November 1910. Sabotage by striking miners against collieries, strike-breakers and the trains attempting to bring them in, as well as extensive looting, led the government to send in troops and more police. Attempts to defend the workings of collieries led to more violence, and a miner was killed in riots at Tonypandy. Disputes arose from pressure on the profitability of pits and on miners' living standards, due in part to geological factors which reduced pit productivity. Employers tried to restrict customary rights and payments and the strike played a major role in the development of anarchist and communist sentiment in Wales, although it was unsuccessful.

Below: The development of higher education for women at Cambridge; scenes from Girton and Newnham Colleges. Girton was founded in 1873; Somerville College and Lady Margaret Hall, Oxford, in 1879.

to vote Liberal or Conservative; ethnic, religious, regional and occupational divisions were as important as class issues.

Britain on the eve of world war was still in many respects an hierarchical society; George V (1910-36) summoned 'my loyal subjects' to war. Hereditary monarchy was still important, and society was scarcely egalitarian. Third-class passengers were not allowed on Great Western Railway expresses until 1882. The aristocracy had

survived as major players in political and social life until the very end of the nineteenth century, but thereafter they suffered major blows. Death duties were introduced in 1894. Greatly-expanded institutions with a meritocratic ethos – the civil service, the professions, the universities, the public schools and the army – were all very significant in the creation of a new social and cultural Establishment to replace the aristocracy in the late nineteenth century. The armed forces played a much less dominant role in Victorian Britain than in the leading continental states, where they served as a base for continued aristocratic, or at least landed, influence. In Britain the old landowning political elite had its dominance of the electoral process challenged in 1832, and, thereafter, provided a steadily decreasing percentage of MPs. Mr Merdle, the great 'popular financier on an extensive scale' in Dickens's *Little Dorrit*, was 'a new power in the country . . . able to buy up the whole House of Commons'. The Liberal Herbert Asquith, a barrister, was in 1908 the first prime minister not to have his own country house, though he was to end up with a country house and an earldom. Successive extensions of the franchise had not brought the vote to women, although they were socially less dependent than is generally assumed and than their legal situation might suggest.

The political, religious, intellectual and educational authority of the Church of England had been challenged, but it still played a major role in a society which was still very much Christian in its precepts. There were numerous clergymen. The principal challenge to the Church of England came not from atheism but from the rise of Dissent, although the re-emergence of 'public'

Catholicism, with the re-establishment of the Catholic hierarchy in 1850-51 and massive Irish immigration, caused tension. The Irish-born population of England and Wales rose to 602,000 in 1861, about 3 per cent of the total population. The equivalent statistics for Scotland in 1851 were 207,000 and 7 per cent. The impact of the Irish was increased by their concentration in a few cities such as Glasgow, London, where the Irish were 5% of the population in 1861, and Liverpool, where the percentage was near 25. The right of the British to rule over other peoples was still taken for granted, and Darwinism, with its stress on natural selection, seemed to give new force to it. The Primrose League, a popular Con-

Above: Interior of Newcastle Central Station by John Dobson; a masterpiece of iron and glass. Dobson's ambitious and original classical design for the facade had to be modified due to the financial crisis that hit the railways in 1849 as the frauds of the 'Railway King', George Hudson MP, were discovered.

Below: The Menai Bridge on the Crewe/Holyhead railway linking Anglesey with the rest of Wales.

Above: Harrowing by H H
La Thangue, *c*.1899.
Agriculture involved hard
physical labour for men and
women alike. La Thangue,
an English painter much
influenced by French *plein-
air* artists, was known
particularly for his studies
of peasant life.

Far right: Pear's Soap
advertisement *c*.1900. Mass
markets were served by
national advertising
campaigns.

servative movement launched in 1883, enjoyed
much support in the 1880s and 1890s for its
defence of Crown, social system and empire.

And yet there had also been major change,
necessarily as both cause and consequence of a
society with a mass electorate, universal compulsory primary education, and widespread
urbanization and industrialization. These had
brought widespread social dislocation, instability
and fears. Deference and traditional social patterns, never as fixed as some thought, had ebbed,
and the new and newly expanded cities and towns
created new living environments in which the
role and rule of the old world were far less signif-
cant. Railways created new economic and social
relationships, new leisure and commuting
options. Their construction destroyed or
damaged many of the most prominent sites of the
past, including Berwick and Newcastle Castles
and Launceston Priory, and wrecked the canal

system. The geography and townscape of London
was changed by the train, including underground
railways, and the tram, and by new roads such as
Kingsway and Northumberland Avenue, which
respectively destroyed a red light district and the
splendour of Northumberland House.

Technology was like a freed genie, bringing
ever more changes. Railway and telegraphy were
succeeded by motor car and telephone, electricity
and wireless. The growth of the genre of 'scientific romance' testified to the seemingly inexorable
advance of human potential through technology.
In *The Coming Race* (1871), by Sir Edward Bulwer
Lytton, one of the leading men of letters of his age
and a former Conservative Secretary for the
Colonies, a mining engineer encountered at the
centre of the earth a people who controlled 'Vril',
a kinetic energy offering limitless powers. The
novel is largely forgotten, other than through
Bo[vine]vril. Science fiction played a greater role

in the work of H G Wells (1866-1946), who had studied under Charles Darwin's supporter, the comparative anatomist T H Huxley. Man's destiny in time and space was a central question for Wells, reflecting in part the intellectual expansion offered by Darwin's evolutionary theory as outlined in his *The Origin of Species* (1859), and by interest in manned flight. His first major novel, *The Time Machine* (1895), was followed in *The War of the Worlds* (1898) by an account of a Martian invasion of England.

Developments were in fact less lurid, but they still changed many aspects of human experience. The first demonstration of electric lighting in Birmingham was in 1882, and the Birmingham Electric Supply Ltd was established seven years later. The first original full-size British petrol motor was produced in 1895; the first commercial motor company established at Coventry in 1896; and motor buses were introduced in about 1898. The first successful powered flight, by the American Wright brothers in 1903, led Lord Northcliffe to remark that 'England is no longer an island'. The Motor Car Act of 1903 extended the rights of the motorist; the motor bus was introduced in London in 1905; and four years later the national Road Board was founded to lend energy and cohesion to road construction. Motor transport led to the widespread tarring of roads from the early 1900s, a visual and environmental change. By 1914, there were 132,000 private car registrations, 124,000 motor cycle registrations and 51,167 buses and taxis on the road. Cars ensured that bicycling, which had boomed following the development of the safety bicycle in 1885, descended the social and age scales. A new world of

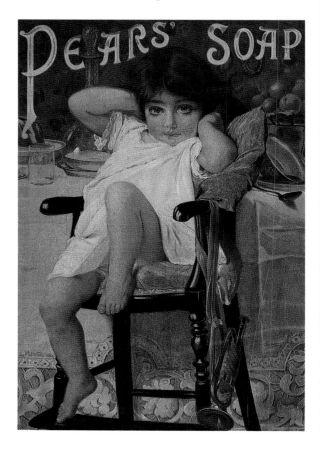

speed and personal mobility, with its own particular infrastructure, was being created. If cars were still a luxury, every such innovation contributed to a sense of change that was possibly the most important solvent of the old order.

Above: Circe Invidiosa, 1892, by J W Waterhouse (1849-1917), illustrates the appeal of the exotic in fin de siècle culture.

9

THE TWENTIETH CENTURY

1914-92

Left: The experience of
war. Old Coventry
Cathedral was destroyed by
German bombing on 14
November 1940; it was hit
by fire bombs, not high
explosives, and so the shell
remained.

WAR AND THE LOSS OF EMPIRE framed the political experience of Britain from the outbreak of the First World War (1914) to the 1960s, but the social and economic context was to be transformed totally as a result of technological innovation and application. The nineteenth century had brought major changes but the contemporary age has witnessed a revolution in theoretical and applied science and technology in most fields, whether transportation, the generation and distribution of power, medicine, contraception, agricultural yields, or the accumulation and manipulation of information. The wealth created made it feasible to suggest that man's lot on earth could be substantially improved. Change was so all-encompassing that fear about permanent damage to the environment became a major issue from the 1960s. Sulphur dioxide from British coal-fired power stations has been blamed for acid rain in Britain and on the Continent. Concern had been expressed earlier; in his *To Iron-Founders and Others*, Yorkshire poet Gordon Bottomley (1874-1948) warned:

When you destroy a blade of grass
You poison England at her roots . . .
Your worship is your furnaces,
. . . your vision is
Machines for making more machines.

In this brave and troubled new world, it was possible for people to travel and transmit ideas as never before, to create and destroy in new ways and on a scale hitherto only graspable in imaginative fiction, to synthesize and manufacture new substances, tastes and sounds, and thus create from the fertile mind of man a world in which man himself, his desires, needs and imagination, seemed the sole frame of reference, the only scale.

For someone aged 80 or over in 1992 (a growing percentage of the population), it was not only the major individual technological innovations of their lifetime, whether atomic energy or contraceptive pill, television or microchip, jet engine or computer, bio-technology or artificial hip, that were of importance in affecting, directly or indirectly, insistently or episodically, their life, but also the cumulative impact of change. The past ceased to be a recoverable world, a source of reference, value and values for lives that changed very little, and became instead a world that was truly lost, a theme-park for nostalgia, regret or curiosity. Al Stewart's song *On the Border* (1976) lamented:

the village where I grew up
Nothing seems the same
. . . the customs slip away
. . . In the islands where I grew up
Nothing seems the same
Its just the patterns that remain,
An empty shell.

Change was first a matter of displacement. Migration had always been important in British history, especially in the nineteenth century, with movement to the new industrial areas and emigration to the colonies, but in the contemporary age population patterns have changed even more radically. Rural England is now like a skeleton, without its people. In 1921-39 the number of agricultural labourers fell by a quarter, and the pace quickened after the Second World War. Horses were replaced by tractors, and local mills fell into disuse. Hand-milking was replaced by machines. W.H. Auden (1907-73), an alienated and left-wing writer, especially prominent in the 1930s, wrote in *The Dog Beneath the Skin* (1935):

I see barns falling, fences broken,
Pasture not ploughland, weeds not wheat.
The great houses remain but only half are inhabited,
Dusty the gunrooms and the stable clocks stationary
. . .
Those who sang in the inns at evening have departed
. . .
Their children have entered the service of the suburban areas; they
have become typists, mannequins and factory operatives; they
desired a different rhythm of life.
But their places are taken by another population, with views about nature,
Brought in charabanc and saloon along arterial roads
. . .

Below: A Westmorland farm labourer with his scythe c.1890; the traditional rural economy relied on manual labour but the technological advances of the twentieth century led to a depopulation of rural areas.

Left: Going to the Meet by Sir Alfred Munnings, 1913. Born and brought up in Suffolk, Munnings studied in Norwich and Paris and initially concentrated on landscapes and paintings of rural life. He was attached to the Canadian Cavalry Brigade in France 1917-18, painting 45 war pictures for the Canadian Government, and thereafter concentrated on equestrian portraits, becoming President of the Royal Academy. Hunting played a major role in the rural life of the upper classes.

Agriculture continues to shed workers. Other non-urban activities, such as forestry, mining and quarrying, have also either declined or dramatically cut their workforces. These changes have led to the depopulation of many rural regions, especially upland areas and those beyond commuting distance from towns. This is not a case of the destruction of age-old lifestyles, for the rural world of 1900 was in many respects no older than the major changes of the period 1500-1800, while the depopulation of some rural areas had been a major problem in Tudor England and earlier.

Left: Piercefield, near Chepstow. Many stately homes were abandoned during the twentieth century, owing to the combined effect of tax changes such as death duties and the lack of a cheap labour force.

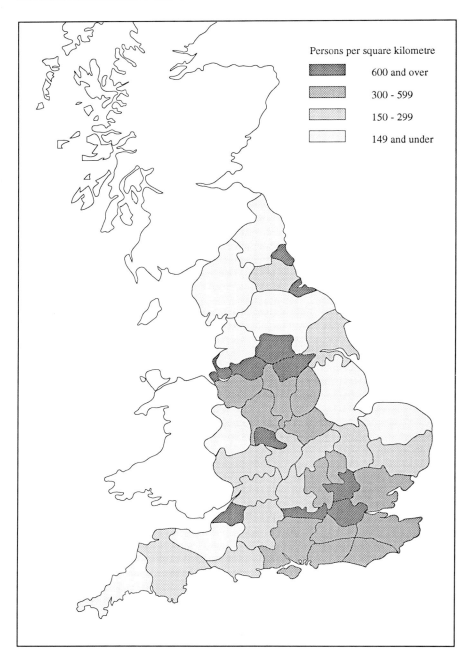

Persons per square kilometre

600 and over

300 - 599

150 - 299

149 and under

Above: Population density, 1990. The areas of nineteenth-century industrial growth are still densely populated, but so are the commuting counties round London. Largely agricultural counties, such as Cumbria, Lincolnshire and Shropshire, have low densities. The new county boundaries date from 1974.

Change is and was constant, and yet, in terms of the sense of place and identity of the British population of this century, the past seemed more fixed and the scale of change therefore revolutionary. The countryside has become, for many of its inhabitants, a place of residence rather than of work, and urban attitudes have been introduced, as in complaints about the noise produced by farm animals. In much of rural England, housing has become scarce and expensive as a result of purchase by commuters, while the problems of the rural economy have led to a large number of rural households living below the poverty line. At the other end of the social scale, while state subsidies for agriculture from the 1940s helped farmers and landowners, Lloyd George's tax changes and the disappearance of the vast labour force of cheap servants had already hit country house life, and many country houses were demolished or institutionalized. Over 600 were destroyed or abandoned in 1920-75; many others were transferred to the National Trust or became

reliant on paying visitors. The dominance of much of rural England by the aristocratic estate became a thing of the past. The influence of landowners in the politics of agriculture was replaced by that of farmers.

Visually and environmentally, rural England has also changed greatly. Redundant farmsteads have fallen into ruin or been destroyed. Amalgamating fields and bulldozing hedges have led since the 1950s to the replacement, as in Essex and Suffolk, of the earlier patchwork of small fields, surrounded by dense hedges, by large expanses of arable land, bounded often by barbed-wire fences. This has had serious environmental consequences, as have changes in the use of more marginal lands. Large plantations of coniferous trees have been established on upland moors and on the Suffolk Breckland. Marshlands have been drained and are now intensively farmed. Upland valleys, such as the North Tyne and the Durham Derwent, have been drowned for reservoirs, and others are threatened as water use and shortage becomes a more acute problem. Pesticides are used extensively in agriculture, and enter the groundwater system. The conquest of nature has become ever more comprehensive and insistent.

People have moved not only off the land, but also away from declining industrial regions. Areas that were collectively the nineteenth-century 'workshop of the world', became industrial museums and regions of social dereliction, designated as problems requiring regional assistance, as under the Special Areas Act (1934). During the slump of the 1930s unemployment in Sunderland rose to 75 per cent of shipbuilders and half of the working population, and was associated with hardship and higher rates of ill-health. In addition, crowded inner-city areas lost inhabitants as slums were torn down and instead, people moved to new developments in 'greenfield' sites, in the countryside or on the edge of older settlements. The former were new towns, the first garden city being Letchworth (1903); the latter suburban sprawl, the suburbia where a far greater percentage of the population than hitherto came to live. The process is still continuing; in July 1992 the government indicated that it expected 855,000 new houses to be built in the south-east between 1991 and 2006.

Designed to allow the expanding middle class to realize their earning potential, to escape from the crowded and polluted conditions of the city, and to join in the expanding hobby of amateur gardening, new housing was both cause and consequence of a massive expansion of personal transportation. Commuting led to an increase in first train and later car use. In the 1920s and 1930s the development of the London tube system allowed a major spread of the city to the north, while national private ownership of cars increased by over 1000% and by 1937 over 300,000 new cars were being registered annually. 'The sound of horns and motors', referred to in T.S. Eliot's *The Waste Land* (1922) was becoming more

Left: An official from Dr Barnardo's Homes pays a visit to the dank slums of Shadwell, 1920. London philanthropist Thomas Barnardo (1845-1905) opened his first home for destitute children in Stepney in 1870.

insistent. The railways had often pioneered feeder bus services, but from the 1920s the competition of road transport became serious for them. After a fall in car ownership during the Second World War it accelerated again rapidly. In terms of thousand million passenger-kilometres, private road transport shot up from 76 in 1954 to 350 in 1974, an increase from 39 to 79 per cent of the

Below: The new town being built at Hemel Hempstead, 24 April 1952, as part of a drive to replace slum dwellings. Government minister Ernest Marples had opened the 1000th flat built by the Hemel Hempstead Development Corporation the previous day.

Right: Rural landscape in modern Worcestershire. Recent agrarian changes have included the removal of hedgerows to produce larger fields more suited to mechanized cultivation and, as in this photograph, the spread of oil-seed rape: a striking contrast with the romanticized scene below.

total. This gain was made at the expense of bus, coach and rail transport. Nationalized in 1948, the railways lost money from the late 1950s and the Beeching Report of 1963 led to dramatic cuts in the network. There were 12.2 million cars in Britain in 1970, 21.9 million in 1990. A motor-way system was created, beginning with the M6 Preston by-pass, opened by Prime Minister Harold Macmillan in December 1958. The latest, the Oxford to Birmingham M40, opened in January 1991. As rural usage grew, it became necessary progressively to supplement existing

Right: Train Landscape by Eric Ravilious, 1940. A Londoner brought up and trained in Eastbourne and influenced by the Italian Primitives, Ravilious was commissioned by Wedgwood in 1936 to execute designs for china, which enjoyed considerable success. He was killed in 1942 in an aeroplane accident while an official war artist with the Royal Air Force. His *Train Landscape* offers, at a time of national challenge, a view of an apparently unchanged England.

roads and build by-passes; Exeter's was an early example, opened in 1938. Car exhaust emissions contributed to growing environmental pollution, while by the early 1990s 45,000 children were being hurt on the roads every year and among those aged five to fifteen, two-thirds of deaths were the result of road accidents.

Greater personal mobility for the bulk, but by no means all, of the population, both facilitated and was a necessary consequence of lower density housing. Employment patterns changed; in place of factories or mines with large labour forces, most industrial concerns were capital intensive and employed less labour. A growing number of the rising percentage of the population who were retired left the cities to live in suburban, rural or coastal areas, such as Colwyn Bay and Worthing. New shopping patterns developed with the rise of the supermarket in the 1950s and the hypermarket in the 1980s. By 1992 16% of the total shopping space in Britain was made up of shopping centres, such as Brent Cross in north London, Lakeside Thurrock in Essex, The Glades in Bromley, Kent, Meadowhall in Sheffield and the Metro Centre in Gateshead. These were moul-

ders of taste and spheres of purchasing activity at the centre of the consumer society. Most of their customers came by car, abandoning traditional high street shopping. Related changes in location were also of great importance in other fields, including education; in 1971 14 per cent of junior school children were driven to school, in 1990 64 per cent. The spatial segregation of the population was scarcely novel but it became more pronounced, while an obvious aspect of what was termed the 'underclass', in both town and countryside, was their relative lack of mobility.

Consumerism and technology, the two closely related, have been crucial features of the contemporary age and their impact has been very varied. The spread in the 1930s of affordable cars with reliable self-starter motors, so that it was not necessary to crank up the motor by hand, led to a wave of 'smash and grab' raids as the criminal fraternity took advantage of the new technology. Greater mobility totally changed the pattern of crime. In response, the Metropolitan Police experimented with mounting ship radios in cars and were able to develop a fleet of Wolseley cars thus equipped with which to launch an effective

Below: New and speedier modes of travel. The M1 motorway under construction near Northampton, 25 March 1959; it was built to provide a faster route for through traffic between London and Birmingham. This photograph shows a junction between the straight motorway and an already established lesser road which follows the curves of the existing land-use pattern.

Above: Changing retail patterns. Marks and Spencer's Original Penny Bazaar, Newcastle, 10 September 1955.

response. The post-war world was to bring computer fraud but also the use of sophisticated forensic techniques. Traffic offences brought middle-class individuals into contact with the police and the courts. Labour-saving devices reduced the burden of housework, easing the struggle with dirt and disease, although they also ensured that household use of water increased considerably. The communication of messages has been revolutionized. Telephone ownership has risen to a high level; fax machines and mobile phones became important facilities in the 1980s; and the growing numbers of personal and company computers have encouraged the growing use of electronic mail.

The number of radio and television channels has multiplied. Radio broadcasts began in 1922; the British Broadcasting Corporation, a monopoly acting in the 'national interest' and financed by licence fees paid by radio owners, was established in 1926; and it began television services in 1936. Commercial television companies, financed by advertising, were not established until 1955. Television ownership shot up in the 1950s, the numbers of those with regular access to a set rising from 38 per cent of the population in 1955 to 75 per cent in 1959. By the early 1990s ownership and access rates were far higher, and the larger number of regular channels had been supplemented for many by satellite channels, the receiving dishes altering the appearance of many houses, as television aerials had done earlier. By

1992 over a million Sky Television dishes had been sold. Over 50 per cent of households had video recorders, giving them even greater control over what they watched.

Television succeeded radio as a central determinant of the leisure time of many: a moulder of opinions and fashions, a source of conversation and controversy, an occasion of family cohesion or dispute, a major feature of the household. A force for change, a significant contributor to the making of the 'consumer society', and a 'window on the world' which demands the right to enter everywhere and report anything, television has also become increasingly a reflector of popular taste. Just as radio had helped to provide common experiences – royal Christmas messages from 1932, Edward VIII's abdication speech in 1938, the war speeches of Churchill, heard by millions as those of Lloyd George could not be; so television fulfilled the same function, providing much of the nation with common visual images and messages. This process really began with the coronation service for Elizabeth II in 1953, which led to many purchasing sets or first watching television, and thanks to television the royals have almost become members of viewers' extended families, treated with the fascination commonly devoted to the stars of soap operas. Indeed, both the 'New Elizabethan Age', heralded in 1952, and present discontents about the position and behaviour of the royal family owe much to the 'media'. Television is central to much else, such

as the advertising that is so crucial to the consumer society, and the course and conduct of election campaigns. Parliament is televized, and much of public politics has become a matter of sound bites aimed to catch the evening news bulletins.

Technological change contributed to an economic situation in which the annual output of goods rose appreciably for most of the century, while personal output, consumption and leisure similarly rose, despite a major growth in population; including Northern Ireland, up from 44.9

Above: The Tesco supermarket at Purley, south London, opened in 1991, reflecting 1990s consumerism, Post-modern architecture and the car.

Left: The Daleks from the BBC's classic children's programme *Dr Who*. These easily-assembled, violent extra-terrestrials first appeared in 1963 and gripped children's imaginations in the 1960s. The Doctor, a modern and very human white knight, travelled through time in a police telephone box and contrasted greatly with American imports such as Batman and Superman.

Right: A comfortable 1930s scene. The Morris Minor four-door family saloon is pictured in an advertisement of 1933 against a backdrop of mock-Tudor houses characteristic of the period – although most houses were in fact more densely packed.

Below: Britain's royal family out in force for the Queen Mother's 90th birthday in 1990; the initial euphoria of the New Elizabethan Age soon subsided and by the 1990s there was widespread indifference, combined with increasing criticism of the expense and apparent irrelevance of the monarchy and of the lifestyle of some of the junior royals.

million in 1931 to 49 million in 1951 and 55.5 million in 1981. Despite the slump, for most of those in work the 1930s were a decade of im-

proved housing, wider consumer choice and a better quality of life. It was a period of new and developing electrical goods, of radio, television

and the 'talkies'. Large numbers of cinemas were constructed: despite its relatively low population, Suffolk had 40 in 1937. This was of scant value to the unemployed, nearly three million in late 1932 and, despite a strong recovery in 1934-37, still above one million until 1941. More than a quarter of the Scottish labour force was out of work in 1931-33, as was about one-third of Derbyshire's miners, and the 1933 Derbyshire march of the National Unemployed Workers' Movement had such slogans as 'We refuse to starve in silence . . . We want work schemes'. Many of those who had work nevertheless faced low wages, a life of shifts and expedients, inadequate food and poor housing, but for many others the 1930s was a period of prosperity, and this helped to account for the victory of the National Government in the 1935 election. The same contrast was true of the recessions at the beginning of the 1980s and the 1990s. Alongside high unemployment, and social strains manifested in rising crime rates and urban riots, many of those in work had high living standards. Ownership of telephones, washing machines, dishwashers, cars and video-recorders all rose. In both recessions, however, the rising ownership of goods was in part met by increased imports, while British industry was harmed by the high exchange rate of sterling as the interests of producers were subordinated to those of finance, not least due to a determination to reduce inflation.

Economic growth and changing political and social assumptions led to the development of national social security and educational provision and, from 1948, of a national health service, ensuring that the indigent and ill were offered a comprehensive safety net, while a range of services were provided free at the point of delivery to the whole of the population. Measures such as free school meals (1907), non-contributory old age pensions (1908), labour exchanges (1909), the National Insurance Act (1911) and the establishment of the Unemployment Assistance Board (1934), were limited, but an improvement on the earlier situation, and the establishment of antenatal screening in the 1920s was an important health measure. Further developments were widely supported in the three decades after the Second World War, a period which reflected a measure of continuity between Conservative and Labour policies.

The creation of the welfare state reflected a conviction that social progress and economic growth were compatible, that indeed a major purpose of the latter was to achieve the former. Stable employment and social security were seen as important goals. Following the 1915 Rent and Mortgage Interest Restrictions (War) Act, which owed something to the Clydeside rent strikes of that year, private landlordship became less profitable, tenants' rights more secure and renting from local authorities, 'council housing', more important; and after 1945 slums were swept aside and their inhabitants moved into new housing

Above: Perhaps a more representative view of the 1930s, showing the misery of unemployment.

Left: Conservative election poster of 1929 seeking the support of workers. Labour won the election but, in the face of a world recession, were even less successful in safeguarding jobs.

Above: A soup kitchen to
help the poor and the
unemployed, 1924.

estates. Extolled at the time, and illustrated alongside castles and cathedrals in guidebooks of the 1960s, these have subsequently been attacked as lacking in community feeling and breeders of alienation and crime. Similarly, there has been disagreement about the social and educational consequences of comprehensive education – the abandonment in the state sector, in the 1950s and especially from 1965, of streaming children by ability into different schools after examination at the age of eleven. The percentage of children in private schools rose markedly in the 1980s, and such schools continue to be perceived as both cause and consequence of class distinction. Major expansions in higher education in the 1960s and early 1990s dramatically increased the percentage of school-leavers continuing in full-time education, and thus eventually the graduate population, but it is not clear that the hopes inspiring this process, especially that of fulfilling the economy's requirements for skills, have been met.

Although for long regarded as one of the triumphs of social welfare policy, the National Health Service, established in 1948, was hampered from the outset by the measures taken to win the consent of interest groups, especially doc-

tors and dentists, and has subsequently suffered from the rising cost of medical treatment, a consequence of the greater potential for medical action and rising expectations of care. Private health care has developed and the state of the NHS was a major issue in the 1992 general election, and yet the NHS has been able to maintain the policy of treatment free at the point of delivery, so that many of the anxieties about the availability and cost of medical treatment that the poor faced earlier in the century have ended. It has established a much fairer geographical and social allocation of resources and skills than existed hitherto, and there has been a positive effort to develop medical education and specialized services spread across the regions rather than concentrated, as earlier, in a few centres, principally London.

Uniform health provision through the NHS has played a major role in the dramatic change in the medical condition of the population that has characterized the twentieth century although other factors, such as improved diet, have also been of great importance. Britain has been in the forefront of medical research and development throughout the century, and as general medical knowledge has increased enormously, so the

Left: Traditional terrace housing, probably back-to-backs, opening directly onto the cobbled street, Liverpool, 1954. The doorstep-scrubbing women reflect an era when men worked to support the family and most married women worked in the home.

ability to identify and treat disease has increased exponentially. These improvements have touched the lives of millions and totally altered the condition of the people; perception and experience of illness have altered radically. The discovery of insulin in 1922 and its use from the

Below. Three concrete prefabricated houses on the Temple Hill council estate in Dartford, Kent, May 1947. This estate, which was to be opened by the Prime Minister, Clement Attlee, in July, was an example of the council-funded housing designed both to free people from slum dwellings and to replace war-damaged stock.

mid-1920s gave life to young diabetics. Britain has played a major role in the understanding and treatment of mental illness. The twentieth century has brought recognition of the importance of psychological and mental processes, and the diagnosis and treatment of mental illness has been revolutionized. The development from the 1940s of safe and effective drugs has helped in the treatment of major psychoses and depression, dramatically improving the cure rate. British scientists such as Sir Alexander Fleming, the discoverer of penicillin, played a major role in the development of antibiotics in the 1930s and especially the 1940s. These were of enormous benefit in dealing with infections which, of one kind or another, were a very common cause of death in the first half of the century. Tuberculosis, which killed one adult in eight at the beginning of the century, was conquered thanks to the use from the 1940s of an American antibiotic, streptomycin, as well as to better diet and the programme of mass BCG vaccination. Antibiotics also helped with other bacterial infections: diarrhoeal diseases have diminished; urinary infections can

Below: The satirical magazine *Private Eye* reflects the sense of national malaise during the mid-1970s. Oil-rich King Faisal of Saudi Arabia appears to have the resources to purchase debt-ridden Britain, then suffering from a high rate of inflation. The 1992 London production of Gilbert and Sullivan's 1870 light opera *Princess Ida* was set in 2002, with Buckingham Palace owned by a Japanese sushi-burger magnate.

be more readily treated. The common childhood diseases which caused high mortality and high morbidity in children in the early part of the century, such as measles, whooping cough, polio, diphtheria, mumps and rubella (German measles), have been dramatically reduced by the post-war introduction of immunization programmes for the entire child population. From the 1970s on screening was introduced for the early detection and treatment of other diseases, such as breast and cervical cancer, while the 1980s saw the increasing development and use of anti-viral agents for the treatment of viral infections.

Surgical treatment has dramatically increased. The two world wars, especially the second, saw a major improvement in surgical techniques, for example, the development of plastic surgery. A major increase in anaesthetic skills, due to greater knowledge and the introduction of increasingly sophisticated drugs, has meant that complex surgical operations can be performed. Once-serious operations, such as appendectomies, have become routine and minor. The range of research and development now encompasses skin grafts and artificial knee joints. There have been major advances in the treatment of the heart, and bypass and transplant surgery have been completely developed since the Second World War.

Medical advances have led to dramatic changes in the pattern of causes of death, although related developments in public health have also been of great importance. The Clean Air Act (1956) and other environmental measures, safety awareness and the Health and Safety at Work Act, and growing understanding of the dangers of working in smoke-filled buildings and with asbestos, have all contributed. The hazards of drinking to excess and, particularly, of smoking have become generally appreciated and been addressed by government action.

Whereas large numbers of children died in the first half of the century and infections were a major cause of death, now later-onset diseases, such as heart disease and cancers, are far more important, and infections mainly kill people who are suffering from associated disorders and are at the extremes of life. Average life expectancy for all age groups has persistently risen this century, the major exception being those aged between 15 and 44 during the 1980s. This has led to a new age structure, as a result of the increasing number of pensioners, and the problems posed by the greater number of people over 85 with the increasing dependencies associated with age. In addition, not all illnesses are in retreat. Possibly as a result of increasing car exhaust emissions, respiratory diseases such as asthma have definitely risen, and others may also be increasing. The massive increase in the import, treatment and burying of hazardous waste in the 1980s has led to concern about possible health implications.

If the age structure of the population has changed totally as a result of medical advances, so also have many aspects of people's lives. Contra-

ceptive developments have vastly increased the ability of women to control their own fertility and have played a major role in the emancipation of women, as well as in the 'sexual revolution', the change in general sexual norms, of the 1960s on. The situation of the approximately 20 per cent of couples who are infertile is changing, thanks to new techniques such as *in vitro* fertilization. Although AIDS has developed as a new killer, antibiotics have dealt with most other sexually transmitted diseases. Pain is increasingly held at bay by more effective and selective painkillers, bringing relief to millions suffering from illnesses such as arthritis and muscular pain. Thus the condition of the people has really changed; they are generally healthier and longer-living. Nutrition has improved, average height has increased for both men and women, and the country is affluent and health-conscious enough to emphasize the newly-perceived problem of the over-weight.

Yet the modern age was also a period when Britain's relative economic performance declined appreciably with reference to both traditional and new competitors. In 1960-81 Britain's annual growth in gross domestic product was lower than that of all the other 18 OECD countries. The average standard of living fell beneath that of Germany, Japan, France and Italy in the post-1960 period. A sense of decline, pervasive at times, was especially characteristic in the 1970s. The cover of the satirical journal *Private Eye* on 10 January 1975 showed the oil-rich King of Saudi Arabia, with the caption 'Britain Sold Shock. New Man at Palace'. Ironically, the discovery of oil in the North Sea shortly beforehand was to help ease Britain's balance-of-payments problem, although it did not prevent continued economic decline relative to competitors who lacked that resource. By seeking, first informally and in 1990-92 formally through the European Monetary System, a fixed exchange rate with the currency of the strongest European economy, Germany, British policy makers surrendered the initiative over economic management, and in September 1992 it proved impossible to sustain the policy. In addition structural changes in the economy created major problems, particularly widespread unemployment, often over two, and in some cases over three, million since 1975; a decline in manufacturing industry with associated regional problems; and difficulties in maintaining a stable currency.

These problems interacted with aspects of the 'political economy', not least the rising power of trade unions with their generally perceived determination to put sectional interests first, the conviction of politicians that they could improve the economy, and a variety of interventionist policies that have generally not had this result. Trade union membership rose from 1½ million (1895) to 11½ million (1975). Union leaders such as Jack Jones, General Secretary of the Transport and General Workers Union 1968-78, wielded great influence in the 1960s and 1970s. They played key roles in what was a corporatist state, with Jones forging a Social Compact with the Labour government of Harold Wilson in 1974: the unions were to moderate wage demands in return for an acceptable legislative programme. Strikes by the National Union of Miners, some of whose leaders were motivated by political hostility, defeated the Conservative government of Edward Heath in 1972 and, crucially, 1974, and that of 1984-85 was only beaten by the government of the determined Margaret Thatcher (Conservative PM 1979-90) after a long struggle, and then in part because the miners were divided and the weather good. Thanks respectively to television and power cuts, people became accustomed to the immediacy of picket-line violence and to baths in the dark. A 'winter of discontent' in 1978-79, in which 'secondary picketing' played a major and disruptive role, helped Mrs Thatcher to victory in 1979. She had little time for discussions with trade union leaders and passed legislation to limit their powers, a task that Harold Wilson had failed to achieve in 1969 when the 'In Place of Strife' white paper was

Below: The resignation of Labour Prime Minister Harold Wilson and his succession by James (Jim) Callaghan, as viewed by *Private Eye*. Britain was widely perceived to be in a mess and Wilson was mistrusted as a fixer who could no longer fix anything. Callaghan had beaten Michael Foot for the leadership by 176 to 137 votes.

No. 373 Friday 2 April '76   15p

PRIVATE EYE

END OF AN ERA

Alright, Jim, you can take over now

withdrawn due to trade union and Labour party opposition. In the late 1980s trade union militancy became less common, and the level of industrial action (strikes) continued to fall in the early 1990s. By 1990 only 48% of employees were union members and only half a million were covered by closed shop agreements, compared to 4 million a decade earlier. Far more wage negotiations were conducted at a local level.

There has been a lack of continuity in economic policy, for example over regional aid. The steel industry was nationalized in 1949 and 1967, and privatized in 1953 and then again after 1979, alongside gas, electricity, telephones, water and much else, as the Conservatives under Mrs Thatcher sought to privatize nationalized industries and to reduce the role of the state in economic management. Economic growth has not matched political expectations, leading to disagreement over expenditure priorities, and the major increase in government expenditure and employment since 1914 has increased the importance of these disputes. The national budget has been unable to sustain the assumptions and demands of politicians on behalf of, for example, social welfare and defence. The devaluation of the pound by 30.5% in 1949 was followed by public expenditure cuts, leading to the introduction of prescription charges and resignations by left-wing Labour ministers. Alongside the often unsuccessful management of the economy by pol-

iticians, for example the delay in devaluing sterling by the government of Harold Wilson, Labour Prime Minister 1964-70, 1974-76, there was also at times a serious neglect of aspects of the economy, symbolized by the remark of Sir Alec Douglas-Home, who renounced his earldom to become Conservative Prime Minister (1963-64), that his grasp of economics was of the 'matchstick variety'. All post-war premiers, with the possible exception of James Callaghan (Labour 1976-79), spent too much time on foreign policy and found it difficult to abandon the habit of seeing Britain as a major international player. These were politicians who cared more about Cape Town than Consett; poor economic management was in part to blame for high rates of inflation, which rose to an average of 15.8% in 1972-75, and for the subsequent need to turn to the International Monetary Fund for assistance (1976).

An overall rate of economic growth is scant consolation to those with diminished experiences and disappointed expectations. And yet a striking feature of the domestic and international problems that Britain has encountered is that they have not led to a radicalization of British politics. The First World War was followed in 1919 by 'Red Clydeside', the British Communist Party was formed in 1920, there was a General Strike in 1926 and the 1930s saw the formation by Sir Oswald Mosley of the New Party, which subsequently evolved into the British Union of

Below: The London General Omnibus Depot during the General Strike, 1926. Volunteers drive buses, protected by police and troops; the buses are bedecked as usual with advertisements.

Left: Sir Oswald Mosley (1896-1981) taking the salute at a Fascist march through the East End of London, 4 October 1936. Conservative, Independent and then Labour MP (1918-31), Mosley founded the British Union of Fascists in 1932. A would-be dictator, whose changing opinions and loyalties revolved around a fixed point of belief in himself, he deliberately staged marches by his Blackshirts in order to provoke violence. As with some other opposition movements in British history, he was discredited not only as a result of his opinions, but also because of demagoguery, violence and links with hostile foreign powers, in Mosley's case Nazi Germany. He was imprisoned 1940-43.

Fascists. Some writers of the period expressed the fear that sinister conspiracies lay behind political and industrial problems; this was the theme of Sapper's [Lieutenant-Colonel H C McNeile] *Bulldog Drummond* (1921). John Buchan (1875-1940), a Scottish writer who served in Intelligence during the First World War before becoming an MP and Governor-General of Canada, discerned in *The Three Hostages* (1924) 'wreckers on the grand scale, merchants of pessimism, giving society another kick downhill whenever it had a chance of finding its balance, and then pocketing their profits . . . they used the fanatics . . . whose key was a wild hatred of something or other, or a reasoned belief in anarchy'. According to *The Big Four* (1927) by the detective writer Agatha Christie (1890-1976), the best-selling British author of the century: 'The world-wide unrest, the labour troubles that beset every nation, and the revolutions that break out in some . . . there is a force behind the scenes which aims at nothing less than the disintegration of civilization . . . Lenin and Trotsky were mere puppets'. Technology is seen as at the service of this force, 'a concentration of wireless energy far beyond anything so far attempted, and capable of focusing a beam of great intensity upon some given spot . . . atomic energy', so that the Big Four could become 'the dictators of the world'. Such sinister threats facing Britain were to be a staple of spy thrillers, such as the novels of Ian Fleming (1908-64), beginning with *Casino Royale* (1952). These were

adventure stories, many of which testified to the imaginative potency of the new technology, but they also revealed a sense of the nation under threat, an imaginative extension of the challenges facing the country.

Yet radicalism was to make little impact in Britain and the continuity of parliamentary government was not overthrown. The General Strike was defeated by the firmness of the Baldwin government and the resulting lack of nerve of the trade union leadership, and the combined total membership of the Communists and the Fascists never exceeded 38,000. The economic upturn of 1934 stemmed rising support for Mosley. Despite their subsequent reputation, far more Cambridge undergraduates of the 1930s were interested in sport than in Communist activism. The limited extent of radicalism was even more true after the Second World War. Nazi activities discredited the extreme right, while the policies and eventual failure of the Soviet Union struck successive blows at the credibility of the far left. The Labour Party drifted to the left in the 1970s and was affected by 'entryism' by far left groups, so that there was little to choose in the 1980s between the views of some Labour MPs and Western European Communists, but this helped to lead to four successive Labour failures in the general elections of 1979, 1983, 1987 and 1992, the most unimpressive record of any political party since the decline of the Liberals after the First World War, and one achieved despite serious economic diffi-

Right: Campaign for Nuclear Disarmament march, London, 3 April 1972. The movement was launched on 17 February 1958 to press for the abandonment of nuclear weapons and a cut in defence expenditure. It achieved wide but temporary popularity in 1958-64 and, in response to the deployment of cruise missiles, again in the early 1980s, but lacked broader appeal. The Labour Party's support for unilateral nuclear disarmament was in part responsible for its loss of the 1983 election.

culties for Conservative governments at the beginning of the 1980s and during the 1992 election. The attempt to create a collectivist society by means of state action, a new model society planned in accordance with socialist principles, was rejected by the electorate, and in the late 1980s by the Labour party under the leadership of Neil Kinnock. Similarly, successive public opinion polls in the 1980s and early 1990s revealed limited support for much of the agenda of

Right: The centre of power. *Waterloo Bridge* by Emile Claus, 1917 shows Westminster, the Houses of Parliament and the bridge from the south bank of the Thames.

the 'New Right', and clear support for the welfare state, especially the National Health Service. The recessions of the early 1980s and 1990s did not lead to a revival of left-wing radicalism, and the circulation of the Communist daily newspaper, the *Morning Star*, fell below 10,000.

The relationship between the absence of a successful challenge to the political system, or at least a major transformation of it, and the lack of sustained defeat abroad is unclear. Germany, Japan, France, Italy and Austria-Hungary all suffered serious defeat in the First and/or Second World Wars, leading to a political and institutional transformation which has been as important for the subsequent success of most of those societies as the rebuilding of economic systems on which attention is usually focused. No such process has taken place in Britain. Indeed in several respects the essential features of the political system are still those of 1914: a hereditary monarchy, albeit one that adopted the British name of Windsor in 1917; a bicameral Parliament, with the House of Commons being the most powerful and only elected chamber; national political parties with recognizably different regional and social bases of support; and a centralized British state without regional assemblies, still less devolved, or independent, parliaments for Scotland and Wales. Britain remains in some respects an elective dictatorship. The social system is still markedly inegalitarian, and the political system, the civil service, the armed forces, the profes-

sions, the banking system, large companies and the universities are disproportionately dominated by those whose background cannot be described as working class. The Conservatives stressed the modest origins and difficult upbringing of John Major, Prime Minister from November 1990, but neither circumstance is true of the bulk of his Cabinet and parliamentary colleagues.

And yet there have also been major changes, which can be summarized under the headings of Ireland, empire, Europe and democratization. War tore the guts out of the British empire, weakening it in resources and morale. The first major loss was Ireland. Half a million men of Irish descent volunteered to fight for George V in 1914, and fewer than 2000 rose in the Easter Rising of 1916 in Dublin, an unsuccessful attempt to create an Independent Irish Republic; but the 1918 general election was largely won in Ireland by Sinn Fein, nationalists under Eamonn de Valera, who refused to attend Westminster and demanded independence. British refusal led to a brutal civil war in 1919-21, followed by partition and effective independence for the new Irish Free State. Vestigial British authority was extinguished by the Republic of Ireland Act (1948). Ulster, which remained part of Britain represented at Westminster, was self-governed and became very much a Protestant state, with its Catholic minority suffering discrimination; this sectarian division led to violence in the 1960s, the intervention of British troops (1969) and the

Above: The 125 train, capable of travelling at up to 125 miles per hour, is the diesel-powered workhorse of British Rail's inter-city network. In January 1993 the Conservative party confirmed plans to privatize much of British Rail. By then 125s had been replaced on some routes by electric 225s, capable of 225 kilometres per hour.

suspension of the regional government (1972). By September 1992 3000 people had died in the 'Troubles', mostly as a result of terrorism by the anti-British Irish Republican Army (IRA), although an increasing number were killed by Protestant paramilitary groups determined to remain part of Britain. IRA terrorism on the British mainland included attacks on the Conservative party conference (1984), and the Cabinet (1991), and led to the deaths of three Conservative MPs.

The loss of Ireland revealed the weakness of the British empire when confronted by a powerful nationalist movement. The First World War (1914-18), in which Britain had played a major role on the victorious side, mobilizing her resources of people and wealth as never before, was followed by the extension of the British empire to its greatest extent. The war began with pistol shots in Sarajevo, the assassination by Serbian terrorists of Archduke Franz Ferdinand, the heir to the Austro-Hungarian empire, and pitted a large coalition, in which Britain, France, Russia and, from 1917, the USA were the major powers, against Germany, Austria-Hungary, Bulgaria and Turkey. The German invasion of Belgium, as a means to out-flank French forces, led Britain, which had guaranteed Belgian neutrality, to declare war on 4 August 1914. The German drive,

first on Paris and then on the Channel ports, was thwarted, and in late 1914 both sides dug in on the Western Front. The concentration of large forces in a relatively small area, the defensive strength of trench positions, particularly thanks to modern field artillery and the machine gun, and the difficulty of making substantial gains if opposing lines were breached, ensured that, until the collapse of the German position in the last weeks of the year, the situation was essentially deadlocked. British attacks at Neuve-Chapelle and Loos (1915), the Somme (1916), and Arras and Passchendaele (1917), led to major losses of men with little gain of territory. The discontent of many soldiers with the situation led to thousands of court martials, while shell-shock affected large numbers. The unimaginative nature of British generalship did not help. Douglas Haig, who was appointed to the command of the British army in France in December 1915, believed that the war would be won on the battlefield, and by determined leadership, superior morale and offensive operations. He saw the British as a chosen race who would be purified by victory. Using British manpower in offensives against the firepower of German defensive positions ensured that it was British rather than German strength that was exhausted by attrition. In fact,

Right: Sledmere, Yorkshire, war memorial for those slain in the First World War. In 1919 a two-minute silence was first instituted on the anniversary of the Armistice to commemorate the dead. In 1920 the Unknown Warrior was buried in Westminster Abbey and the Cenotaph was unveiled in Whitehall.

although the blocking of German offensives in 1914, 1916 and 1918 were essential preconditions of victory, the war was won as a result of the collapse of Austria-Hungary and the growing military, economic and domestic problems facing the Germans, which destroyed their will to fight.

Although the Western Front dominated British strategy and was responsible for most of their 750,000 dead, there were attempts to search out a weaker front and to strike at Germany's allies. These led to the disastrous expedition to the Dardanelles (1915), whose forceful advocate, the energetic First Lord of the Admiralty, Winston Churchill, resigned, and to failures in Iraq and at Salonika (1916), but also to Allenby's successful campaign in Palestine (1917-18). The German colonies were overrun. The threat from the German surface fleet was blocked at the indecisive battle of Jutland (1916), but their submarines took a heavy toll of British merchant shipping, although their impact was lessened by the use of convoys and the entry of America into the war. The scale and duration of the struggle led to an unprecedented mobilization of national resources, including the introduction of conscription (1916), after over two million men had volunteered to fight for king and country, and state direction of much of the economy. The war gave a tremendous boost to the role of the state and the machinery of government. The Cabinet Office was created in 1916. The allocation of resources led to a rise in civilian living standards and an improvement in the life expectancy of those of the worst-off sections of the pre-war working class who were exempt from war service.

The defeat of the German empire meant that its place in the sun was distributed among the victors, Britain gaining League of Nation mandates for Tanganyika, part of Togo and a sliver of the Cameroons. War with Germany's ally Turkey led to the annexation of Cyprus and Egypt (1914), and the gaining of mandates over Palestine, Transjordan and Iraq when Turkey's empire was partitioned at the end of the war. Ardent imperialists, such as Lord Milner and Leo Amery, wanted to strengthen of the empire, partly in the hope that this would mean that Britain need never be dragged into the continental mire again. British influence increased in both Persia and Turkey, and British troops operating against the Communists in the Russian civil war that followed their coup in 1917 moved into the Caucasus, Central Asia, and the White Sea region and were deployed in the Baltic and the Black Sea.

This high-tide of empire was to ebb very fast. The strain of the First World War, the men lost, for example ten per cent of male Scots between the ages of 16 and 50, the money spent, the exhaustion produced by constant effort, left Britain unable to sustain her international ambitions, and this was exacerbated by political division. Lloyd George had split the Liberal party when, in order to bring more decisive war leadership and further his own ambition, he had replaced

Above: The Spithead Review, May 1937. George VI reviews the fleet; a general view of the rocket display.

Asquith as Prime Minister at the end of 1916, and he was dependent on Conservative support, which in turn strained postwar Tory unity. Thus, despite Lloyd George's strutting the imperial stage, there was an absence of stable leadership. In 1922 there was a Conservative revolt from below, by backbenchers, junior ministers and constituency activists, leading at a meeting of the parliamentary Conservative party at the Carlton Club to a decision to abandon the coalition. This led to the fall of both Lloyd George and the Conservative leader Austen Chamberlain, who had sought continued support for the coalition. The new leader, Andrew Bonar Law, formed a totally Conservative government and easily won the 1922 general election. Far from breaking the mould of British politics, Lloyd George was consigned to the political wilderness. When in power, he had been unwilling to support electoral reform, the proportional representation discussed in 1918 that would have helped the Liberals in the 1920s, and once out of power could not obtain it.

Liberal disunity assisted in the rise of Labour, which became the official opposition after the 1922 election. Its trade union alliance allowed Labour to identify itself as the natural party of the working class, and thus to benefit from the extension of the franchise and the doubling of trade union membership from 1914 to 8 million in

1920. The 1918 Reform Act gave the vote to men over 21 fulfilling a six months' residence qualification and to women over 30, increasing the electorate from 8 to 21 million. A Redistribution Act was based on the principle of equal-size constituency electorates. The new larger electorate was potentially volatile and winning its support posed a considerable challenge to politicians, similar to that which had confronted Disraeli and Gladstone. The complex manoeuvres of three-party politics led to minority Labour governments under Ramsay MacDonald in 1924 and 1929-31, but the second was badly affected by the world economic crisis that began in 1929, and divided over the cuts believed necessary to balance the budget in order to restore confidence in sterling. A cut in unemployment benefit was rejected by the TUC and the bulk of the Labour party, but MacDonald and a few supporters joined the Conservatives and some Liberals in forming a National Government, which continued in power until the wartime coalition was formed in 1940. MacDonald was succeeded by Baldwin (1935) and Chamberlain (1937) and the government won the general elections of 1931 and 1935. Labour lost working-class voters as a result of the economic problems of 1929-31, while the Conservatives benefited from the economic upturn of 1934.

The 1920s were a period in which British governments drew in their horns. At home spending was cut, the Geddes Axe (1922) making cuts in education, housing and the armed forces. The homes promised to those 'heroes' who had survived the mud and machine guns of the Somme and Passchendaele, and the other mass graves of humanity on the Western Front, were not all built, as Treasury opposition thwarted some of the aspirations of the 1919 Housing Act. Abroad, intervention in Russia had been a failure; in the Middle East, revolt in Egypt (1919) and Iraq (1920-21) led to Britain granting their independence in 1922 and 1924 respectively; while British influence collapsed in Persia (1921) and the British backed down in their confrontation with Turkey (1922-23), the last a crucial factor in Lloyd George's fall. Unable to maintain Ireland or their extra-European pretensions in the 1920s, the British were also to fail to sustain the Versailles settlement in Europe and the League of Nations outside it. These failures were a consequence both of what had already been obvious in the decades prior to the First World War, the problems created by the rise of other states and Britain's global commitments, and the particular strains arising from that conflict and from subsequent developments.

And yet the empire was still very much a living reality in the interwar period. In some respects links developed further, a process given concrete form in the majestic buildings designed by Sir Edwin Lutyens and Sir Herbert Baker for the official quarter in New Delhi and finished in the 1930s. Economic links between Britain and empire became closer. Imperial Airways, a company founded with government support (1924), provided new routes for the empire. Weekly services began to Cape Town (1932), Brisbane (1934) and Hong Kong (1936); in contrast, thanks to the problem of flying the Atlantic, they only began to New York in 1946. It took nine days to fly to Cape Town in 1936, 14 to Adelaide, but

Below: The Blitz in London with St Paul's Cathedral in the background, December 1940. Indiscriminate German bombing, planned to destroy civilian morale, began 7 September 1940 and spread over the whole country from October, with severe attacks continuing on London. 43,000 were killed in the raids but, although morale was shaken in some places, generally it held up very well.

these were far shorter than sailing times. Commitment to the empire was demonstrated in a different form by the major new naval base built at Singapore for the defence of the Far East.

The empire faced serious problems in the 1930s, not least pressure from the Indian National Congress and serious disturbances in Palestine. As with Ireland in 1914, it is not clear what would have happened in India had there not been war. The Government of India Act (1935), though bitterly opposed by Conservatives such as Churchill who saw its moves towards self-government as a step towards the abandonment of empire, was designed to ensure British retention of the substance of power, but the provincial elections of 1937 were a success for Congress. Nevertheless it was the Second World War (1939-45) that undermined the empire, even as it brought British occupation of yet more territory, Somaliland and Libya, both formerly Italian, and led Churchill to consider the annexation of the latter.

The Second World War cost fewer British lives than the First, and spared the British army from being put through the mangle of the trenches, but in several respects it was much more close-run for Britain. As in 1914, she went to war to resist German aggression and to fulfil the logic of her alliance politics, but in 1939-40 Hitler's Germany destroyed the British alliance system. The East-

ern Front was ended within weeks as Poland was defeated (1939) and Stalin's Russia took its share, while the Western Front was rolled up in a German *Blitzkrieg* that overran the Netherlands, Belgium and France (1940); Denmark and Norway had fallen earlier that year. Expelled from the Continent, though able by bravery and skill to save much of the army in the evacuation from Dunkirk, Britain had the valuable support of the empire and control of the sea, but the latter was challenged by the potent threat of German air power and still more by German U-boats (submarines). She appeared to have lost the war, and it is not surprising that several major politicians were willing to consider a negotiated peace with Hitler. In May 1940 Viscount Halifax, the Foreign Secretary, was ready, if Hitler made one, 'to accept an offer which would save the country from avoidable disaster'. Hesitation was ended by the replacement of Neville Chamberlain, a Prime Minister identified with the appeasement of Germany in the 1930s and with failure in war, by Churchill (1940). Convinced of the total rightness of the British cause and the utter untrustworthiness of Hitler, he was determined to fight on, however bleak the situation might be. The blunting of German airpower in the Battle of Britain led Hitler to call off Operation Sealion, his planned invasion of Britain (1940), but

Above: Londoners shelter from the Blitz – *Women and Children in the Tube* by celebrated sculptor and graphic artist Henry Moore. Many children were evacuated to other parts of the country or even abroad for safety.

British successes against the Italians in North
Africa that winter were followed by a German
offensive there and by their conquest of Yugoslavia and Greece, the latter entailing the defeat
of British forces in Greece and Crete.

The loss of Crete in May 1941 was the last
major defeat for an isolated Britain. Hitherto her
European allies had offered little, as London had
become a collecting house for governments in
exile. The German attack on Russia (June 1941)
and the Japanese attack on Britain and the
United States, followed by the declaration of war
on the Americans by Japan's ally Germany
(December 1941), totally altered the situation.
There were still to be serious blows, especially in

early 1942, and the Battle of the Atlantic against
U-boats was not won until early 1943, but Britain
was now part of an alliance system linked to the
strongest economy in the world, and as Britain
and her new allies successfully blunted German
and Japanese offensives in late 1942, the long and
stony path to victory appeared clearer. In May
1943 the Germans surrendered in North Africa.
In September 1943 the British and the Americans
landed in Italy, and Italy surrendered uncon-
ditionally. The following June Anglo-American
forces landed in Normandy, and in May 1945 the
Germans surrendered. As with the last campaigns
against Napoleon, Russian strength had played a
crucial role, but the Anglo-American achieve-

ment had also been considerable, particularly given that they were also bearing the brunt of the war with Japan, a conflict that ended with Japanese surrender in September 1945 following the dropping of American atom bombs the previous month. Nuclear weapons were the most spectacular application of technology to warfare, but in both world wars British technology, especially in metallurgy and electronics, had made major contributions to advances in weaponry, notably tanks in the First World War and radar in the Second.

The war had fatally weakened the empire. Britain had lost prestige and resources, her dominion allies, especially Australia, had had to look to America for support, and there was a loss of confidence in the legacy of the past within Britain. The surrender of 'impregnable' Singapore to the Japanese on 15 February 1942, after a poorly-conducted campaign in Malaya, and the loss of the *Prince of Wales* and the *Repulse* to Japanese bombers was the most humiliating defeat in modern British history, one to rank with Cornwallis's surrender at Yorktown in 1781. Cornwallis's army had marched out to the tune of 'The World Turned Upside Down', and their surrender led directly to the loss of the American empire. That of Singapore destroyed British prestige in Asia. Combined with the need for Indian support in the war against advancing Japanese forces, it spelled the end of empire in the Indian subcontinent, the heart of the British imperial experience. In 1942 the Congress was offered independence after the war in return for support during it, an offer they spurned with their 'Quit India' movement. The Labour party first and unexpectedly became a majority government, in 1945, as a result of a reaction against the Conservatives as the party of privilege and pre-war division and in favour of the collectivism and social welfare offered by Labour. Labour was committed to Indian independence and this was achieved in 1947, although at the cost of partition and about a million deaths in Hindu-Muslim clashes.

Despite Indian independence, that of Burma and Ceylon (1948), and the ending of the Palestine mandate in 1948, Britain was still a major imperial power and the Labour government, especially its Foreign Secretary Ernest Bevin (1945-51), had high hopes of using imperial resources, particularly those of Africa, to strengthen the British economy and make her a less unequal partner in the Anglo-American partnership. Bevin acted in a lordly fashion in the Middle East, but empire ran out in the sands of rising Arab nationalism and a lack of British resources. The British faced a number of imperial problems in the early 1950s, including the Malayan Emergency (a Communist uprising which was tackled successfully), but it was the Suez Crisis of 1956, an attempt to destabilize the aggressive Arab nationalist regime of Gamul Abdul Nasser in Egypt, which clearly exposed

HOLDING THE LINE!

— COPYRIGHT by HENRI GUIGNON. —   Printed in the United States of America.

their weakness. Just as echoes of the appeasement of dictators in the 1930s were initially to be voiced, misleadingly, when the Argentinians invaded the Falklands in 1982, so in 1956 the Prime Minister, Anthony Eden (1955-57), who had himself resigned as Foreign Secretary in 1938 in protest at appeasement, was determined not to repeat such mistakes and accept Nasser's nationalization of the Suez Canal. Acting in concert with France and Israel, Eden sent British forces to occupy the Canal Zone. The invasion was poorly planned, but it was American opposition and its impact on sterling that was crucial in weakening British resolve and thus leading to a humiliating withdrawal. A lack of American support had been a major problem for the empire ever since the Second World War; in 1956 American anger made Britain's dependent status obvious.

The following 14 years saw the rapid loss of most of the rest of the British empire. The British

Above: This American poster of 1940 by Henri Guignon shows Churchill as the British bulldog acting as the last bulwark against totalitarianism.

Above: Summer at Largs by
Leslie Hunter (1879-1931).
Coastal holidays flourished
from the Victorian period,
but from the 1960s were
increasingly replaced by
foreign tourism, Blackpool
for many losing its appeal
to Benidorm.

people might not have been European minded
after 1950; but neither were they imperial
minded, and after Suez many leading Conservatives, especially Harold Macmillan, Prime Minister 1957-63, and Iain Mcleod, whom he
appointed Colonial Secretary, became deeply
disillusioned with the empire and ready to dis-
mantle it, a process that was hastened by colonial
nationalist movements, though criticised by
some right-wing Conservatives. Empire was
proving too expensive, too troublesome, and too
provocative of both the USA and the USSR. By
1969 none of Africa remained under British rule,
and the east of Suez defence policy had fallen victim to the impact of the devaluation of sterling in
1967. British forces withdrew from Singapore in
1971. Britain's status as a major power was no
longer territorial, no longer a consequence of
empire, let alone economic strength, but rather a
consequence of her being, from 1952, one of the
few atomic powers, and of her active membership
both of American-led international organiza-

tions, especially NATO (the North Atlantic
Treaty Organization of which she was a founder
member in 1949) and, from the 1970s, of the EEC
(European Economic Community), which she
joined in 1973.

NATO was designed to defend western Europe
against the Soviet Union, for the defeat of Germany in the Second World War was followed by
fears of Soviet plans and by a 'Cold War' that
lasted until the late 1980s. Already in mid-1944
planners for the Chiefs of Staff were suggesting a
post-war reform of Germany and Japan, so that
they could play a role against a Soviet Union
whose ambitions in eastern Europe were arousing
growing concern. On 14 March 1946 the British
embassy in Moscow asked if the world was now
'faced with the danger of the modern equivalent
of the religious wars of the sixteenth century',
with Soviet communism battling against Western social democracy and American capitalism
for 'domination of the world'. By January 1947
Clement Attlee, Labour Prime Minister 1945-51,

had decided to develop a British nuclear bomb. The Berlin Crisis (1948) led to the stationing of American B-29 strategic bombers in Britain, and British forces played a role in resisting Communist aggression in the Korean War (1950-53). In 1951 the Chiefs of Staff warned that the Russians might be provoked by Western rearmament into attacking in 1952. Under American pressure, Britain embarked in 1951 on a costly rearmament programme that undid the economic gains that had been made since 1948, and helped to strengthen the military commitment that has been such a heavy economic burden on post-war Britain. Defence spending has taken a higher percentage of gross national product than for any other western European power. The anti-Soviet political and strategic alignment was continued by subsequent governments, both Conservative (1951-64, 70-74, 79-) and Labour (1964-70, 74-79). From 1960 American nuclear submarines equipped with Polaris missiles began to operate from the Holy Loch in Scotland, and in 1962 Macmillan persuaded President Kennedy to provide Britain with Polaris, which offered Britain a global naval capability. That year *Dr No*, the first of the James Bond adventure films, had the hero of the British secret service saving American missile tests. In the 1980s, despite the protests of the Campaign for Nuclear Disarmament, American cruise missiles were deployed in Britain, and American bombers attacked Libya from British bases.

Empire was replaced by NATO, Commonwealth and Europe. The dominion status given to the 'white' colonies was a preliminary to the establishment of the British Commonwealth as an association of equal and autonomous partners (1931). In 1949 the prefix British was discarded and it was decided that republics might remain members, a measure that allowed India to stay in. The Commonwealth was seen for a time as a source of British influence, or as the basis for an international community spanning the divides between first and third worlds, white and black, and its unity was fostered by a Secretariat, established in 1965, and by Heads of Government meetings. Relations with South Africa, immigration policies and the consequences of British concentration on Europe have all led to differences between Britain and her Commonwealth partners, but the absence of common interests and views has been of greater significance. Economic, military and political links with former imperial possessions became less important. New Zealand and, even more, Australia now look to Japan as an economic partner, while Canada is part of a free trade zone with the United States and Mexico. America replaced Britain as Canada's biggest export market after the Second World War, and as the biggest source of foreign investment there in the 1920s. The British share of this investment fell from 85% in 1900 to 15% in 1960, while the American rose from 14 to 75. The percentage of the Australian and Canadian popu-

lations that can claim British descent has fallen appreciably since 1945. Britain had little role to play as the Pacific became an American lake; in 1951 Australia and New Zealand entered into a defence pact with the United States.

The United States has in some respects served Britain as a surrogate for empire, providing crucial military, political, economic and cultural links, and offering an important model. Part of the attraction is ideological. The American stress on the free market has appealed to more groups in British society, not least to commercial interests, than the more statist and bureaucratic continental societies. In the last quarter-century Anglo-American links have slackened, because anglophilia has become less important in America and Britain has had less to offer in terms of any special relationship. On the other hand, America remains very important to Britain, especially to British culture in the widest sense of the word, through the role of American programmes on British television, American or American-derived products in British consumer society, the American presence in the British economy and the more diffuse, but still very important, mystique of America as a land of wealth and excitement. For linguistic and, to a certain extent, commercial reasons, post-war American cultural

Above: Charles de Gaulle rejects the Common Market application by Harold Macmillan. Britain was seen by the French as too closely linked to America.

'hegemony' has been stronger in Britain than elsewhere in Europe, and has thus accentuated differences. The Atlanticism of the 1960s led to the creation of Schools of English and American Studies in new universities such as East Anglia and Sussex, separate from those of European Studies. Few Victorians would have thought it sensible to study their literature and history within this sort of a context. British film audiences have for long been under the sway of Hollywood, and American influence on television has been considerable. When 'J R', the leading character in the television series *Dallas*, was shot, it was reported on the BBC news, the fictional world displacing its less exciting real counterpart.

The postwar movement towards western European unity reflected the particular interests of the participant states. Britain did not share the concern of Italy and Germany to anchor their new democracies, nor the willingness of France to surrender a portion of her sovereignty in order to restrict German independence, and was not one of the founding members of the EEC. The different nature of British commerce and investment was also important. Joining the EEC would be far more disruptive for Britain than it was for the other states, because their trade was overwhelm-

ingly Euro-centric, while this applied to less than half of Britain's trade. Thus joining entailed a major economic dislocation, which for a country whose foreign trade was so vital to her, was bound to make her adjustment to membership more difficult.

It soon became clear, however, that the EEC was going to be a success, and the costs of staying out seemed greater than those of joining. As a result successive governments, both Conservative and Labour, applied to join in 1961 and 1967, only to be rejected by the veto of the French leader, Charles de Gaulle, who argued that Britain's claim to a European identity was compromised by her American links. De Gaulle's departure and a fresh application in 1970, by the Conservative government under Edward Heath (1970-74), led to the successful negotiation of British entry. Britain joined in January 1973, and in the sole national referendum ever held 67.2 per cent voted to remain in the EEC (1975), although voters' interest in and knowledge of the issues was limited and they were more influenced by the support for membership displayed by most politicians. The only areas showing a majority against staying in were the Shetlands and the Western Isles. Protestant suspicion of continental Catholicism was probably responsible for the

Below: Edward Heath, Conservative Prime Minister, signs the Common Market Membership Treaty, 22 January 1972, to his right Foreign Secretary Sir Alec Douglas-Home, to his left treaty negotiator Geoffrey Ripon. The signing was delayed because Heath was hit with black ink thrown by a demonstrator and had to change his clothes.

very low *pro* vote in Ulster. In contrast, far smaller percentages voted for devolution for Scotland and Wales in 1979. Thus the electorate appeared to favour both membership of a European body, with supra-national institutions, rationales and pretensions, and the retention of the configuration of the traditional British nation state. Concern about the European dimension has grown as the limited objectives of most of the politicians who constructed the EEC have developed in more ambitious directions, with the call to create stronger institutions, to transfer a considerable measure of authority and thus sovereignty from the nation states. Changing nomenclature has registered the perception of new objectives. The European Community has developed from being an economic organization; the EEC has become the EC.

The 'duality of ocean and continent' in British foreign policy, discerned by Burrow and by a later Oxford Professor of Modern History, Wernham, depended on the 'defence of insularity' and 'the shield of sea power', but as these were torn away first by air-power and then by nuclear weapons, it was necessary to rethink totally Britain's strategic situation and policy. This was a crucial component in Anglo-American relations during the decades of defence from the 1940s to the late

1980s. This defence was not, however, simply bilateral, but part of a strategy for the whole of western Europe. The largest sector allocation in the Defence White Paper of May 1989, 39 per cent, was to the British forces in what was then West Germany. The close of the Cold War may have brought an end to the decades of defence, and writers of spy stories will have to search elsewhere than Moscow for villains, but international uncertainty remains acute and at present the EC is unable, and is not intended, to meet Britain's international and strategic requirements.

The extent to which Britain is 'truly' part of Europe has vexed commentators since the Second World War. In some respects Britain and the societies of western Europe have been becoming more similar over the last 20 years. This is a consequence of broadly similar social trends, including secularization, the emancipation of women and the move from the land. Sexual permissiveness, rising divorce rates, growing geographical mobility, the decline of traditional social distinctions and the rise of youth culture are all shared characteristics. Deference, aristocracies, and social stratification have all declined, although differences in wealth, both capital and income, remain vast. The gradual virtual dis-

Below: The suffragette movement. Emmeline Pankhurst being arrested outside Buckingham Palace, May 1914. The emancipation of women has been the most important social change of the century.

Summer 1981

Yugotours

Super sunshine selection

YUGOSLAVIA
ROMANIA
GREECE
AUSTRIA
ITALY

SUN & SEA HOLIDAYS
LAKES & MOUNTAINS
COACH TOURS
ISLANDS &
NATURIST
HOLIDAYS
2 CENTRE
HOLIDAYS

Price Guarantee on all holidays
from February to November 1981

Above: Travel sales literature, 1981. Foreign tourism boomed in the 1980s; British tourist expenditure abroad in 1987 was £7,255.2 million.

they had been in the nineteenth century, and as a result the number of children in an average family fell from three in 1910 to two in 1940. Despite a post-war birth-peak in 1947 and another in 1966, population growth-rates continued to decline in the 1950s and 1960s, almost to a halt in the 1970s and early 1980s, before a slight upturn from the mid-1980s. The population of surburban, commuter and southern England has increased more rapidly than that of the north and of London.

Immigration, especially from former colonies, has altered the ethnic composition of many continental societies. In Britain much of the immigration was from Europe: Irish after the potato famine of 1845-49; Russian and Polish Jews from the 1880s until the Alien Act of 1905; Poles and Ukrainians in the 1940s. Thereafter large scale immigration was from the 'New Commonwealth', especially the West Indies and the Indian sub-continent. A labour shortage in unattractive spheres of employment, such as foundry work and nursing, led to the active sponsorship of immigration, but concern about its scale and growing racial tension led to immigration acts (1962, 1968, 1971, 1981) that progressively reduced Commonwealth immigration. Successive waves of immigrants faced poor housing and took on the less attractive jobs, the 'sweated' trades, such as tailoring, and casual labour in the docks and the building trade.

While some immigrants have sought assimilation, others have striven to retain a distinctive identity, in certain cases linked to a lack of sympathy for generally accepted values. Over some issues, such as the education of Asian Islamic women in co-educational schools, this has created administrative and legal problems. Britain has both 'multi-culturalism' and a degree of racial tension; while racial discrimination is illegal under the Race Relations Act (1976), which is supported by the work of the Commission for Racial Equality, racial violence has played a role in the harrassment of non-whites, especially in attacks on housing estates. Black crime is a serious problem, with high rates of drug-dealing and muggings, and black hostility to the police played a major role in the 1981 riots in south London and Liverpool and in subsequent violence. While the effects of immigration have become more of an issue in Britain, emigration has fallen. It was still a major factor in the first quarter of the century, and net emigration, rather than net immigration, was the situation until the 1930s and then again after the Second World War, but is no longer the case.

As increased numbers have travelled for pleasure, a consequence of greater disposable wealth among the bulk of the population, the development of the package holiday, the use of jet aircraft and the spread of car ownership, so many more inhabitants of Britain than ever before have visited the Continent and far more than ever before make a regular habit of doing so. In 1991 there were 2.45 million British visitors to the

establishment of the Anglican Church, a process that really began with the Catholic Emancipation Act of 1829, has gathered pace in recent years, a parallel to the process of disestablishment on much of the Continent. In both Britain and the Continent social paternalism, patriarchal authority, respect for age and the nuclear family, and the stigma of illegitimacy, have all declined in importance, while rights to divorce, abortion and contraception are established across most of western Europe (reducing the numbers available for adoption), and homosexual acts in private between consenting adults have been decriminalized, in Britain by the Sexual Offences Act of 1967. Cohabitation and one-parent families have both become more common, while the proportion of lifetime celibates has fallen. Working hours and birth rates have both fallen; populations have 'aged', decreasing the economically active percentage.

Average rates of population growth in Britain as a whole were far lower in the inter-war period, when they fell to below replacement levels, than

USA, but far more to the Continent. If many visit 'little Britains' in nondescript Mediterranean resorts such as Benidorm, others do not. The metropolitan middle-class household that would have had servants 60 years ago may now have a second home in France, and *The Times* carries regular articles on where best to purchase such properties. The opportunity of learning at least one foreign language is offered to all school-children, and a certain number benefit. Economically and politically, Britain has become closer to the Continent. The societies of western Europe have felt threatened first by Soviet power and then by the chaos in eastern Europe that has followed the collapse of Communism; their economies have been challenged by the staggering development of the 'dragon' countries of east Asia. Economically, Britain is more closely linked to continental markets and suppliers than she was in 1973, while her attraction for 'inward investment', especially from Japan, America and the other countries of the EC, has largely arisen as a consequence of her access to what is now the largest trading system in the world. Such investment is of growing importance. In the North of England, for example, manufacturing employment in foreign-owned companies rose between 1979 and 1989 from 11.8% to 17.1%, and between January 1985 and June 1992 such investment

there secured 34,388 jobs and an associated capital spend of £2.8 billion, much focused on serving EC markets. The adoption of the Single European Act in 1987 committed Britain to remove all barriers to the creation of the Single European (EC) Market, and also altered the framework of British economic activity. The EC and the domestic market have been legally joined and it is necessary to comply with the SEM in order to operate in the EC and therefore in Britain. Politically, most British politicians proclaim their commitment to Europe and the EC even when criticizing the practices or the objectives of the latter.

And yet there are also important strains in the relationship. Affinity is not the only reason for closeness or union; complementarity is also involved. That was certainly believed to be the case with the British empire in the later nineteenth century. The bases of imperial union were supposed to be twofold; there was a stress on common origins, customs, race and constitutions, but also an emphasis on the degree to which each complemented the others, especially economically. Thus the dominions and crown colonies could exchange primary products for manufactured goods with industrial Britain, their common interests resting on the differences between the parts. This was also the relationship with trans-

Below: Rock concert, Isle of Wight, 1 September 1969. The emergence of the youth consumer as a market force has been one of the most significant developments of the last 40 years.

Right: Carnaby Street and the King's Road, London, became the high fashion spots of the 1960s. Miniskirts made their first appearance, and an irreverent nostalgia for the heyday of imperialism inspired Union Jack waistcoats, hats and bags.

oceanic trading partners that were not part of the empire, most obviously South America. The EC is also less amenable to this reciprocity, because of the similarities between Britain and her neighbours, which makes for a union of competitors rather than of partners.

There are also important political problems affecting the relationship. Scepticism about the notion of a European 'super state' and 'Eurofederalism' is widespread, and some of the support for the European ideal in the 1980s was tactical and opportunistic, designed to attack Mrs Thatcher (Prime Minister 1979-90) who, though she signed the Single European Act, was not the most ardent admirer of European unity. Two very different indicators are the scarcity of the European flag in Britain, and the markedly patriotic response of the British public to the Falklands Crisis of 1982, when British forces drove out invading Argentine troops. In contrast, there is not much willingness to kill or be killed for Europe, and there has been little enthusiasm for the deployment of British troops in Bosnia. Political identity is clearly national, not international.

The ambivalent response to European unity has been matched, over a much longer time span, by an ambivalence towards the democratization of society. This has different sources and takes different forms. Few were as sweeping as Halifax, an old Etonian who, aside from serving as Foreign Secretary (1938-40), was also Viceroy of India and Chancellor of Oxford. He wrote to his father, 'what a bore democracy is to those who have to work it . . .'. H A Gwynne, editor of the *Morning Post* (1910-37) and President of the Institute of Journalists (1929-30), hated democracy and regarded the First Reform Act as the greatest error in recent British history; 'when we handed over the pistol to our masters in 1832 we let ourselves in for all the evils that pursued us'. Lady Bathurst, the paper's owner from 1908 to 1924, stated in 1918 that 'democracy is idiotic'. Hostility to democratic accountability has also been demonstrated in the unwillingness of often self-defining elites to accept popular beliefs and pastimes as worthy of value and attention, and their conviction that they are best placed to manage

society and define social values. Social and cultural condescension can thus be linked to contempt for popular views on such matters as capital punishment or immigration. Most institutions resist unwelcome pressures, while political parties temper their desire for popular support with their wish to maintain their ideological inheritance.

At the same time, however, there have been powerful forces democratizing society. The most important has been the emancipation of women. Their legal and social position was limited at the beginning of the century, not least because most adult women did not have an independent income. In general women lacked good jobs, and the employment rate among women with children was low by modern standards. The change this century has been legal, economic and social. Prior to the First World War the suffragette movement won attention rather than support, as the Pankhursts urged their followers to acts of violence, but the war saw a substantial increase in the female work force as society was mobilized for total war. While men were conscripted, nearly five million women were in employment at the start of 1918, although their wages remained much lower than men's. That year the vote was given to all men over 21 and to women over 30; a decade later the voting age for women was dropped to 21. Progressive changes in the law made divorce easier and removed the formal structure of discrimination. The Equal Pay Act

Below: Poll tax riot, Trafalgar Square, London, 31 March 1990. Although only a small minority took part in violent demonstrations, government unpopularity stemming in part from the Poll Tax (or, more correctly, Community Charge) led Conservative MPs to reject the leadership of Mrs Thatcher later that year.

Right: Still from the Beatles' animated film *Yellow Submarine*, 1968, part of the explosion of pop culture that characterized the 1960s. Intended as a spin-off from the chart-topping album of the same name, the film was poorly received at the time and denied a general release, but has since acquired cult status.

(1970) was made more important by the major expansion of the female work force from the 1940s.

The expansion of the First World War had been partly reversed thereafter as men returned from the forces, but that of the second conflict was not, and the economic shift from manufacturing to service industries helped to create more opportunities for women workers. Whereas previously most women had given up work when they married, older married women entered the labour force as clerical workers in large numbers from the 1940s. Clerical occupations remain today the largest single occupational category for women. There was opposition; the National Association of Schoolmasters was founded in 1922 from a splinter group of male teachers opposed to the National Union of Teachers' support for equal pay. Its leaflets included such titles as *Making Our Boys Effeminate* (1927). The National Union of Foundry Workers only represented men during its history (1920-46), despite there being about 50,000 foundrywomen in the 1940s. Changes in the position of women cannot, however, be separated from other social questions. Class affected the recruitment for different tasks of women in both world wars. The mixture of classes in munitions work during the first war, though stressed in propaganda, was limited. Similarly, in the second war there was little mingling in the factories; social distinctions were maintained. 'Positive discrimination' in favour of hiring and promoting women in recent years has worked largely to the benefit of middle-class women, and the practice of endogamy (marriage within the clan) may therefore ensure that social differences are fortified.

As with other movements lacking a centralizing structure, the women's liberation movement of the 1960s and 1970s was a diverse one. It included pressure for changes in lifestyles and social arrangements that put women's needs and expectations in a more central position. The Abortion Act of 1967 was followed by a situation close to abortion on demand. Employment and its material rewards became more important as aspirations for women, complementing rather than replacing home and family. The range of female activities expanded: the Women's Rugby Football Union was formed in 1983; the first Briton in space was Helen Sharman. While full-time male undergraduates at universities increased by 20 per cent between 1970 and 1989, females increased by 30 per cent. As with other developments of that period which led to pressure for change, the impact of the women's liberation movement diminished in the 1980s, which was ironically that of the first British woman Prime Minister, Margaret Thatcher. Her rise showed that there was no ceiling of opportunity above which women could not rise; her determination and success demonstrated that a woman was easily capable of the job. Never rejected by the electorate, Mrs Thatcher was toppled by disaffection among her MPs, who feared defeat in the light of the government's unpopularity; she was the longest serving Prime Minister of the century and the premier with the longest consecutive period in office since Lord Liverpool (1812-27).

Capitalism has been another force shaping the democratization of society; at the same time as the differing wealth and income of individuals ensures that their purchasing power varies, each is a consumer able to make his or her own purchasing decisions. This element of choice, and the need to shape and cater to it, have combined to ensure a whole range of social shifts, among

How does 1913 sound to you?

Left: The heritage industry. Beamish Open Air Museum, County Durham, partly recreates the year 1913, with the Mahogany Drift coal mine, the abacus in the classroom, the working forge, and the Methodist Chapel. Period dramas on television, such as *Upstairs Downstairs* (first screened 1971), were very successful in the 1970s and 1980s, and critics claimed that they were a sign of dangerous escapist nostalgia, reflecting a lack of confidence in present and future. In fact this was not a recent development; Galsworthy's *Forsyte Saga* had been a great success on television in 1967, and nostalgia for the past can be found in much popular fiction of the century, for example the novels of Georgette Heyer and her many successors. Attitudes to religion, sex and the role of women in the 1990s harldly suggest a yearning for an earlier era.

which the most striking has been the emergence over the last 40 years of the youth consumer, and the development of cultural and consumer fashions that reflect the dynamism and volatility of this section of the market. It is easy to focus on 'pop culture', rock to drug culture via the Beatles and the Sex Pistols, psychedelia and punk, but more significance can be attached to the wish and ability of youth, first, to create an adolescent identity – not to be younger copies of their elders – and, secondly and more specifically, to reject the opinions of their parents. Pop culture is only one manifestation of this. The willingness to try different foods, to holiday in different places, to move away from parental religious preferences, to go on to higher education or to purchase property, are as interesting and possibly more important.

Certainly the interrelationship between the aspirations of youth and socio-economic changes must be seen to play a role in the major expansion of the middle class that has been such a marked feature of the last three decades. In 1900 75 per cent of the labour force were manual workers, members of the working class. By 1974 the percentage had fallen to 47, by 1991 to 36. The manufacturing base has declined; the service sector grown. White collar has replaced blue collar, and average incomes for those in work have risen appreciably. The longterm impact of the social revolution of recent years, crucial aspects of which are falling union membership (the TUC had more than 12 million members in 1979, fewer than 8 million in 1992), and rising home ownership (three-quarters of trade unionists by the late 1980s), is still unclear; but the basic lineaments of society for the foreseeable future are of a capitalist, consumerist, individualist, mobile, predominantly secular and urban, property-owning democracy, with a substantial underclass. 'Who governs Britain?' was the slogan of the Heath government that, although it won more votes than Labour, was nevertheless defeated in February 1974. The defeat of the miners' strike of 1984-85 answered the question. The substantial increase in individual and corporate debt in the 1980s, however, as a consequence of the liberalization of the financial system and government encouragement of the widespread desire to own property, combined with structural economic problems, have ensured that many who are not in the underclass are in a vulnerable situation. By June 1992 repossessions of houses by creditors were at an annual rate of about 75,000, while 300,000 mortgage-holders were six months or more in arrears. A more general problem is posed by rising crime figures, the related perception of a more lawless and less safe society, and the difficulties of policing contemporary British society. Widespread refusal to pay the unpopular poll tax, introduced by Mrs Thatcher, indicated a willingness to reject laws deemed unfair. The unpopularity of the tax, combined with a worsening economic situation, helped to lead to the crisis in confidence in her leadership in the parliamentary Conservative party which led to her fall in November 1990.

There is little confidence in central planning; limited support for state collectivism. More prefer to shop than to go to church on Sundays, and fewer of the population express their religious faith through the Church of England than ever before. Social differences remain, the working class eating less well, having poorer housing, fewer children and less access to higher education than the middle class. Class mortality differences have widened from the late 1950s. Nevertheless, although there are clear variations between and within regions in many fields, including political preference, crime patterns, nuptiality, fertility and house ownership, these are less marked than in the past. National broadcasting, state education and employment, nation-wide companies, unions, products and pastimes have all brought a measure of convergence that can be seen in the

Below: The Thames flood barrier under construction. A major feat of civil engineering, this is designed to protect London from disastrous flooding such as that of 1953, which overwhelmed much of the east coast.

decline of dialect and distinctive regional practices, for example cooking. Wales and England appear indissolubly linked; nationalism has failed to make much headway in Scotland; but the future of Ulster continues to be a major problem for its own citizens and for Britain as a whole. Britain is an active member of the European Community, but the future trajectory of that body, and Britain's relations with it, are both unclear.

The threat of Russian power has markedly diminished, and although many other regions of the world are unstable and pose challenges to British interests, western Europe appears safe for liberal democracy. The future of the environment is a growing concern, global warming and ozone depletion both being themes of the early 1990s; but the British can look back on over four decades without a major war. The experience of serving or losing loved ones in the two world wars, which greatly affected major politicians, such as Attlee, Eden and Chamberlain, as well as millions of their contemporaries, is one that has not been repeated. History is so often a story of the move from one crisis to another, and that of modern Britain is no exception, but crisis can be seen as an integral part of the functioning and development of any sophisticated society. Despite its serious problems, British society still has many attractive features and there is still a clear sense of national identity and loyalty.

History is like travel. To go back in the past and then to return is to have seen different countries, other ways of doing things, various values. The traveller may not have the time or resources to appreciate fully what he or she is seeing, but is nevertheless made aware of variety and change. To travel today is to be made aware of some of the strengths and weaknesses of Britain and the British, and also serves to confirm a sense of identity with place and people. A distinguished recent collective study of the history of the country concluded by stressing continuity. Using the structural image of geological constancy, it emphasized a constant expression of a deep sense of history, an organic, closely-knit society, capable of self-renewal, as earlier the rooted strength of its institutions and its culture had been mentioned. Writing nine years later, in 1992, it is possible to stress the role of chance. Much of the relative stability of this century was due to victory in both world wars. Most Continental countries were defeated and occupied, with the accompanying strains. Many right-wing political groupings were contaminated, or at least stained, by collaboration; their left-wing counterparts affected by the rise of Communism. In Britain, in contrast, there was no foreign invasion, no seizure of power by undemocratic forces from left or right. Similarly, it was far from inevitable that Britain would survive French invasion attempts in the eighteenth century and the Napoleonic period. There have also been dom-

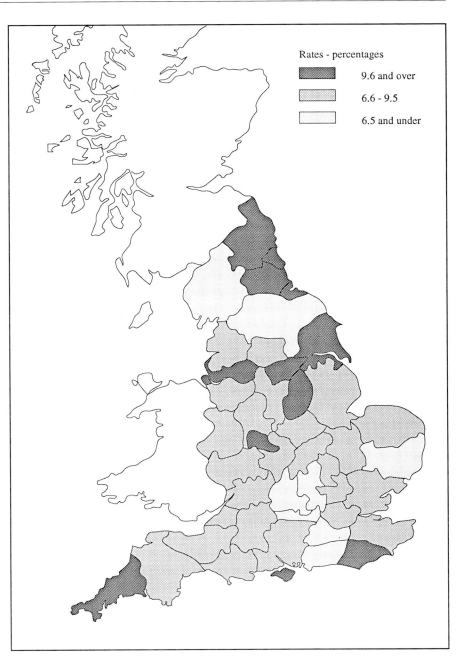

Rates - percentages

■ 9.6 and over

▦ 6.6 - 9.5

□ 6.5 and under

estic crises whose peaceful resolution was far from inevitable; as well as civil conflicts whose outcome was far from certain to contemporaries. The result of the English Civil War and the 1745 Rebellion are obvious examples.

While stressing chance, therefore, it is also necessary to draw attention to those who were unsuccessful. British society can be presented as both organic and divided. The Glorious Revolution, for example, plays a major role in the British public myth, but many were not comprehended within the Whig consensus, and both the Revolution settlement and the Hanoverian regime were only established by force. For all their talk about being the natural party of government, only twice this century (the Tories in 1900 and 1931) has either the Labour or the Conservative Party gained more than 50 per cent of the popular vote. Deterministic approaches to the past are suspect, and it is necessary to qualify any emphasis on patterns by stressing the role of chance and contingency.

Above: Unemployment rates, January 1992. Unemployment was heavily concentrated in the old industrial areas, but the recession was more widely spread, and in 1992 unemployment also rose appreciably in London and the Home Counties as the financial services industry and other service sector employers shed staff. By January 1993 the national average was 10.6% and over three million were unemployed. In December 1992 average EC unemployment was 9%.

INDEX

SELECTED BIBLIOGRAPHY

The following is necessarily a selective list, concentrating on recent books. Other works and articles can be traced through the bibliographies of these books.

General Works
C Bayly (ed), *Atlas of the British Empire* (1989)
M Falkus and J Gillingham (eds), *Historical Atlas of Britain* (1981)
C Haigh (ed), *The Cambridge Historical Encyclopedia of Great Britain and Ireland* (1985)
P Jenkins, *A History of Modern Wales 1536-1990* (1992)
H Kearney, *The British Isles: A History of Four Nations* (1989)
R Mitchison (ed), *Why Scottish History Matters* (1991)
K Morgan (ed), *The Oxford Illustrated History of Britain* (1984)
B Short (ed), *The English Rural Community* (1992)

Britons and Romans
M W Barley and R P C Hanson (eds), *Christianity in Britain 300-700* (1968)
A R Birley, *The People of Roman Britain* (1979)

B W Cunliffe, *Iron Age Communities in Britain* (1974)
B Jones and D Mattingly, *An Atlas of Roman Britain* (1990)
M Todd, *Roman Britain* (1981)

Anglo-Saxon England
J Campbell (ed), *The Anglo-Saxons* (1982)
B Goulding, *The Normans in England 1066-1100: Conquest and Civilization* (1993)
D Hill, *Atlas of Anglo-Saxon England* (1981)
D Kirby, *The Earliest English Kings* (1990)
J Morris, *The Age of Arthur: A History of the British Isles from 350 to 650* (1973)
C Thomas, *Britain and Ireland in Early Christian Times* AD 400-800 (1972)

Medieval England
M T Clancy, *England and its Rulers, 1066-1272* (1983)
A Curry, *The Hundred Years War* (1993)
J Le Patourel, *The Norman Empire* (1976)
H R Loyn, *The Norman Conquest* (1982)

A J Pollard, *The Wars of the Roses* (1988)
M Prestwich, *English Politics in the Thirteenth Century* (1990)
M Prestwich, *The Three Edwards* (1980)
R R Davies (ed), *The British Isles 1100-1500: Comparisons, Contrasts and Connections* (1988)
W L Warren, *Henry II* (1973)

Tudor England
P Collinson, *The Religion of Protestants: The Church in English Society 1559-1625* (1982)
C S L Davies, *Peace, Print and Protestantism, 1450-1556* (1977)
J Guy, *Tudor England* (1988)
C Haigh (ed), *The Reign of Elizabeth I* (1984)
C Haigh, *Elizabeth I* (1988)
D Loades, *The Mid-Tudor Crisis* (1992)
D MacCulloch, *The Later Reformation in England 1547-1603* (1990)
D Palliser, *The Age of Elizabeth* (1983)
R Rex, *Henry VIII and the English Reformation* (1992)
C Russell, *The Crisis of Parliaments, 1509-1660* (1974)
J J Scarisbrick, *Henry VIII* (1983)
P Williams, *The Tudor Regime* (1979)

Stuart England
K Fincham (ed), *The Early Stuart Church 1603-1642* (1993).
A Hughes, *The Causes of the English Civil War* (1991)
R Hutton, *The British Republic 1649-1660* (1990)
R Hutton, *Charles II* (1989)
J R Jones, *County and Court, 1660-1714* (1978)
P Laslett, *The World We Have Lost* (1972)
P Seaward, *The Restoration, 1660-1688* (1991)
K Sharpe and P Lake (eds), *Culture and Politics in Early Stuart England* (1993)
M Spufford, *Contrasting Communities: English Villagers in the Sixteenth and Seventeenth Centuries* (1974)
K Wrightson, *English Society 1580-1680* (1982)

Hanoverian England
J Black, *Robert Walpole and the Nature of Politics in Early Eighteenth-Century Britain* (1990)
J Black, *Culloden and the '45* (1990)

J Black, *War for America* (1991)
J Black, *The Elder Pitt* (1993)
J Derry, *Politics in the Age of Fox, Pitt and Liverpool* (1990)
P Langford, *A Polite and Commercial People: England, 1727-1783* (1988)
K Perry, *British Politics and the American Revolution* (1990)
R Porter, *English Society in the Eighteenth Century* (1982)
J Rule, *Albion's People: English Society 1714-1815* (1992)
J Rule, *The Vital Century: England's Developing Economy 1714-1815* (1992)
F M L Thompson (ed), *The Cambridge Social History of Britain 1750-1950* (1990)

Victorian England
A Briggs, *Victorian Things* (1988)
G Crouzet, *The Victorian Economy* (1982)
E J Evans, *The Forging of the Modern State 1783-1870* (1983)
R Pope (ed), *Atlas of British Social and Economic History since 1700* (1989)
K G Robbins, *Nineteenth-Century Britain: Integration and Diversity* (1988)
G R Searle, *The Liberal Party: Triumph and Disintegration* (1992)
R Stewart, *Party and Politics 1830-1852* (1989)
F M L Thompson, *The Rise of Respectable Society: A Social History of Victorian Britain, 1830-1900* (1988)

Modern England
C J Bartlett, *British Foreign Policy in the Twentieth Century* (1989)
D G Boyce, *The Irish Question and British Politics 1868-1986* (1988)
R Floud and D McCloskey (eds), *The Economic History of Britain since 1700* (1981)
T R Gourvish and A O'Day (eds), *Britain since 1945* (1991)
P Hennessy, *Never Again: Britain 1945-51* (1992)
K Jefferys, *The Labour Party since 1945* (1993)
R Lowe, *The Welfare State in Britain since 1945* (1993)
A Marwick, *British Society since 1945* (1982)
H Perkin, *The Rise of Professional Society: England since 1880* (1989)
D Powell, *British Politics and the Labour Question, 1868-1990* (1992)
M Pugh, *The Making of Modern British Politics, 1867-1939* (1982)
D Reynolds, *Britannia Overruled* (1991)
K G Robbins, *The Eclipse of a Great Power: Modern Britain 1870-1975* (1983)
K G Robbins, *Churchill* (1992)
J Stevenson, *British Society 1914-1945* (1983)
J Young, *Britain and European Unity since 1945* (1993)

ACKNOWLEDGMENTS

The publisher would like to thank the author for picture suggestions; picture researchers Suzanne O'Farrell and Stephen Small; designer Martin Bristow; and the following institutions, agencies and individuals for illustrative material.

AA Photo Library, Basingstoke: pages 21, 28, 48, 78 (top left), 149 (below). **Art Gallery of South Australia, Adelaide:** pages 2, 78 (top right), 78 (below), 87, 98 (below), 102 (above), 104, 126 (below), 127, 146 (above), 147, 150, 151 (right), 170 (below), 178. **Beamish Open Air Museum, Northumberland:** page 187. **Bettmann Archive, New York:** pages 30, 76, 88, 93, 116 (below), 120, 123 (above), 128 (above), 129, 131 (above),132, 141 (above), 141 (below), 143 (below), 143 (above), 148 (above), 148 (below), 154, 161 (below), 163 (above), 165 (above), 168, 169, 176, 180, 181, 188. **Blenheim Palace, Woodstock** (Reproduced by kind permission of His Grace the Duke of Marlborough. Photography by Jeremy Whitaker): pages 95, 107, 109. **Bodleian Library, Oxford:** pages 49, 146 (below), 163 (below). **Bridgeman Art Library, London:** pages 70;/Goodwood House, Sussex: 103 (above);/Guildhall Library, London: 130;/Manchester City Art Gallery: 134;/National Gallery, London: 126 (above); /Wallington Hall, Northumberland: 135. **British Architectural Library:** page 105. **British Film Institute:** page 186. **British Library:** pages 8, 16, 19 (below), 24 (below), 25, 31 (below), 34, 35 (above), 36, 37 (above), 37 (below), 39 (above), 39 (below), 40, 42 (above), 43 (above), 43 (below), 44 (above), 45 (left), 46 (above), 51, 52, 56 (above), 56 (below). **British Museum:** pages 18, 44 (below), 64 (below), 68, 69, 81 (above), 89 (above), 94 (below), 100, 116 (above), 117, 128 (below), 131 (below), 132. **Brompton Picture Library:** pages 1, 32, 119, 175, 177,/British Rail: 171. **Brown University Library, Anne S K Brown Military Collection Rhode Island:** pages 82, 139 (above). **City of Aberdeen Art Gallery:** page 158 (below). **City of Bristol Record Office:** page 125 (below). **Clayton, Peter:** page 11 (above). **Corpus Christi College, Cambridge, UK:** page 55. **Department of the Environment, London:** page 14 (below). **Environment Picture Library, London:** page 158 (above). **Giraudon/Art Resource, New York:**

page 26. **Guildhall Art Gallery, London:** page 103 (below). **Hereford Cathedral, Dean & Chapter:** page 47 (below). **Hever Castle Ltd:** pages 58, 63 (above). **House of Lords, Record Office:** pages 84, 94 (above). **Hulton Deutsch, London:** pages 72, 73 (above), 157 (above), 157 (below), 159, 160, 164, 165 (below), 170 (above), 173, 174, 183, 185. **Hussein, Anwar, London:** page 162 (below). **Ironbridge Gorge Museum, Telford, Shropshire:** pages 114 (above), 122, 124. **Jeffery, Sally:** pages 46 (below), 47 (above), 73 (below), 77 (below), 106, 108, 155 (below). **Lichfield Cathedral:** page 144. **Life File, London:** pages 54, 153. **Manchester University Museum, Dept of Archaeology:** page 13 (below). **Mansell Collection, London:** pages 23 (above), 53, 57, 64 (above), 65, 66 (above), 67 (above), 80, 97 (above), 101, 113 (below),114 (below), 123 (below), 125 (above), 140, 145 (above), 145 (below). **Mary Evans Picture Library, London:** pages 77 (above), 97 (above), 113 (above), 151 (left). **Museum of London:** page 91. **National Army Museum, London:** pages 83 (above), 96, 136, 137, 139 (below). **National Gallery, Washington DC:** page 118. **National Maritime Museum, London:** pages 71 (below), 89 (below), 102 (below). **National Motor Museum at Beaulieu, UK:** page 162 (above). **National Portrait Gallery, London:** pages 61, 62, 66 (below), 67 (below), 79, 86, 90, 110, 111. **Photo Resources, Canterbury:** pages 6, 10 (below), 12, 14 (above), 15 (above), 15 (below), 19 (above), 20, 23 (below), 24 (above), 31 (above), 35 (below), 50, 71 (above), 81 (below), 83 (below), 172. **Private Eye, London:** pages 166, 167, 179. **Public Records Office, London:** pages 38, 45 (right). **Skyscan, Cheltenham:** page 10 (above). **Tesco Creative Services, Wolverhampton:** pages 161 (above). **Thomas Photos Oxford:** page 74. **Trinity College, Cambridge, UK:** pages 33, 99 **Tyne and Wear Museums, Laing Art Gallery:** pages 142, 149 (above), 155 (above). **Ulster Museum, Northern Ireland:** page 85. **Unichrome:** page 98 (above). **University and Society of Antiquaries, Newcastle upon Tyne Museum of Antiquities:** page 13 (above). **Vintage Magazine Company:** page 184. **Ward, Andrew:** page 11 below). **Windsor Castle, Royal Library,** c.1992 Her Majesty The Queen: page 63 (below), 115, 138. **York Archaeological Trust:** page 9. **Yugotours, London:** page 182.